D0453541

MENORCA

Ciutadella •

Alaior •

Maó •

Pollença •
• Alcúdia

Inca •

Artà •

MALLORCA

• Manacor

Llucmajor •

• Felanitx

Campos •

Santanyí •

CABRERA ISLAND

MENORCA
Pages 90–111

MALLORCA
Pages 42–89

0 km   20

0 miles   20

EYEWITNESS TRAVEL GUIDES

MALLORCA
MENORCA & IBIZA

EYEWITNESS TRAVEL GUIDES

MALLORCA
MENORCA AND IBIZA

GRZEGORZ MICUŁA

DK

LONDON, NEW YORK,
MELBOURNE, MUNICH AND DELHI
www.dk.com

Produced by Wydawnictwo Wiedza i Życie S.A., Warsaw

SENIOR GRAPHIC DESIGNER Paweł Pasternak
EDITORS Robert G. Pasieczny, Anna Moczar-Demko
GRAPHIC DESIGN Paweł Kamiński, Piotr Kiedrowski
TYPESETTING AND LAYOUT Paweł Kamiński,
Piotr Kiedrowski, Elżbieta Dudzińska

CARTOGRAPHY Magdalena Polak
PHOTOGRAPHY Bartłomiej Zaranek
ILLUSTRATIONS Bohdan Wróblewski,
Michał Burkiewicz, Monika Żylińska

CONTRIBUTORS Grzegorz Micuła, Katarzyna Sobieraj,
Robert G. Pasieczny, Eligiusz Nowakowski
CONSULTANT Carlos Cassas Marrodan

For Dorling Kindersley

TRANSLATOR Magda Hannay
EDITOR Matthew Tanner
SENIOR DTP DESIGNER Jason Little
PRODUCTION CONTROLLER Sarah Dodd

Reproduced by Colourscan, Singapore
Printed and bound in Italy by Graphicom s.r.l.

First published in Great Britain in 2004
by Dorling Kindersley Limited, 80 Strand, London, WC2R 0RL

Copyright © 2004 Dorling Kindersley, London
A Penguin Company

A CIP CATALOGUE RECORD IS AVAILABLE FROM THE BRITISH LIBRARY.

ISBN 1 40530281 X

FLOORS ARE REFERRED TO THROUGHOUT IN ACCORDANCE WITH BRITISH
USAGE; IE THE "FIRST FLOOR" IS THE FLOOR ABOVE GROUND LEVEL.

**The information in every
Dorling Kindersley Travel Guide is checked regularly.**
Every effort has been made to ensure that this book is as up-to-date
as possible at the time of going to press. Some details, however,
such as telephone numbers, opening hours, prices, gallery hanging
arrangements and travel information are liable to change. The
publishers cannot accept responsibility for any consequences arising from
the use of this book, nor for any material on third party websites, and
cannot guarantee that any website address in this book will be a
suitable source of travel information. We value the views and
suggestions of our readers very highly. Please write to:
Publisher, DK Eyewitness Travel Guides
Dorling Kindersley, 80 Strand, London, WC2R 0RL, Great Britain

◁ **Cala Morell, the most beautiful bay on the north coast of Menorca**

CONTENTS

**Baroque sundial in one of
Palma's palaces**

INTRODUCING THE BALEARIC ISLANDS

**Horse-cab ride through the streets
of the old town, Palma**

A sunny morning on the beach near S'Arenal harbour

A stall selling watermelons
at the weekly market in Inca

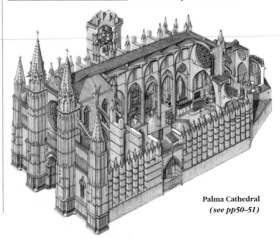
Palma Cathedral
(see pp50–51)

HOW TO USE THIS GUIDE

THIS GUIDE WILL HELP you to make the most of your visit to the Balearic Islands. The first section, Introducing the Balearic Islands, locates the islands geographically and gives an outline of its rich history and culture. Individual sections describe the main historic sights and star attractions on each of the four archipelago islands. Help with accommodation, restaurants, shopping, entertainment and many recreational activities can be found in the *Travellers' Needs* section, while the *Survival Guide* provides useful tips on everything you need to know, from money and language to getting around and seeking medical care.

THE BALEARIC ISLANDS AREA BY AREA

In this guide, each of the islands has been given its own chapter. Within each chapter there is an introduction, a pictorial map, and a detailed listing of all the best sights.

Colour-coded thumb tabs identify pages devoted to individual islands.

1 Introduction
This section provides a brief overview and history of each island, describing its history, geographical features and cultural characteristics as well as main tourist attractions.

A locator map indicates the position of the island within the archipelago.

2 Pictorial Map
This shows the main roads and topography of the island. It also locates all the sights that are later described in detail.

Boxes contain information about events and people associated with an area.

3 Detailed Information
All the important sights on the islands are described individually. The address, phone number, opening hours, admission charges, how to get there and disabled access are given for each sight.

4 Major Towns
At least two pages are devoted to each major town, with a detailed description of the historic remains and local curiosities that are worth seeing.

A Visitors' Checklist provides tourist and transport information, including opening hours of tourist attractions, admission charges, and details of local festivals and market days.

A Town Map shows the location of all the main sights within the town centre and provides tourist information on post offices and car parks.

5 Street-by-Street Map
This gives a bird's-eye view of a particularly interesting sightseeing area described in the section.

Photographs illustrate the most interesting areas and the most impressive sights within an attraction.

Tourist information details length of suggested tour plus good stopping places.

6 Star Sights
At least one page is dedicated to each major sight. Historic buildings are dissected to reveal their interiors, and parks are illustrated to show the main attractions.

Star Attractions point out the best sights or exhibits that no visitor should miss.

Cut-outs show the sight in its surroundings and some parts of the interior.

INTRODUCING THE BALEARIC ISLANDS

Putting the Balearic Islands on the Map

THIS LITTLE GROUP OF ISLANDS off the east coast of Spain is the Mediterranean's westernmost archipelago. An autonomous province, the Balearic Islands are 82 km (51 miles) from the Iberian Peninsula, a three-hour journey by ferry. The total area of the islands is slightly over 5,000 sq km (1,930 sq miles). Mallorca, the largest island, has an area of 3,640 sq km (1,405 sq miles). The smallest of the four main islands is Formentera.

Northern Coast of Mallorca
The northern shores of the Balearic Islands descend steeply via craggy cliffs. There are few beaches here, but cliff-top trails are highly recommended.

Bird's-eye View of Eivissa, Ibiza
The old town at the centre of Ibiza is particularly interesting when viewed from above. A bird's-eye view reveals its maze of narrow streets and the layout of the city walls.

Barcelona

Barcelona, Tarragona

SA DRAGONERA

Sóller

Palma

Andratx

Valencia, Alicante, Denia

IBIZA

Sant Antoni de Portmany

Santa Eulária des Riu

Eivissa

Formentera
El Mirador's restaurant terrace provides a stunning island view.

Valencia, Denia

La Savina

Sant Francesc

FORMENTERA

KEY

✈	Airport
▬	Motorway
▬	Major road
⚓	Ferry port
----	Ferry route

0 km   15

0 miles   15

◁ **Hill-top village of Deià, where writer Robert Graves once lived**

Rocky coast near Coves d'Artà in Mallorca

TOURIST PARADISE

It was in the early part of the 19th century that tourists first began to arrive on the Balearic Islands, and since that time the local economy has taken full advantage of the opportunities these new arrivals offered. Over 10 million visitors arrive every year to enjoy the islands' many attractions.

Mallorca, the largest island, is by far the most culturally rich, but the other islands are not short of attractions. Ibiza is famous as the clubbing capital of Europe; Menorca is an ideal resort for families, while those in search of peace and quiet head for Formentera.

Sweet and fragrant oranges from the Balearics

You may even spot the occasional celebrity – Annie Lennox, Claudia Schiffer and Michael Schumacher all have homes on Mallorca, while Elle MacPherson, Roman Polanski and Noel Gallagher (to name but a few) have opted for life on Ibiza. The Balearic Islands are also very popular with politicians and royalty, including the Spanish royal family with their summer residence in Palma.

The Balearics have many fascinating historic sights ranging from Neolithic remains and castle ruins to stunning cathedrals and fine examples of British colonial architecture. Gourmets can delight in the famous Menorcan cheeses and Mallorcan wines, as well as sample the products of the local distilleries, including gin (inherited from the English) and the potent Ibizan herbal liqueurs. The famous *Caldereta de llagosta* (Menorcan lobster stew) is not to be missed.

NATURAL TREASURES

The greatest riches of the archipelago are its landscape and natural beauty. The local authorities, hoping to

Portal of the main entrance to Palma's cathedral

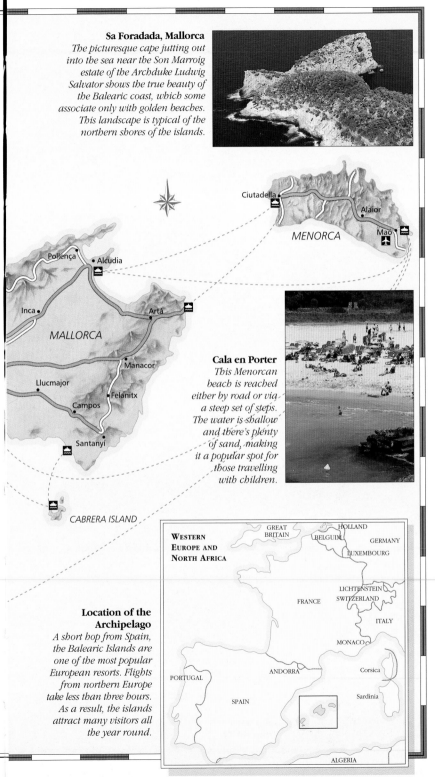

Sa Foradada, Mallorca
The picturesque cape jutting out into the sea near the Son Marroig estate of the Archduke Ludwig Salvator shows the true beauty of the Balearic coast, which some associate only with golden beaches. This landscape is typical of the northern shores of the islands.

Cala en Porter
This Menorcan beach is reached either by road or via a steep set of steps. The water is shallow and there's plenty of sand, making it a popular spot for those travelling with children.

Location of the Archipelago
A short hop from Spain, the Balearic Islands are one of the most popular European resorts. Flights from northern Europe take less than three hours. As a result, the islands attract many visitors all the year round.

WESTERN EUROPE AND NORTH AFRICA

A PORTRAIT OF THE BALEARIC ISLANDS

THE BALEARIC ISLANDS *are blessed by a hot Mediterranean sun that is tempered by cool sea breezes. Holidaymakers crowd onto the beaches every summer while the young make the most of the clubs and bars. Away from the resorts, time has moved at a gentler pace and inland the islands are quiet and undeveloped.*

An ideal staging post between Europe and Africa, these beautiful islands have had their fair share of invaders, including the Phoenicians and the Romans who made the islands part of their Empire. In recent times, the islands have fallen to a full-scale invasion of tourists, which began in the 1960s.

The islands' nightlife, particularly on Ibiza and Mallorca, is legendary and attracts a young crowd. There is far more on offer than clubs however, and if chic cafés are more your thing, the Balearic Islands can supply these too. Indeed, the islands have proved to be popular with the rich and famous, many of whom have homes on the hillsides, away from the prying lenses of the paparazzi.

A clay whistle from Mallorca

Even before the influx of tourists, the islands' climate attracted celebrities. The composer Frédéric Chopin journeyed to Mallorca with his lover George Sand in the winter of 1838–9. Other artists, including the painter and sculptor Joan Miró and the poet Robert Graves liked it so much that they settled down here.

Menorca is quieter than Mallorca or Ibiza. It has low-key resorts, golden beaches and rocky landscape that is rich in fascinating prehistoric remains.

Formentera, 4 km (2 miles) south of Ibiza, is the smallest of the Balearic Islands. Tourism is still light though the island's population doubles in the summer as daytrippers come to enjoy what is still a rural haven.

Cala Tarida on the western shores of Ibiza

◁ **Stone windmills and olive trees, typical features of the Mallorcan landscape**

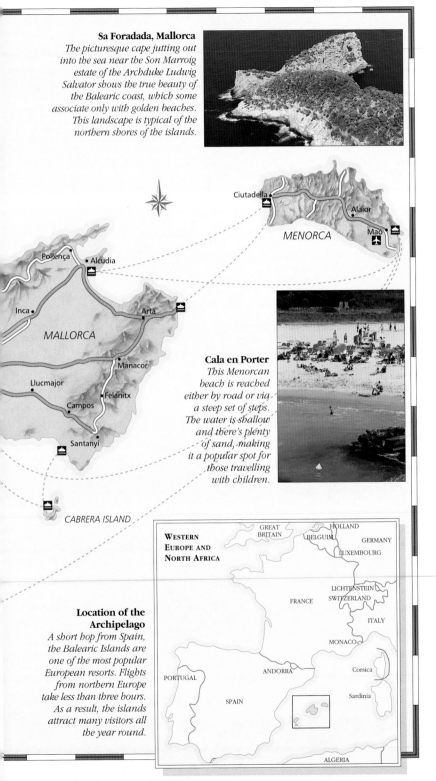

Sa Foradada, Mallorca
The picturesque cape jutting out into the sea near the Son Marroig estate of the Archduke Ludwig Salvator shows the true beauty of the Balearic coast, which some associate only with golden beaches. This landscape is typical of the northern shores of the islands.

Ciutadella

Alaior

MENORCA

Maó

Pollença

Alcudia

Inca

Artà

MALLORCA

Manacor

Llucmajor

Felanitx

Campos

Santanyí

Cala en Porter
This Menorcan beach is reached either by road or via a steep set of steps. The water is shallow and there's plenty of sand, making it a popular spot for those travelling with children.

CABRERA ISLAND

WESTERN EUROPE AND NORTH AFRICA

GREAT BRITAIN

HOLLAND

BELGIUM

GERMANY

LUXEMBOURG

LICHTENSTEIN
SWITZERLAND

FRANCE

ITALY

MONACO

ANDORRA

Corsica

PORTUGAL

SPAIN

Sardinia

Location of the Archipelago
A short hop from Spain, the Balearic Islands are one of the most popular European resorts. Flights from northern Europe take less than three hours. As a result, the islands attract many visitors all the year round.

ALGERIA

A PORTRAIT OF THE BALEARIC ISLANDS

THE BALEARIC ISLANDS *are blessed by a hot Mediterranean sun that is tempered by cool sea breezes. Holidaymakers crowd onto the beaches every summer while the young make the most of the clubs and bars. Away from the resorts, time has moved at a gentler pace and inland the islands are quiet and undeveloped.*

An ideal staging post between Europe and Africa, these beautiful islands have had their fair share of invaders, including the Phoenicians and the Romans who made the islands part of their Empire. In recent times, the islands have fallen to a full-scale invasion of tourists, which began in the 1960s.

A clay whistle from Mallorca

The islands' nightlife, particularly on Ibiza and Mallorca, is legendary and attracts a young crowd. There is far more on offer than clubs however, and if chic cafés are more your thing, the Balearic Islands can supply these too. Indeed, the islands have proved to be popular with the rich and famous, many of whom have homes on the hillsides, away from the prying lenses of the paparazzi.

Even before the influx of tourists, the islands' climate attracted celebrities. The composer Frédéric Chopin journeyed to Mallorca with his lover George Sand in the winter of 1838–9. Other artists, including the painter and sculptor Joan Miró and the poet Robert Graves, liked it so much that they settled down here.

Menorca is quieter than Mallorca or Ibiza. It has low-key resorts, golden beaches and a rocky landscape that is rich in fascinating prehistoric remains.

Formentera, 4 km (2 miles) south of Ibiza, is the smallest of the Balearic Islands. Tourism is still light though the island's population doubles in the summer as daytrippers come to enjoy what is still a rural haven.

Cala Tarida on the western shores of Ibiza

◁ **Stone windmills and olive trees, typical features of the Mallorcan landscape**

Rocky coast near Coves d'Artà in Mallorca

TOURIST PARADISE

It was in the early part of the 19th century that tourists first began to arrive on the Balearic Islands, and since that time the local economy has taken full advantage of the opportunities these new arrivals offered. Over 10 million visitors arrive every year to enjoy the islands' many attractions.

Mallorca, the largest island, is by far the most culturally rich, but the other islands are not short of attractions. Ibiza is famous as the clubbing capital of Europe; Menorca is an ideal resort for families, while those in search of peace and quiet head for Formentera.

Portal of the main entrance to Palma's cathedral

Sweet and fragrant oranges from the Balearics

You may even spot the occasional celebrity – Annie Lennox, Claudia Schiffer and Michael Schumacher all have homes on Mallorca, while Elle MacPherson, Roman Polanski and Noel Gallagher (to name but a few) have opted for life on Ibiza. The Balearic Islands are also very popular with politicians and royalty, including the Spanish royal family with their summer residence in Palma.

The Balearics have many fascinating historic sights ranging from Neolithic remains and castle ruins to stunning cathedrals and fine examples of British colonial architecture. Gourmets can delight in the famous Menorcan cheeses and Mallorcan wines, as well as sample the products of the local distilleries, including gin (inherited from the English) and the potent Ibizan herbal liqueurs. The famous *Caldereta de llagosta* (Menorcan lobster stew) is not to be missed.

NATURAL TREASURES

The greatest riches of the archipelago are its landscape and natural beauty. The local authorities, hoping to

King Juan Carlos, a frequent visitor to the Balearics

the English King Edward VII and the German Emperor Wilhelm II. This high-society tourism reached its peak in the 1930s, when the poet Adam Diehl built the luxurious Hotel Formentor on Pollença Bay. In the 1960s, Ibiza was "discovered" by hippies. Soon after, charter flights began operating to Mallorca. Mass tourism developed rapidly after the death of General Franco, in 1975.

In 1983, the islands became an autonomous region of Spain. The authorities made Catalan and its local dialects (*Mallorquín* on Mallorca, *Menorquín* on Menorca and *Eivissenc* on Ibiza) the joint official language with Spanish and introduced strict control of the local economy.

Following a string of environmental protest marches in 1998 and 1999 an "eco-tax" was introduced in 2002. The tax, levied on visitors to the islands, was intended to tackle some of the environmental havoc that had been wreaked by un-regulated tourism over the last 30 years. In its first year the tax's bene-fits included funding the demolishing of a number of unsightly hotels. The "eco-tax" was always controversial, however, and the government has finally decided to scrap it.

Bullfights *(corridas)*, popular in mainland Spain, enjoy more limited popularity in the Balearics. A bullfight can be seen in one of the arenas in Mallorca, but the standard of shows is not high.

The true local passion is *fútbol* (football). Real Mallorca, based in Palma, is one of the leading Spanish sides and won the 1998 Spanish Cup. It is worth attending a match, not just as a sporting event but to enjoy the good-natured enthusiasm of the crowd.

HIPPY MARKET
TODAS LAS NOCHES - EVERY NIGHT

Banner advertising a hippy market

Other sports strongly associated with the islands include yachting, windsurfing, horse riding and golf. Excellent golfing conditions exist in the islands, even in winter.

PRESENT-DAY BALEARICS
Once removed from the mainstream of international life, the Balearic Islands have now found themselves drawn in, thanks to tourism. Before World War I, they were visited by

Bullfight in the Mallorcan arena

Architecture of the Balearic Islands

T HE BALEARIC ISLANDS boast a rich and diverse architectural heritage. The sights worth seeing range from prehistoric chamber tombs to magnificent aristocratic mansions and palaces. Palma has the most to see, notably the fine Gothic cathedral which was renovated by Antoni Gaudí, while Menorca has many remains from the Talayotic period. Ibiza's houses, influenced by the Arabs, have inspired some of the greatest architects of the 20th century including Le Corbusier and Walter Gropius.

Main entrance to a residence in Els Calders in Mallorca

COUNTRY HOUSES

The typical village landscape is marked by low, often whitewashed houses. Built of the local stone, many have aged to a yellow-brown colour, blending with their surroundings. Thick walls and few openings ensure that the interior stays cool even on the hottest days. A farmstead often also includes some modest outbuildings; the whole surrounded by a garden and fields.

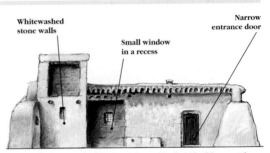

Whitewashed stone walls

Small window in a recess

Narrow entrance door

More modest homes are often adjoined by farm buildings, with a small granary on top. Village houses are almost always single-storey dwellings.

COUNTRY ESTATES

At the centre of each country estate was a fine *hacienda*. Their owners vied with each other by building ever more extravagant dwellings attesting to their wealth and importance. The interiors were furnished with magnificent furniture and paintings. The accommodation included formal apartments, private rooms and domestic quarters. Some are now available to rent as holiday lets.

Great country houses, such as La Granja on Mallorca's southwest coast, belonged to wealthy landowning families and were run according to a feudal system.

VILLAS

This form of architecture appeared on Mallorca in the 19th century. Villas, serving as summer residences, were built in line with the fashion of the day. Their numbers rose with the increasing popularity of the island.

Modern villas are often owned by the rich and famous. They stand in beautiful, secluded spots on many of the islands.

Old villas, with their delightful architecture, can be seen in many large town centres and in seaside resorts on Mallorca.

CHURCHES

Whitewashed churches are typical of Ibiza, although they can also be seen on Menorca and Formentera. Often they stand at the centre of the village or on a hillside at its outskirts. The entrance to the dark interior is usually preceded by a triple arcade.

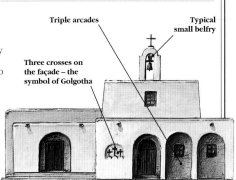

Triple arcades

Typical small belfry

Three crosses on the façade – the symbol of Golgotha

The belfry on a village church is usually a simple affair. It consists of a distinctive arcade rising above the façade, crowned with an iron cross and housing a bell.

A church is often adjoined by single-storey parish building or a vestry. It may be surrounded by a low stone wall and feature an enclosed forecourt.

WATCH TOWERS

The stone towers that can be seen along the coastline were built to protect the islands from attacks by pirates, mainly from North Africa, who raided the ports and inland towns. The towers stand in secluded, inaccessible spots, so that they could be easily defended. Most of the towers are deserted, and closed to visitors. A few are used as viewpoints.

Towers on Mallorca are slender. For extra protection, their entrances were high above the ground. Their walls feature narrow loop-holes.

Towers on other islands are lower. Built of stone, they resemble the fortresses built in the Canary Islands.

WINDMILLS OF THE BALEARIC ISLANDS

Stone-built windmills are another typical feature of the Balearic landscape. Early mills were used to grind grain; later they were used to pump water. Most stone-built mills are no longer in use and are slowly falling into disrepair. Some have lost their sails, and they now resemble watchtowers. Others have been converted into restaurants, with the machinery and millstones serving as tourist attractions.

Windmills were built mostly on the plains among green fields, and were used to grind corn or to drive the pumps of deep-water wells. Because they are cheaper to run than petrol-driven pumps, some farmers still use wind power to pump water even today.

Typical windmills were built near towns with food markets, and were used for grinding grain. Often the miller would actually live in the tower.

Handicrafts in the Balearic Islands

A hippy earring

CERAMICS ARE EXTREMELY POPULAR in the Balearic Islands, just as in the rest of Spain. One of the most characteristic items of Mallorcan handicrafts is the *siurell* – a statuette-whistle made of painted clay. Sa Cabaneta, one of the Mallorcan parishes, is known as "clay country" due to the large number of pottery workshops found there. Weaving and embroidery are also popular and leather goods are plentiful, especially in Menorca. Mallorca has become famous for its production of simulated pearls.

Ceramic lamps on display in one of Mallorca's markets

CERAMICS

THE ART OF MAKING pottery on the Balearic Islands goes back thousands of years. It was greatly influenced by the art of the Moors, who ruled the archipelago for several centuries.

The item you are most likely to see is the *siurell*, a statuette-whistle made of clay and painted white, with green and red decorations. It usually depicts a man sitting on a donkey or playing a guitar; but it can be styled as a bull, a dog, a peacock, a rooster or even the devil. The origin of the *siurell* is uncertain; already known in Moorish times, it was most likely inherited from the Phoenicians. The Spanish artist Joan Miró was particularly taken with these little toy whistles and drew inspiration from them. The

siurell was once a highly important item; a man would hand it to the lady of his choice – if she blew on it, it meant "yes", but if she put it aside it meant that the suitor had been rejected. The Fira dels Siurells, a lively fair held at the end of June in Sa Cabaneta, is dedicated to these clay whistles *(see p27)*.

Original ceramic products with distinctive yellow and green glazing are produced in Felanitx in Mallorca. At the busy Sunday market in this small town you can also buy blue-and-white bowls and jugs, decorated with floral or arabesque motifs.

In Pòrtol, near the small town of Santa Maria del Camí, there are a few remaining potters who produce bulging pots made

of red clay *(ollas)* and shallow bowls *(greixoneras)*.

In Ibiza, in the small village of Sant Rafael situated on the route from Eivissa to Sant Antoni de Portmany, there are many pottery workshops producing lovely bowls, vases and jugs based on ancient Carthaginian designs. Ceramic copies of terracotta figurines dating from the Punic era (3rd century BC) displayed in archaeological museums in Eivissa – particularly busts of women – are popular as souvenirs from Ibiza.

GLASSWARE

THE EARLIEST GLASS vessels found on the Balearic Islands date from Roman times. In the 16th century, glassware from Mallorca competed successfully with Venetian products. Even today, the best-selling products are copies of ancient designs.

Traditional condiment pot

There are three factories of artistic and household glass in Mallorca; the best known of these is the Can Gordiola glass museum near Algaida, on the road from Palma to Manacor. The oldest glassworks on the island, it has been run by the same family since 1719. Here, you can watch the glassblowers at work. Using

Clay pot production in a pottery workshop

long, thin pipes they can produce a variety of objects, from lovely small trinkets to large vases.

SIMULATED PEARLS

THE PRODUCTION METHOD for simulated pearls was patented in 1925 by Edward Heusch, a German engineer. The recipe for producing a thin bead-coating layer is kept secret to this day, for obvious reasons, though it is said to contain fish scales mixed with resin.

Three factories in Manacor and Montuïri produce these simulated pearls, which are of good quality and, to the untrained eye, virtually impossible to distinguish from the real thing.

The beads are immersed repeatedly in a liquid compound, which imitates the natural process of pearl production. Afterwards, each pearl is polished by hand and weighed. The production process can be seen during a visit to the factory. The factory shop sells them at much lower prices than those charged by shops elsewhere.

**Straw hat, popular
in the islands**

WOOD AND
WICKER PRODUCTS

ARTIFACTS MADE OF olive wood are very popular in the Balearic Islands and are distinguished by their rich colour and unusual grain. La Casa del Olivio, a shop in Palma, produces many household goods, such as bowls and mortars, as well as ornamental items and souvenirs.

The dwarf palm, or palmito, grows on many of the islands' mountain slopes. Its

Inside the Gordiola glass factory in Mallorca

leaves are used, particularly in Artà, to weave chair seats, baskets, bags and the soles of the *espadrille* or *alpargatas*. In addition, local craftsmen produce a wide variety of bags and baskets woven from strong grass or jute, and hats that are popular with the locals and tourists alike.

**An olive wood
household bowl**

OTHER LOCAL
PRODUCTS

THE BALEARIC ISLANDS, and Menorca in particular, are famous for their production of excellent footwear. In Menorca the centre of the leather industry is Ferreries. Here, you can buy relatively inexpensive shoes, bags and leather clothes. It is worth taking a closer look at some of the sandal designs, which are unique to this island. In Mallorca the cheapest place to buy leather products is Inca.

Weaving and embroidery have a long local history. The traditional *robes de llengues* – print-decorated heavy linen fabrics – are often found in Mallorcan homes, even today. They are sometimes used for curtains and

bedspreads, wall linings and furniture upholstery.

Clothes imitating hippy fashions from the 1960s are still in vogue, and designs produced in this style continue to create a stir at the annual fashion shows. The three-day fashion show Moda Ad Lib is held in June, at Passeig de Vara de Rey, in Eivissa, Ibiza. Clothes that are shown here can later be bought in Eivissa's fashionable boutiques – at high prices.

Traditional gold and silver jewellery has been produced in the islands for centuries. Less fashionable now, it is almost exclusively used as an addition to folk costumes. Similar to the fashion in clothes, the designs of gold jewellery are inspired largely by hippy culture. Silver and metal items can be bought at "hippy markets", particularly in Ibiza and Formentera.

A cobbler at work

Landscape and Wildlife of the Balearic Islands

THANKS TO THE HUGE variety of habitats, from mountains and cliffs to sandy beaches and wide plains, the Balearics have a wide diversity of wildlife including some rare birds and reptiles. Mallorca's characteristic terrain is *garrigue*, an open scrubland, interspersed with small pockets of forest. At higher altitudes the scrub is replaced by *maquis* – a mix of mainly rosemary, broom and laurel. Menorca, in particular, is noted for its wild flowers and shrubs while large swathes of Ibiza are covered by forests of pine.

Lilac crocus flower

The craggy cliffs, sharp-edged and forbidding, appear inaccessible. Consisting of limestone, they are sparsely covered with vegetation.

Forests are rare on the islands. The largest woodland areas can be found in Mallorca. These are mainly pine forests, featuring Aleppo pine mixed with holm oak.

Olive groves are seen mainly in Mallorca, inland as well as near the coastline. Tree trunks and boughs are sometimes twisted into curious shapes.

The northern shores *of the islands are mostly steep and craggy. Inland, the vegetation is dense and lush. There are few beaches and those that are accessible are rocky or pebbly. The northern shores have been less affected by tourism, and provide stunning views as well as excellent natural areas to explore.*

BALEARIC LANDSCAPE

Of all the Balearic Islands, Mallorca's landscape is the most diverse. As well as its many secluded coves, it has magnificent green plains and the Serra de Tramuntana mountain range.

Cove beaches *are one of the features that make the islands so attractive. Some are now resorts. Others can be difficult to reach, but their soft sands, gentle waves and clear water attract a steady supply of visitors.*

High mountains are found only in the northern part of Mallorca. Puig Major – the highest peak in the Serra de Tramuntana – rises to a height of 1,445 m (4,740 ft).

FLORA

There are some 1,500 species of flowering plant on the islands, of which 50 or so are native. Some of them grow only in Mallorca and the Cabrera archipelago. Most flower in spring and at this time the islands are a blaze of colour. For the rest of the year, the islands are green, but the sun-bleached foliage is no longer quite so lush.

Common broom is typical of Mediterranean flora. Its bright yellow flowers, which blossom in March, can be seen from afar.

Small foxglove, with its distinctive, thimble-like flower, is a highly ornamental plant. It is one of the plants native to the Balearic Islands. Few people realize that the species is also poisonous.

Holm oak is widespread throughout the islands. Its tough, evergreen leaves protect it against water loss.

Coves with sandy beaches are typical of the Balearic Islands' landscape.

Macchia, an evergreen shrub, grows on the rocky mountain slopes.

FAUNA OF THE BALEARIC ISLANDS

Fauna on the Balearic Islands includes a handful of native species, such as the rare Lilford's wall lizard. The islands are also home to some rare species of birds, including the black vulture, rock falcon and the Balearic shearwater. Several smaller mammals such as rabbits and hedgehogs are commonplace in the lowlands of the archipelago.

The Lilford's wall lizard is one of the few endemic species living on the islands.

The Silver gull is the most common bird inhabiting the coastal regions of the archipelago.

Rabbits have easily adapted to the wide variety of landscapes on the islands, particularly since they have no natural predators.

The Underwater World

SOME FOUR MILLION YEARS AGO, the Balearic archipelago was joined to the continent. The sinking seabed caused the islands to become separated from the mainland by the Balearic Sea. The coastline is topographically varied, featuring sandy beaches with shallows stretching far out into the sea, and cliffs with distinct layers of rock, full of cracks, niches and caves. Facing them, rising up from the sea, are small rocky islands and solitary rocks created by sea abrasion. In the coastal and offshore waters there is a rich variety of marine life.

Cardinal fish *live in small shoals. The tiny red fish can be seen mostly among sea grass or hiding near the entrances to underwater caves and grottoes.*

MARINE SPECIES

The waters surrounding the archipelago are too cold for coral reefs. The only variety found here is the soft gorgonia. The sea grass meadows are home to a variety of animals, from lugworms to fish. The rocky sea bed supports the richest variety of life. Here, you will find varieties of molluscs, starfish, lobster and fish – from the smallest goby to the giant grouper.

Ray fish eggs   **Cuttle-fish shells**   **Sea grass**   **Shark eggs**

The great pipefish *hides among sea grass. It feeds on small marine animals, including crustaceans and fry, which it sucks in with its long snout. Pipefish eggs hatch inside the male's pouch.*

Sea horse

Psi shark

The cuttle-fish *is a predator that uses its long tentacles to catch its prey. It hunts while swimming or lying buried in the sand, almost invisible to its victim. The cuttle-fish can change its colour to blend in with the background. When threatened, it ejects an inky fluid that disorientates the attacker.*

Pinna are huge, long-lived molluscs that dig into the sand with the sharp end of their shells.

Starfish *inhabit the coastal regions of the Balearic Islands, up to a depth of 35 m (115 ft). They live mainly on the rocky bottom, and are conspicuous by their red colour.*

The Lilford's wall lizard *can be seen everywhere, even close to beaches, in dry, sunny places. There are 22 known subspecies, which are spread throughout the archipelago.*

The Balearic shearwater*, also known as the "Moresque shearwater", is a common sight. It gathers food by sitting on the water and catching crustaceans, squid and small fish. The shearwater is native to the Balearic Islands and nests in large colonies.*

The Mediterranean monk seal was once a common sight in the archipelago but is now almost extinct.

Red clingfish *have no scales and attach themselves to the surfaces of rocks with a sucker situated between their ventral fins.*

The Haliotis clam prefers rocky bottoms close to the shore. This primitive snail is highly valued by gourmets.

The species of moray *found in the Mediterranean has no venom, but its bite can be dangerous. Hidden amid rocks, it springs surprise attacks, feeding on fish and crustaceans.*

Mediterranean scallop

Gorgonia

Link wrasse

Amarela

The slipper lobster *is not as common as the cicada lobster, which is twice its size. Its body is covered with a hard shell and is armed with spikes, while its antennae have evolved into short, wide plates.*

The Dusky grouper *is, despite its fearsome size, a gentle fish. Because of this, and its sheer bulk, it presents an easy target for spear-fishing.*

THE BALEARIC ISLANDS THROUGH THE YEAR

Children enjoying a fiesta in Mallorca

THE INHABITANTS OF the Balearic Islands are deeply attached to their traditions, a fact that is reflected in the many religious feast days, or fiestas, they celebrate. Fiestas are generally associated with the cult of saints, particularly the patron of the local parish or the island. Though mostly religious, fiestas are an opportunity for people to enjoy themselves, with parades, music and much dancing.

The most spectacular of these is the Festa de Sant Joan, which has been celebrated in Ciutadella, Menorca, since medieval times. In the resorts, fiestas are less conspicuous, but elsewhere everybody joins in the fun. During the fiesta, normal life stops and only minimal bus services run. It is also difficult to find hotel accommodation, so book in advance. Tourist information offices can provide details of local fiestas.

Princess Sofia Cup yachting regatta

Almond blossom in early spring in Mallorca

SPRING

WITH THE ADVENT of spring, life in Spain moves out into the streets, and the café terraces fill with guests. This is a very beautiful time of year. Before the arrival of the summer heat, trees, flowers and wild herbs burst into flower. The famous Semana Santa (Holy Week) before Easter is a time of religious processions.

MARCH

Semana Santa
On Maundy Thursday in Palma, a procession leaves the church of La Sang at Plaça de Hospital, carrying a crucifix. On Good Friday,

solemn processions are held in many towns, including Palma and Sineu (Mallorca) and Maó (Menorca). The sombre ceremony of laying in the tomb (*Davallament*) is held at the church of Nostra Senyora del Àngels, in Pollença. In Monastir de Lluc the faithful conduct a penitential Way of the Cross.

APRIL

Festa Sant Francesc (*2 Apr*). The popular feast of St Francis is celebrated throughout the islands, in parishes of which the saint is the patron.
Festa Sant Jordi (*23 Apr*). Feast day of the patron saint of many towns and villages, celebrated on all the islands.
Princess Sofia Trophy, Palma. One of the most important yachting regattas in the Balearic Islands.

MAY

Festa de Maig (*1st Sun in May*), Santa Eulàlia, Ibiza. This springtime flower festival is one of the most colourful and beautiful fiestas in the Balearic Islands.
Festa de Nostra Senyora de la Victòria (*2nd Sun in May*), Sóller and Port de Sóller, Mallorca. Mock battles pit Christian against Moor, and are staged to mark the raid by Turkish pirates, on 11 May 1561.
Eivissa Medieval (*2nd Sun in May*), Eivissa, Ibiza. A new festival to celebrate the declaration of Dalt Vila as a World Heritage site in 1992 with dancing and concerts.
Festa de Primavera de Manacor (*27 May*), Manacor. Spring Festival, the most important festival in Manacor, lasting until early June.

AVERAGE DAILY HOURS OF SUNSHINE

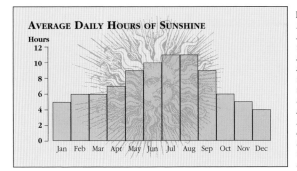

Hours

12
10
8
6
4
2
0

Jan Feb Mar Apr May Jun Jul Aug Sep Oct Nov Dec

Hours of Sunshine
During July and August, there are nearly 11 hours of sunshine daily. Not surprisingly, these months coincide with the peak of the tourist season. Fewer sunny days occur in November, December and January. At this time of the year the islands are at their least attractive.

SUMMER

JUNE MARKS THE beginning of the peak tourist season in the Balearic Islands, which will last until September. It is ushered in by numerous cultural events, including concerts, festivals and folk group performances. The latter half of summer features various fiestas associated with gathering the harvest.

Beaches of Cala Millor, in Mallorca, crowded with holidaymakers

Festa de Nostra Senyora de la Victòria in Sóller

JUNE

Corpus Christi, Pollença, Mallorca. The Dance of Eagles, performed in the main square of the town, is followed by a procession.
Sant Antoni de Juny *(13 Jun)*, Artà, Mallorca. A local feast featuring parades of people dressed as horses.
Sant Joan *(24 Jun)*, Ciutadella, Menorca. King Juan Carlos's name day. Horses are a major feature.

At its climax the horses rear up and the crowd attempts to support them.
Romeria de Sant Marçal *(30 Jun)*, Sa Cabeneta, Mallorca. A fair where they sell *siurells*. Similar fairs are also held in Campos, Sineu, Felanitx and Manacor.

JULY

Día de Virgen de Carmen *(15–16 Jul)*. The feast of the patron saint of sailors and fishermen, celebrated all over the islands with parades and a blessing of the fishing boats.
Passejada dies Bou i Carro Triunfal *(27–28 Jul)*, Valldemossa, Mallorca. The feast of Catalina Thomàs. A bull is led through the streets of this small town, followed the next day by a procession of carts, with one girl playing the role of St Catalina.

AUGUST

Copa del Rey *(1st wk in Aug)*, Palma, Mallorca. International yachting regattas held under the patronage of King Juan Carlos.

Sant Ciriac *(8 Aug)*, Ibiza, Formentera. A feast commemorating the Spanish recapture of these islands.
Festa de Sant Lorenç *(2nd wk in Aug)*, Alaior, Menorca. Riding displays in the streets.
Assumption of the Virgin *(15 Aug)*. A festival celebrated throughout Spain.
Sant Bartomeu *(24 Aug)*. Horse races in Capdepera; devil dances in Montuïri.
Sant Agustín *(28 Aug)* Felanitx, Mallorca. A joyful fiesta in honour of St Augustine, with dancing and horse-riding shows.

Busy fruit stalls at Pollença market in Mallorca

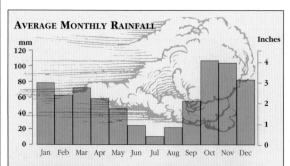

AVERAGE MONTHLY RAINFALL

Rainfall
The lowest rainfall is in July; the highest between October and December. Storms are rare in the summer. Visitors should bear in mind that in the mountainous regions clouds may be thicker and rain more frequent than in the coastal areas.

Procession with crops, during Festa des Vermar in Binissalem

AUTUMN

AFTER THE summer scorchers, autumn brings cool air and rain. With the passing of the peak holiday season, the resorts empty out. Harvest fiestas continue and the wine festivals come to the fore, particularly in Binissalem, Mallorca. The first juice extracted from the grape harvest is blessed and in some places wine is served free.

SEPTEMBER

Processió de la Beata *(1st Sun in Sep)*, Santa Margalida, Mallorca. A procession of floats and people dressed in folk costumes honouring Sant Catalina – known as *beata* – the blessed one.
Diada de Catalunya *(11 Sep)*. Catalonian National Holiday throughout the islands, marking the occasion, in 1714, when Felipe V became ruler of Catalonia and the region lost its autonomy.

Festa des Vermar *(last Sun in Sep)*, Binissalem, Mallorca. A grape-harvest festival with floats and open-air concerts.
Festa des Meló *(last Sun in Sep)*, Vilafranca de Bonany, Mallorca. Watermelon Festival, marking the end of harvest.

OCTOBER

Día de la Hispanidad *(12 Oct)*. Spanish National Holiday celebrating the

Es Vedrà on the coast of Ibiza, shrouded in clouds

discovery of the "New World" by Christopher Columbus, in 1492.
La Beateta *(16 Oct)*. Fancy-dress procession in Palma. Fairs in Alcúdia, Campos, Felanitx, Porreres and Llucmajor. Raft races in Porto Portals.
Festa de Virgin *(21 Oct)*, Palma. Festival where enormous quantities of *buñelos de vientyo* cakes are consumed and young people sing serenades in honour of Santa Ursula and the 11,000 virgins.
Festa dies Butifarró *(3rd Sun in Oct)*, Sant Joan, Mallorca. This fairly recent festival includes dancing and music to accompany the eating of large amounts of sausages *(berenada de butifarra)* and vegetable pies *(coca amb trampó)*.

NOVEMBER

Todos los Santos *(1 Nov)*. All Saints' Day and the following day – *Día dels difunts* (All Souls) – are a time when people visit the graves of relatives and friends.
Sant Carles *(4 Nov)*, Ibiza. Patron saint's day, celebrated throughout the island.
Dijous Bó *(3rd Thu in Nov)*, Inca, Mallorca. Important agricultural feast in Mallorca, featuring fairs and revelry.
Birthday of Junipero Serra *(24 Nov)*. Celebrated throughout the archipelago as the birthday of this Franciscan monk who founded the cities of San Diego, Los Angeles and San Francisco *(see p77)*.

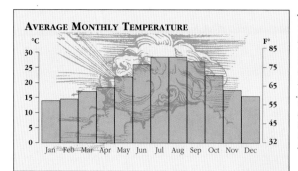

AVERAGE MONTHLY TEMPERATURE

°C / F°
Jan Feb Mar Apr May Jun Jul Aug Sep Oct Nov Dec

Temperature
Temperatures in the Balearic Islands rarely fall below zero. This happens only occasionally in December and early January. For this reason, many people enjoy out-of-season visits. Summer temperatures may soar to 40° C (104° F).

WINTER

THE BALEARIC WINTER is not particularly severe. Nights are cold, but days are often sunny and mild. Christmas is a time of special celebration throughout Spain, with families gathering to participate in religious festivities.

Working in the fields during early spring

DECEMBER

Noche Buena *(24 Dec)*. Christmas Eve is celebrated within the family circle, and often includes midnight mass. Numerous nativity plays and scenes are organized in Palma. **Santos Inocentes** *(28 Dec)*. The Spanish equivalent of Britain's April Fool's day. **Festa de l'Estandard** *(31 Dec)*, Palma, Mallorca.

Feast commemorating the town's conquest by Jaume I, in 1229.

JANUARY

Revelta i Beneídes de Sant Antoni Abat *(16–17 Jan)*, Mallorca. Fiesta with bonfires, parades and the blessing of animals. People wander between the bonfires, dressed in costumes, dancing and consuming large quantities of eel and vegetable pies. **Processo dels Tres Tocs** *(17 Jan)*, Ciutadella, Menorca. The Procession of the Three Strikes marks the victory of Alfonso III over the Muslims, in 1287. **Festa de Sant Sebastià** *(20 Jan)*, Pollença, Mallorca. Procession carrying a banner with the image of the saint and with two dancers, called *cavallets*, mounting wooden horses.

FEBRUARY

Carnival Parades *(Feb/Mar)*. Fancy dress balls marking the end of Carnival, before Lent. The most

Carnival in Palma, Mallorca

spectacular fiesta, called *Sa Rua* (the Cavalcade), takes place in Palma and its surrounding resorts.

PUBLIC HOLIDAYS

Año Nuevo *New Year's Day (1 Jan)*
Día de Reyes *Epiphany (6 Jan)*
Jueves Santo *Maundy Thursday (Mar/Apr)*
Viernes Santo *Good Friday (Mar/Apr)*
Día de Pascua *Easter (Mar/Apr)*
Fiesta de Trabajo *Labour Day (1 May)*
Corpus Christi *(early Jun)*
Asuncíon *Assumption of the Virgin (15 Aug)*
Día de la Hispanidad *National Day (12 Oct)*
Todos los Santos *All Saints' Day (1 Nov)*
Día de la Constitución *Constitution Day (6 Dec)*
Inmaculada Concepción *Immaculate Conception (8 Dec)*
Navidad *Christmas Day (25 Dec)*

Autumn fishing from a traditional Balearic boat

THE HISTORY OF THE BALEARIC ISLANDS

T HE BALEARIC ISLANDS *were often a target for conquest and this turbulent history has left behind numerous reminders. Consecutive waves of raiders continually destroyed the heritage of their predecessors and it was not until the conquest of the islands by Jaume I, in 1229, that a period of relative stability began. But even the centuries that followed were not a period of calm.*

EARLIEST INHABITANTS

The earliest inhabitants of the Balearic Islands probably arrived from the Iberian Peninsula. Archaeological findings indicate that the islands were occupied by 4000 BC. Archaeological remains include flint tools, primitive pottery and artifacts made of horn, giving evidence that these early settlers were shepherds and hunters. As well as herding sheep, the earliest inhabitants of the Balearic Islands hunted the local species of mountain goat *(Myotragus balearicus)*, now extinct. Most archaeological finds were discovered in caves, which were used for shelter and also for ritual burials. The best-preserved complex of caves, developed and extended by the Talayotic settlers, are the Cales Coves discovered near Calla en Porter, in Menorca.

The Beaker ware found in Deià, in Mallorca, represents a style known throughout Western Europe. Beaker People are so named because of their custom of placing pottery

Terracotta bust dating from the Punic era

beakers in graves. The representatives of this culture were capable of producing excellent bronze tools and artifacts. They appeared in the islands around 2300 BC.

TALAYOTIC PERIOD

The mysterious structures made of giant stones found on the islands date from around 1300 BC. The most typical of the time, which also gave the period its name, is the *talayot* derived from the Arabic word *atalaya* meaning observation tower. These structures appear in greatest numbers in Menorca, with somewhat fewer in Mallorca. None has been found in Ibiza. Other common sights are *taulas* and *navetas (see p99)*. In southern Europe similar structures can be found only in Sardinia *(nuraghi)*.

These early inhabitants of the islands represented a relatively advanced civilization. Some of them lived in fortified settlements, such as Capocorb Vell, Mallorca, where over 30 stone houses and four massive *talayots* have been found.

TIMELINE

4000 BC Human occupation well established on the Balearic Islands	2300 BC Beaker culture flourishes in the Iberian Peninsula	1300 BC Beginning of the Talayotic civilization; development of Cales Coves

6000 BC	4000 BC	3000 BC	2000 BC

Around 5000 BC Probable arrival of man can be dated from finds around Sóller and Valldemossa

Arrowhead dating from the Talayotic era

◁ **A painting of Maó harbour, Menorca, in the early 19th century**

Figurine, 5th century BC, from Torralba d'en Salord

PHOENICIANS, GREEKS AND CARTHAGINIANS

The Phoenicians arrived in the islands in the early part of the 1st millennium BC. They founded a trading settlement, Sanisera, on the northern coast of Menorca. Two hundred years later, the islands attracted the attention of the Greeks, who were exploring the western regions of the Mediterranean. The Greeks did not settle in the Balearics, as they lacked the metal ores that would have made the islands suitable for colonization. They were also discouraged by the hostile reception from the local inhabitants. But the archipelago owes its name to the Greeks. It derives from the Greek word *ballein* (to throw from a sling). The islanders were famed as outstanding sling-shots and, more than once, made life a misery for various raiders.

The Carthaginians also took an interest in trade in the western region of the

Clay oil lamp from Roman times

Mediterranean. Carthaginian sailors started to explore the Balearic Islands in the early 7th century BC. In 654, they took Ibiza, where they founded the fortified capital of Eivissa (the famous Carthaginian general, Hannibal, was born on Ibiza). After conquering the entire archipelago, they founded new towns, including Jamna (Ciutadella) and Maghen Maó in Menorca.

The Balearic Islands played a strategic role during the Punic Wars. Following their defeat at Zama in 202 BC, the Carthiginians were crushed. Soon afterwards, they left Mallorca and Menorca but remained in Ibiza for a further 70 years.

ROMAN EMPIRE AND BYZANTIUM

The Romans conquered Ibiza in 146 BC. Meanwhile, the inhabitants of Mallorca and Menorca, taking advantage of the political upheavals, turned to piracy. This lasted until 123 BC, when the Roman Consul Quintus Metellus occupied the islands. He was awarded the honorary title of *Balearico* for his

Ruins of the Christian basilica in Son Bou, Menorca

TIMELINE

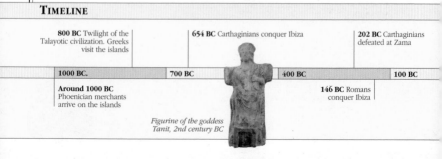

800 BC Twilight of the Talayotic civilization. Greeks visit the islands

654 BC Carthaginians conquer Ibiza

202 BC Carthaginians defeated at Zama

| 1000 BC. | 700 BC | 400 BC | 100 BC |

Around 1000 BC Phoenician merchants arrive on the islands

146 BC Romans conquer Ibiza

Figurine of the goddess Tanit, 2nd century BC

deeds. Roman rule lasted for over 500 years and the islands were renamed: Balearis Major (Mallorca), Balearis Minor (Menorca) and Ebusus (Ibiza). The *Pax Romana* brought prosperity: Roman settlers planted vineyards, built roads and founded Palmeria and Pollentia, a settlement near Alcúdia in Mallorca. They also founded Portus Magonis (Maó) in Menorca, which subsequently became the island's capital and extended the Phoenician port, Sanisera, making it one of the biggest harbours of the empire.

A mosaic from the Calvià library, Mallorca, showing the conquest of Mallorca by Arabs in 904

By the 3rd century AD, the expansion of Christianity had begun on the islands. Roman rule was already in decline when, in 425, the Vandals invaded and destroyed both the Roman and Christian cultural heritages.

Subsequently, the Byzantine army led by Belisarius expelled the Vandal tribes from the Balearic Islands. For over 100 years the islands remained within the sphere of influence of the Byzantine Empire. This ensured their stability until the declining empire came under attack from the Arabs.

THE MOORS

The conquest of Menorca and Mallorca by the Emir of Cordoba at the beginning of the 10th century marks the beginning of Moorish influence over the islands, which lasted for more than three centuries. During this period the Muslims transformed the Balearic Islands, introducing new irrigation techniques, planting crops like rice and cotton and, on terraced hillsides, oranges, limes and olives. In 1114, Muslim rule was interrupted when an army of 70,000 Italian and Catalan soldiers attacked Ibiza and Mallorca. Supported by the pope, the Christian troops slaughtered most of the Muslims and set sail, filling their ships with spoils. The Moors quickly re-established themselves, however, and flourished once again under the rule of the Almoravids, a Berber dynasty from North Africa. Reminders of Moorish presence on the islands include the agricultural terraces, architecture and designs for embroidery and ceramics.

Arab Bath in Palma, one of few surviving relics of Muslim culture on the islands

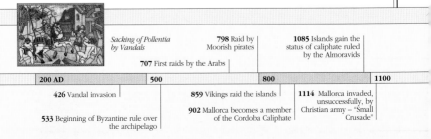

	Sacking of Pollentia by Vandals	**798** Raid by Moorish pirates	**1085** Islands gain the status of caliphate ruled by the Almoravids	
		707 First raids by the Arabs		
200 AD	**500**	**800**		**1100**
	426 Vandal invasion	**859** Vikings raid the islands	**1114** Mallorca invaded, unsuccessfully, by Christian army – "Small Crusade"	
	533 Beginning of Byzantine rule over the archipelago	**902** Mallorca becomes a member of the Cordoba Caliphate		

JAUME I

In September 1229, on the beach near Santa Ponça, Mallorca, the Catalan King Jaume I, later known as "El Conqueridor", landed with his army, which consisted of 16,000 soldiers and 1,500 cavalry. The pretext for the attack was the seizure of several Catalan vessels by the Emir of Mallorca. In the ensuing battle, Jaume I captured the capital and conquered the entire island. In 1232, he returned to Mallorca with a handful of soldiers. From there he sent delegates to Menorca, who were to negotiate a surrender. Meanwhile, Jaume I built a camp on the mountain slopes near Capdepera. In the evening he ordered numerous bonfires to be lit, to look as

Cross in Santa Ponça, marking Jaume I's conquest

though a large army was preparing to attack. The ruse worked and the Moors surrendered Menorca to the king, who left them to rule the island as his vassals.

In 1230, Jaume I had issued the *Carta de Població* (People's Charter), which encouraged Catalans to settle on the conquered islands, granting them exemption from taxes and guaranteeing equality before the law to all its citizens. Special privileges were granted to the Jews, in an effort to stimulate trade. After the king's death, his successors fought for the inheritance, which was finally won by Alfonso III.

ALFONSO AND HIS SUCCESSORS

Despite being nicknamed "The Liberal", Alfonso III massacred the rebels of Palma and the remaining fortresses after he had conquered them, a bloody deed that led to his excommunication from the Catholic church. Worse was to follow. In 1287, Alfonso III's army attacked and conquered Menorca. The Moslem defenders were sold into slavery or slaughtered. Medina Menurqua was renamed Ciutadella and its mosques turned into churches or destroyed. Following the death of Alfonso III in 1291 at the age of 25, Jaume II took control of Mallorca and Menorca. Jaume II, who had been crowned king of Mallorca and Menorca in 1276 before being deposed by Alfonso III, was an altogether more enlightened ruler. He and his successors presided over a "Golden Age" that saw great advances including the building of the Castell de Bellver and Palau de

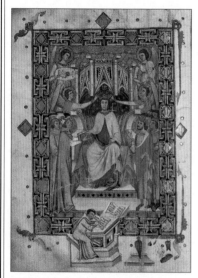

Miniature with the image of Jaume I

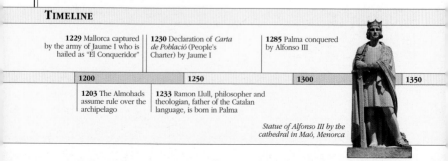

L'Almudaina, the establishment of a weekly market in Palma and the reintroduction of gold and silver coinage to stimulate trade. The next ruler of the archipelago was Jaume II's son, Sancho, who built a strong fleet to defend the islands against pirates. After his death, in 1324, control passed into the hands of his nephew, Jaume III, whose two-decade reign also marked a period of great prosperity. The "Golden Age" came to an abrupt end in 1344 when an Aragonese conquest, led by Pedro IV, landed on Mallorca and took it in only a week. The islands of Menorca and Ibiza soon suffered the same fate.

Painting of Saint George slaying the dragon, by Francesca Comesa

armed conflict. The economic position of the Balearic Islands was worsened further by the discovery and colonization of the Americas at the end of the 15th century, which shifted the hub of European trade to the shores of the Atlantic Ocean. This downturn led, in 1521, to a bloody revolt by peasants and craftsmen in Mallorca, which ended in the slaughter of many of the nobility and their supporters.

Throughout the 16th and 17th centuries, there were frequent pirate attacks. Many of the islands' fortifications date from this period including Eivissa's surviving defences and Maó's Fort San Felipe.

DECLINE AND FALL

Now part of the kingdom of Aragón, the Balearic Islands found themselves to be outside major politics. The economy soon suffered as a result of high taxes and in 1391 Mallorca was the scene of an uprising by the poorest parts of the community. In Menorca, the rivalry between Ciutadella and Maó ended in

Ideal fortification layout of 16th-century Palma

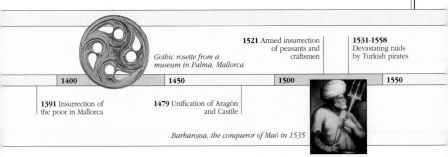

Gothic rosette from a museum in Palma, Mallorca

1521 Armed insurrection of peasants and craftsmen

1531-1558 Devastating raids by Turkish pirates

| 1400 | 1450 | 1500 | 1550 |

1391 Insurrection of the poor in Mallorca

1479 Unification of Aragón and Castile

Barbarossa, the conqueror of Maó in 1535

Junipero Serra setting up a mission in California

UNDER BRITISH AND FRENCH RULE

During the 17th century, Menorca's harbours became the subject of Anglo-French rivalry. In 1708 the British occupied Maó's harbour, and subsequently the whole of Menorca. In 1756, the island was captured by the French, although they soon returned it to the British, in 1763, in exchange for Cuba and the Philippines. The government of the island changed hands several more times until, finally, in 1802, Menorca was handed over to Spain. The town of Sant Lluís, founded by the French, stands as a reminder of French rule.

The British colonial legacy on Menorca includes the building of the garrison town of Georgetown (now known as Villacarlos) and major improvements to the roads. The choice of Maó as Menorca's capital is thanks to the British governor, Richard Kane. Reminders of Georgian architecture, including the sash windows in Hanover Street, Maó, can still be seen today.

Composer Frédéric Chopin

THE 19TH CENTURY

The 19th century proved extremely difficult for the islands. The inhabitants were plagued by periods of famine and epidemics, Spanish was declared the official language, and many inhabitants of the Balearic Islands decided to emigrate. During the 19th century the islands acquired scheduled links with Barcelona and Valencia and the situation began to improve. In 1838, Chopin visited Mallorca and in 1867 Archduke Ludwig Salvator *(see p68)* settled here. At the same time, the development of agriculture, particularly almond-growing in Mallorca, and footwear production in Menorca led to a rise in the standard of living. Catalan culture was also becoming popular and *Modernista* buildings, including designs by Antoni Guadí, began to appear in Palma and other town centres.

FRANCO'S DICTATORSHIP

During the Spanish Civil War (1936–39), which spread as far as Morocco, the Balearic Islands were

Monument to the pirates defending Ibiza

TIMELINE

1652 Islands devastated by horrific plague	**1713** Juniper Serra born in the small town of Petra, in Mallorca		**1756** Menorca conquered by the French

1600 — **1660** — **1720** — **1780**

Baroque stone tablet from 1672

1708 Menorca conquered by the British

1763 British regain Menorca

1802 Menorca passes into the hands of the Spanish

divided. Mallorca became an important base for the Fascists, while Menorca and Ibiza declared themselves for the Republicans. In retaliation, Italian planes bombed Ibiza. Menorca was the last stronghold of the Republicans.

Following a peace deal, negotiated with the help of the British, 450 refugees left the island aboard *HMS Devonshire*, and the island was left under the

Monument at Monte Toro for those killed in Morocco in 1925

control of Franco. Formentera, which had backed the Republicans, became the site of a concentration camp established by the Fascists, where some 1,400 people were imprisoned. Throughout the entire 40 years of Franco's dictatorship, the Catalan language and culture were suppressed, as elsewhere on the mainland.

MODERN TIMES

After Franco's death in 1975, a process of decentralization began. In 1983, the inhabitants of the islands succeeded in creating the Comunidad Autónoma de las Islas Baleares, and the islands became an autonomous region. This led to the introduction of Catalan in schools and offices and greater control of the local economy. Most of the money earned by the islands now remains here and is reinvested locally.

Initially, the most important factor driving the local economy was tourism. Where the hippies led, others followed. In 1966 Mallorca received one million tourists. By 2000 this number had grown to eight million and the islands, so poor until fairly recently, now boast the highest income per capita in the whole of Spain. This economic achievement has come at a price. Large numbers of foreigners, mainly German and British, have settled here, pushing up the cost of real estate, while the construction of a number of poor quality resorts has left a blot on the islands' otherwise idyllic landscape. Many jobs on the island are now seasonal and there has been a general decline in traditional forms of employment. Factors such as these gave rise to a growing environmental movement and the introduction of an "eco tax" *(see p17)*, designed to sustain the islands' tourism. The tax has recently been scrapped.

Hippy in colourful head gear

Mallorcan beaches filled with tourists

Archduke Ludwig Salvator

1926 Argentinian poet Adan Diehl opens the Hotel Formentor

1975 Death of General Francisco Franco

1983 Creation of the Autonomous Community of the Balearic Islands

| 1840 | 1900 | 1960 | 2020 |

1867 Mallorca visited by Habsburg Archduke Ludwig Salvator, subsequent promoter of the island

1936-1939 Spanish Civil War

1950 The first charter plane, from Germany, lands in Mallorca

Tourists in a hotel bar

THE BALEARIC ISLANDS AREA BY AREA

The Balearic Islands at a Glance

THE HOT CLIMATE, cooling sea breezes, lively resorts and excellent beaches make the Balearic Islands an ideal holiday destination. Those who want to rave choose Ibiza, with its frenetic clubs and all-night entertainment. Those who prefer a more sedate holiday can find peace and quiet on all the islands, where charming little towns and miles of empty trails are perfect for walking, riding and cycling. Mallorca's caves and grottoes can provide interesting exploration while Menorca's prehistoric structures offer a fascinating glimpse into life on the islands many thousands of years ago.

Palma is the capital of Mallorca and of the Balearic Islands. Full of historic sights and throbbing with life, it is the archipelago's finest city.

Cala Bassa's Blue Flag beach is typical of Ibiza's beaches. Small, with fine, golden sand, it is hidden in a sheltered cove.

IBIZA
(see pp112–131)

Santa Eulària des Riu is one of the loveliest resort towns in Ibiza. It has good restaurants and bars, plenty of shopping and a beautiful beach.

FORMENTERA
(see pp132–139)

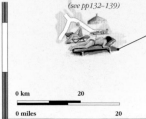

Platja Migjorn is a narrow sandy beach, stretching over 5 km (3 miles) along the southern coast of Formentera; it is always possible to find an isolated spot.

0 km   20

0 miles   20

◁ **Dawn over yachting marina in Port de Pollença in Mallorca**

Cap de Cavalleria *is the northernmost point of the Balearic Islands and one of Menorca's wildest regions. The road to the lighthouse on the headland runs through an undulating area. The steep cliffs here provide a nesting ground for a number of sea birds including the sea eagle and kite.*

MENORCA
(see pp90–111)

MALLORCA
(see pp42–89)

Poblat de Pescadors, Binibeca Vell, Menorca, *with its distinctive development of white houses, was purpose-built for holidaymakers to resemble a Mediterranean fishing village.*

Aquacity, *in S'Arenal near Palma, is one of several water parks in Mallorca. With pools, water flumes and plenty of space to run around, it provides a fun day out for the children.*

Cap de Formentor *is Mallorca's northernmost peninsula. It makes a good destination for a day-long excursion during which you can take in the cliff-top views or swim in one of the coves below. At the very tip of the peninsula is a lighthouse, which also serves at a viewing point.*

MALLORCA

MALLORCA'S LANDSCAPE IS *incredibly diverse for such a small island, ranging from the fertile lowlands of the central region to the high peaks of the Serra de Tramuntana. Its warm climate, fine beaches and historic capital, Palma, make it one of the main European holiday centres. Venture away from the resorts and you also find picturesque inland villages, pine forests and peaceful coves.*

With an area of 3,640 sq km (1,405 sq miles), and a population of around 676,000, of which nearly half live in Palma, Mallorca is the largest island of the Balearic archipelago. Consisting mainly of limestone, the terrain has a large number of cave systems, particularly in the wild central region of the Serra de Tramuntana and on the east coast. Some of these, such as the Coves d'Artà, can be visited as part of a guided tour. Elsewhere on the island, there is much to enjoy from stunning nature reserves and charming fishing villages to picturesque ruins and impressive country estates.

Wind-powered water pump

The climate here is typically Mediterranean, with dry summers and up to 650 mm (26 inches) of rainfall during the autumn-winter season. Cold winters are rare.

The island has unique flora and fauna, which includes a wide variety of birds. Native species of flowers and flowering shrubs are also much in evidence though the cultivation of fields, vineyards and olive groves has partly displaced the natural vegetation.

The island has been known since ancient times and traces of Roman and Arab civilizations can still be seen. Once an independent kingdom, Mallorca became part of Aragón in the 14th century, and was later incorporated into Spain. Since 1983, the Balearic Islands have been an autonomous region of Spain.

Much of the island is virtually untouched by tourism. Mallorca offers wonderful beaches and nightlife for visitors who want a lively holiday, and rural retreats, peaceful coves and historic ruins for those seeking quiet.

Crowded beach in Cala Millor, the destination for many sun-seeking visitors

◁ Yacht moored in the shelter of Port d'Andratx, with dwellings rising steeply behind it

Exploring Mallorca

MOST VISITORS TO MALLORCA come in search of sun and make the most of the nightclubs, discos, waterparks and the plentiful supply of clean beaches. Many also enjoy the historic towns and villages, particularly the winding streets of the island's capital, Palma, which has lots to see and a wide range of shops and restaurants. Visitors looking for the best beaches go to the Badia de Palma region or to the northeastern shores of the island.

PALMA
MEDITERRANEAN SEA

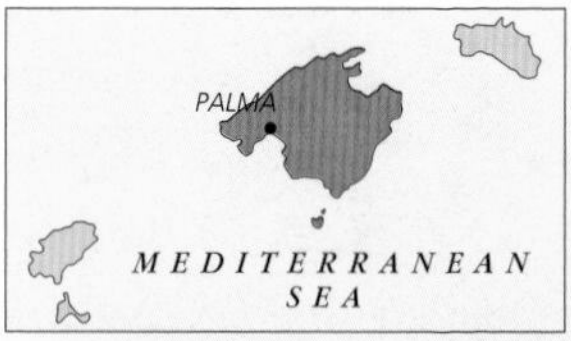

Locator Map

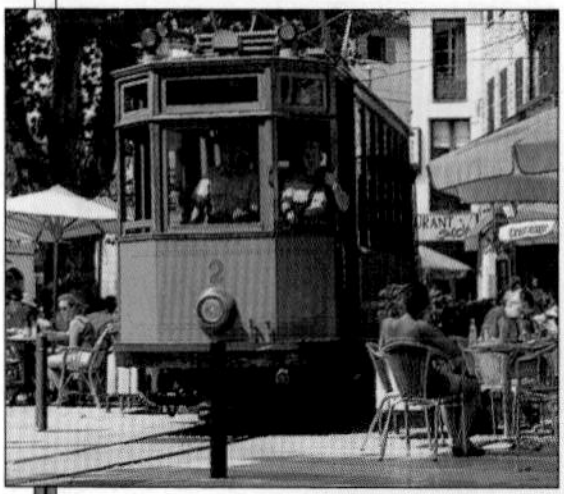

Historic tram in the main square in Sóller

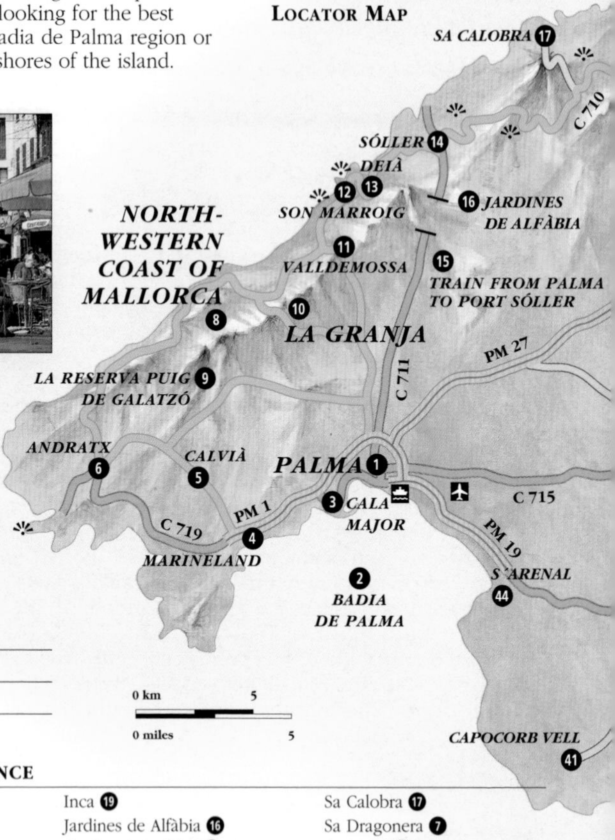

SA CALOBRA 17
C 710
SÓLLER 14
DEIÀ
12 13
SON MARROIG
16 JARDINES DE ALFÀBIA
NORTH-WESTERN COAST OF MALLORCA
11
VALLDEMOSSA
15
TRAIN FROM PALMA TO PORT SÓLLER
8
10
LA GRANJA
PM 27
C 711
LA RESERVA PUIG 9 DE GALATZÓ
7
SA DRAGONERA
ANDRATX
6
CALVIÀ
5
PALMA 1
3 CALA MAJOR
C 715
PM 1
C 719
4
MARINELAND
PM 19
S'ARENAL
44
2
BADIA DE PALMA
0 km 5
0 miles 5
CAPOCORB VELL
41

See Also

- ***Where to Stay*** pp144–8
- ***Where to Eat*** pp158–161

Sights at a Glance

CAP DE FORMENTOR
21

POLLENÇA
20

C 710

PM 221

22 ALCÚDIA

PM 220

18 MONASTERI DE LLUC

C 713

PM 213

PARC NATURAL S´ALBUFERA
23

SA POBLA

MURO 24

PM 341

C 712

19 INCA

PM 324

CALA RAJADA
29

ARTÀ   C 715
27

28
CAPDEPERA

PM 404

SINEU 25

PETRA 26

30 CALA MILLOR

ALGAIDA
43

33   **MANACOR**
VILAFRANCA   **32**
DE BONANY   PM 402

C 715

31 PORTOCRISTO

UIG DE 42
RANDA

40 LLUCMAJOR

C 717

FELANITX
34

C 714

CAMPOS

SANTANYÍ
35   **36 PARC NATURAL**
MONDRAGÓ

37
SES SALINES

COLÒNIA 38
DE SANT JORDI

39 CABRERA ISLAND NATIONAL PARK

GETTING THERE

Mallorca has air links with all the islands of the archipelago and with many Spanish towns and cities. However, the majority of visitors arrive by chartered flights. Mallorca's airport is 11 km (7 miles) east of Palma. It is also possible to get here by ferry, from one of the Spanish mainland ports. A new high-speed ferry linking Valencia, Ibiza and Palma has reduced the journey time considerably. When travelling around Mallorca, you can use its efficient bus service or the one or two railway lines connecting Palma with Sóller and also with Inca, Sa Pobla and Manacor. However, the best way to explore the island is by car.

KEY

▦	Motorway
▬	Major road
═	Minor road
▬	Scenic route
✈	Airport
⚓	Ferry port
☀	Viewpoint

Beach in Palma Nova on the Badia de Palma

Street-by-Street: Palma ❶

IN 1983, PALMA BECAME the capital of the newly created Autonomous Community of the Balearic Islands and transformed itself from a provincial town into a metropolis. Today, it has over 300,000 inhabitants and captivates all visitors as it once captivated Jaume I, who, after conquering it in 1229 described it as the "loveliest town that I have ever seen". It is pleasant to stroll along the clean, attractive streets past renovated historic buildings. The town and harbour are full of life while bars and restaurants, busy with locals and tourists, remain open late into the night.

Fundació la Caixa
Built in 1902, this is the most beautiful 20th-century building in Palma. Formerly the exclusive Grand Hotel it now houses a cultural centre.

★ Palau de l'Almudaina
This former royal residence was the home of Jaume II and was built after 1309, on the site of an Arab fortress.

La Llotja
The elevation of this small Gothic building, which once housed the stock exchange, is decorated with magnificent sculptures.

KEY

– – – Suggested route

PLAÇA REI JOAN CARLES

CARRER UNIO

PASSEIG D'ES BORN

AVINGUDA D'ANTONI MAURA

CARR

CARRE

Parc de la Mar

★ Cathedral
The Gothic cathedral, standing near the shore and towering over the town, is built of golden sandstone excavated in Santanyí.

0 m ————— 100
0 yards ————— 100

★ **Basílica de Sant Francesc**
This magnificent church took almost 100 years to build. Its façade is decorated with a rosette and a Baroque portal.

Plaça Major

Plaça del Marquès de Palmer

VISITORS' CHECKLIST

325,000. Son Sant Joan, 9 km (6 miles) to the east. Plaça d'Espanya, 971 177 777. Parque Estaciones s/n. Muelle de Peraires, 902 454 645. Plaça Reina, 2, 971 712 216. Sant Sebastià (20 Jan), Carnival (Feb), Easter (Mar/Apr), Festes patronales de Sant Pere (29 Jun), Festa de l'Estendard (31 Dec). Sat.

Museu de Mallorca
This has one of the Balearic Islands' best collections.

STAR SIGHTS

★ **Basílica de Sant Francesc**

★ **Cathedral**

★ **Palau d'Almudaina**

Banys Àrabs
The main room of these 10th-century Arab baths is covered with a dome resting on 12 columns. This is one of the few architectural reminders of a Moorish presence on the islands.

City walls

Bishop's Palace

Horsedrawn cabs in Palau de l'Almudaina

Exploring Palma

Of all the Balearic towns, Palma is the richest in historic sights. Christian kings, Arab rulers and Jewish merchants have all left their mark on the Balearic capital and it is a genuine pleasure to stroll through its narrow streets and quiet courtyards.

✠ Cathedral (La Seu)

Plaça Almoïna, s/n.
[*971 723 130.*
After the capture of Palma by Jaume I, the town's main mosque was used as its cathedral church. Work on the present cathedral *(see pp50–51)*, known in Catalan as La Seu, began in 1230, immediately after the fall of Palma. The main work lasted for almost 400 years and resulted in a monumental Gothic church, visible from afar.

It has three entrances, each framed with a portal. The most beautiful of these is the 14th-century Portal de Mirador, overlooking the Bay of Palma to the south. It is topped with a pediment depicting the Last Supper. Built above the Gothic Portal de l'Almoina is a fortified belfry. The main Portal Major (Great Door), facing the Almudaina palace, has a Neo-Gothic finish and is the least successful of the three.

The splendid interior features 14 slender octagonal pillars

supporting the vault. The 44-metre (145-ft) central nave is one of the highest in Europe. The eastern rose window, measuring over 12 m (40 ft) in diameter, is made of 1,200 pieces of stained glass.

The cathedral features stalls made of walnut, an interesting stone pulpit and 14 chapels including Nostra Senyora de la Corona with statues of allegorical angels.

In the oldest part of the cathedral, hidden behind the altar is the Trinity Chapel, containing the tombs of Jaume II and Jaume III (not open to visitors). In the early 20th century, Antoni Gaudí removed the Baroque altar and put in its place an alabaster table, with an illuminated canopy symbolizing the crown of thorns suspended overhead.

⛪ Palau de l'Almudaina

Carrer de Palau Real. **[** *971 214 134.* 📷 🎫
"Almudaina" means "citadel" in Arabic. This royal residence of Jaume II was built after 1309, using the walls of an Arab fortress. The remodelling work was carried out by Pedro Selva, the king's favourite architect.

The Gothic palace includes Moorish-style arches and intricate, carved wooden ceilings. Now the building houses the army headquarters (a uniformed guard stands at the entrance) and is King Juan Carlos's official residence in Palma.

The building's museum section includes the Santa Ana chapel with a Romanesque portal and a Gothic drawing room, which is sometimes used for official receptions. The palace offers guided tours. The interior is hung with with a small number of 17th-century Flemish paintings and tapestries.

⚜ Parc de la Mar

The Parc de la Mar was established in the 1960s in the area between the southern section of the city walls and Ronda Litoral – the street running along Badia de Palma. Its designers, Josep Lluís Sert and Joan Miró *(see p58)*, built the park on several levels and its central points include a man-made lake in which you can see a reflection of the cathedral, and a giant mural by Miró. The nearby **Sas Volves** is an exhibition space, providing a venue for art exhibitions and concerts.

Gothic portal of La Llotja

⚜ La Llotja

Plaça Llotja
This late-Gothic building (a former stock exchange) was erected between 1426–56 after plans by Guillem Sagrera – the designer of the Portal del Mirador in La Seu. In later years the building was used as a granary, and until recently as

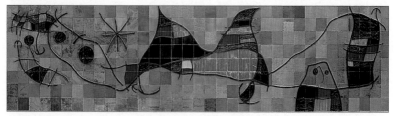

A section of the giant mural by Joan Miró, adorning one of the walls in Parc de la Mar

East frontage of Passeig des Born

an exhibition and concert hall. The vault rests on slender spiral pillars, the walls are pierced by tall windows. The entrance from the square, framed by a portal, is adorned with a pediment featuring a statue of the Guardian Angel. La Llotja's interior is open only for special exhibitions.

Consolat de Mar

Passeig de Sagrera

Not far from La Llotja on the other side of a small garden is an elegant Renaissance-Baroque building, erected in 1614–26. Originally intended as the offices of a shipping tribunal, it is now the seat of the Balearic Islands' government.

The façade facing the harbour features a magnificent covered arcade. The interior has a beautiful coffered ceiling (1664–69). The Consolat building joins with La Llotja via **Porta Vella del Moll** – a former harbour gate, brought here in the late 19th century.

Passeig d'es Born

This is one of the most beautiful corners of Palma. During Arab times it featured a moat that guarded access to the walls. Now this wide avenue, which gets its name from jousting tournaments held here in the 17th century, is Palma's main promenade and is planted with plane trees. It forms the axis of the entire city and is similar in many respects to Barcelona's

famous Ramblas. Set among the trees are flowerbeds and seats for the weary. It is also a venue for book fairs and large-scale cultural events.

At the southern end of the avenue is **Plaça de la Reina**. The entrance on this side is guarded by stone sphinxes. At the north end of the Passeig d'es Born is **Plaça del Rei Joan Carles I**, with a stone obelisk resting on bronze turtles standing at its centre. Of the houses that line both sides of the avenue, the most noteworthy is the **Can Solleric** residence (No. 27). It was built in 1763 as the family home of a merchant who traded in cattle and olive oil and has a beautiful Baroque courtyard. Now it is used as a cultural centre, and has a bookshop, an art gallery and a trendy café.

Avinguda Unió and Plaça Weyler

The avenue, running up to Plaça Weyler and almost reaching Plaça Major, is an eastern extension of Passeig d'es Born. This is a lively area and the street is full of shops. In the squares and streets leading off Avinguda Unió there are numerous cafés where you can sit and take refreshment.

Entrance to Forn des Teatre

In **Plaça Mercat** two identical buildings stand side by side. These fine examples of *Modernista* architecture were built by a wealthy banker, Josep Casasayas in 1908.

The real gem of the district's architecture, however, is **Fundació La Caixa** in Plaça Weyler. The former Grand Hotel was given its present name after the Fundació La Caixa savings bank financed its restoration. It was reopened in 1993 by King Juan Carlos and Queen Sofia. Built in 1903, this early example of Catalan architecture is the work of Lluís Domènech i Montaner. When first built it was considered the smartest hotel in the Balearic Islands. Now, as an outstanding masterpiece of the *Modernista* style, it has been included on the UNESCO World Heritage list and houses, among other things, a restaurant and exhibition rooms (which includes a permanent collection of paintings by the important *Modernista* artist Hermengildo Anglada-Camarasa).

Almost opposite Fundació La Caixa is the **Forn des Teatre** (theatre bakery). This is a small, eye-catching patisserie where you can buy deliciously flaky spiral pastries *(ensaïmadas)*. Adjacent to the bakery is the **Teatre Principal** (1860). This is one of the most important ballet, opera and theatre venues in town.

Jaume I (1208–69)

Jaume I, king of Aragón, landed in Mallorca near Santa Ponça, in 1229. Following a three-month siege and subsequent defeat of the Muslims, he took Medina Mayurqa – the Arab capital of the island. In 1232 he accepted the surrender of Menorca and, in 1235, conquered Ibiza, thus completing the reconquest of the Balearic Islands. In 1230, Jaume I proclaimed the *Carta de Població* (People's Charter), guaranteeing citizens equality in the eyes of the law.

Portrait of Jaume I on the façade of the library in Calvià

Cathedral – La Seu

Palma's cathedral, La Seu, is the most precious architectural treasure of the Balearic Islands and is regarded as one of Spain's most outstanding Gothic structures. Begun on the site of the city's main mosque by Jaume II after the conquest of 1300, the work took some 300 years. In the first half of the 15th century, the building works were supervised by the prominent Mallorcan sculptor and architect Guillem Sagrera. Partly destroyed during the 1851 earthquake, the cathedral was subsequently repaired by Juan Bautista Peyronnet. In the early 20th century, its interior was modernized by Antoni Gaudí. An integral part of the cathedral is its museum, which stores precious works of sacral art.

Belfry
The mighty belfry was built in 1389. The biggest of its nine bells is called Eloi.

Palma Cathedral
Towering over the former harbour in Palma, the cathedral looks most beautiful when viewed from the sea, or at night, when it is illuminated.

Star Sights

★ **Baldachin (canopy)**

★ **Giant Rose Window**

19th-century pinnacle

Entrance to the Cathedral Museum

Portal Major (1601)

Flying buttress

Cathedral Museum
One of the masterpieces on display in the Old Chapter House, now housing the museum, is the reliquary containing wood from the Holy Cross, encrusted with jewels.

★ Giant Rose Window
The largest of the seven rose windows, measuring 12 m (40 ft) in diameter, is filled with 1,200 pieces of stained glass.

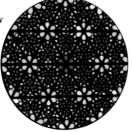

VISITORS' CHECKLIST

Plaça Almoïna, s/n. 📞 971 723 130. ☐ Apr–Oct: 10am–5:30pm Mon–Fri; Nov–Mar: 10am–6:15pm Mon–Fri; 10am–2:30pm Sat. ● public holidays. 📷 ✝ 9am, 7pm daily, (Oct–Mar: 9am, 5:30pm; Sat–Sun 9am, 7pm).

The great organs, built in 1795, stand within a Neo-Gothic enclosure; they were restored in 1993 by Gabriel Blancafort.

Trinity Chapel
The chapel, built in 1329, contains the tombs of the Mallorcan kings, Jaume II and Jaume III.

The Capella Reial (presbytery) was remodelled by Gaudí during 1904–14.

Bishop's Throne
Made in 1346, of white marble, the Bishop's Throne stands on a dais, in a niche.

Stalls made from the dismantled *corro*

Portal del Mirador (1420)

Central Nave
Nineteen metres (62 ft) wide and 44 m (145 ft) high, the central nave, with its vault supported by 14 pillars, is one of the world's biggest.

★ Baldachin *(1912)*
Antoni Gaudí's ceremonial canopy with lights and a multi-coloured crucifix is suspended above the main altar.

Museu de Mallorca

THE BEST MUSEUM in the Balearic Islands can be found close to La Seu, in Palau Ayamans, a residence built around 1630. The palace was erected on the foundations of an Arab house (12th–13th century), which is still visible in the underground rooms of the museum. Opened in 1968, the museum houses a superb collection of works of art associated with Mallorcan history. The collection comprises several thousand exhibits and includes prehistoric artifacts found during archaeological excavations, stone fragments of fallen buildings, priceless Moorish ceramics and jewellery, and medieval and Baroque paintings

★ Votive Painting
This work (c.1792), by an unknown artist, was painted as thanksgiving for saving the life of Joan Maid during a shipwreck.

St Catherine
(17th century)
Painted in the Venetian style, by an unknown Mallorcan artist.

★ Almohad Treasure
Items of Arab jewellery are among the museum's most precious exhibits. They are kept in the treasury room, behind bullet-proof glass.

Ground floor

KEY

- [ ] 20th-century art
- [ ] Secession
- [ ] 19th-century art
- [ ] Modern art
- [ ] Medieval art
- [ ] Islamic art
- [ ] Treasury room
- [ ] Prehistoric art
- [ ] Non-exhibition rooms

GALLERY GUIDE

The museum's collection is arranged on four floors, in chronological order. The oldest relics, including archaeological finds, are kept in the underground vault. The most recent art, including 19th- and 20th-century paintings, is exhibited on the top floor. The second floor is occupied by offices.

Ceramic Vase (11th century)
Discovered during excavations near Pollença, the vase is the work of Arab artists, who lived in Mallorca.

Entrance

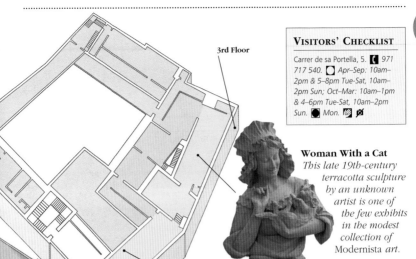

3rd Floor

VISITORS' CHECKLIST

Carrer de sa Portella, 5. 971
717 540. Apr–Sep: 10am–
2pm & 5–8pm Tue-Sat, 10am–
2pm Sun; Oct–Mar: 10am–1pm
& 4–6pm Tue-Sat, 10am–2pm
Sun. Mon.

Woman With a Cat
*This late 19th-century
terracotta sculpture
by an unknown
artist is one of
the few exhibits
in the modest
collection of
Modernista art.*

1st Floor

El Suspiro del Moro (1856)
*The Moor's Sigh is the work of Benito Soriano i Murillo,
a native of Mallorca. This vast picture is kept as an
example of an academic style of painting.*

Crucifixion
(1353)
*This exquisite
Gothic altarpiece
was painted by
Ramon Destorrents
and commissioned
by the Catalan
King Pedro IV.*

★ **Statuette of
a Warrior**
*This 4th-century
BC bronze figure
is one of several
exhibited in the
section devoted
to the island's
prehistoric
times.*

STAR EXHIBITS

★ **Almohad Treasure**

★ **Statuette of a Warrior**

★ **Votive Painting**

Vaults

⚜ Plaça del Marquès de Palmer

This square lies at the end of Carrer Colom – a shopping street running from Plaça Cort, the site of the Ajuntament (Town Hall). It features a five-storey *Modernista* apartment building, Can Rei (20th century). Equally interesting is the nearby building – L'Aguila.

⚜ Plaça Major

This pedestrianized 19th-century square has a number of souvenir shops and lively cafés. Many of the square's restaurants have outdoor tables under its arcades.

The centre of the square is given over to stalls that sell a wide variety of handicrafts. There's also a stage that is frequently used by musicians and jugglers who entertain visitors to the city.

The porticoed square was laid out in 1823 following the demolition of the headquarters of the Inquisition. The new square became the main food market until the 1950s. A large underground shopping centre and car park have since been added.

🏛 Santa Eulàlia

Plaça Santa Eulàlia. ⏱ 7:30am–1pm & 5:30–8pm Mon–Fri, 8am–1pm & 6–8pm Sat–Sun.

The vast Gothic church, standing at the end of Carrer Morey, was built on the site of a mosque in the 13th century on the orders of Jaume II. It was completed in just 25

Modernista-style oriel window of Can Rei, at Plaça del Marquès de Palmer

years. Renovations in the 19th century involved adding the belfry and remodelling the central nave. The aisle chapels feature magnificent original Gothic paintings.

The most precious relic in the church is the crucifix kept in Capella de Sant Crist. Jaume I is supposed to have carried this when he conquered Mallorca in 1229.

Another dramatic event is associated with this church. In 1435, it was the site of a mass baptism of Jews, who converted to Christianity in order to escape being burnt at the stake.

🏛 The Templar Chapel

Plaça Pes de la Palma. ⏱ 9:30am–1pm & 3:30–7pm Mon–Fri, 9:30am–1pm Sat.

The Knights Templar was a 12th-century religious and military order, founded to support the Crusades. Later it turned to banking and became so rich that it made enemies of both the ecclesiastical and secular authorities. In 1312, the pope disbanded the order and seized its assets. The Templars' Palma base was given to a rival order, the Hospitallers of St John, who remained here until the early 19th century when the order was itself dissolved.

Access to the former fortress monastery is through a fortified 13th-century gate. The dim nave, once Gothic in style, was remodelled in the 19th century. Divided into three parts, it is covered with rib vaulting. The entrance chapels, with slender columns supporting their vaults, are decorated with geometric and plant motifs.

⚜ Plaça Sant Jeroni

Standing in a small square, with a central fountain, is the church of **Sant Jeroni**. Its elaborate doorway is all swirls and grinning gargoyles while the church's tympanum depicts the tale of Sant Jeroni and his trials in the desert. A hermit who lived mostly in Bethlehem, this holy man translated the Bible from Hebrew into Latin. Inside the church is *Sant Jeroni*, a late 15th-century altarpiece by Pere Terrencs. There is also a vast organ, though this is rarely heard as the church is often closed.

⚜ Casa Olesa

Carrer Morey, 25.

Built in the mid-16th century, this Renaissance residence is one of Palma's most beautiful. The house is private but you can admire its courtyard through the wrought-iron gate.

Plaça Mayor, the main town square, with live entertainment

Monastery courtyard of Basilica de Sant Francesc

🔒 Basilíca de Sant Francesc
Plaça Sant Francesc. ◯ *9:30am–12:30pm & 3:30–6pm Mon–Sat, 9:30am–12:30pm Sun.* 🖻

The building of the Gothic church and Franciscan monastery started in 1281 and lasted 100 years. During the Middle Ages, this was Palma's most fashionable church and to be buried here was a major status symbol. Aristocratic families competed with each other by building ever more ostentatious sarcophagi in which to place their dead.

The church was remodelled in the 17th century after being damaged by lightning. Its severe façade, with giant rose window, was embellished around 1680 with a Baroque doorway, decorated with stone statues and the Triumphant Virgin Mary in the tympanum. Next to the Madonna is the carved figure of the famous medieval mystic Ramón Llull *(see p87)*, who is buried in the church.

The dark interior (its Gothic windows have been partially bricked up) contains many fine works of art, which are mainly Baroque in style. Particularly eye-catching (if you can see in the dimness) are the vast altarpiece, dating from 1739, and the organ. The delightful Gothic cloisters, planted with orange and lemon trees, offer light relief.

Standing in front of the basilica is a statue of Junipero Serra *(see p77)*, a Franciscan monk and native of Mallorca, who was sent to California in 1768 and founded Los Angeles and San Francisco.

🛁 Banys Àrabs
Carrer Can Serra 7. ☎ *971 721 549.* ◯ *9am–8pm daily.* 🖻

The brick 10th-century *hammam* (bath house) is one of the few architectural reminders of a Moorish presence on the islands. A small horseshoe-arched chamber, with a dome supported by irregular columns and what would once have been under-floor heating, it has survived in its original form. There's not a lot to see but the pleasant garden has tables, where you can sit and rest.

🛁 Palau Episcopal and Museu Diocesà
Carrer Mirador 5. ◯ *Apr–Oct: 10am–1pm & 3–6pm Mon–Thu; Nov–Mar: 10am–1:30pm & 3–6pm Mon–Thu, 10am–1pm Fri.* ● *Sat, Sun.* 🖻

Just behind the cathedral, the Palau Episcopal (Bishop's Palace) is mostly 17th century, though work began

Sundial from Palau Episcopal

in 1238, initiated by Bishop Ramon de Torell. The palace, which is built around a large courtyard, adjoins the city walls. Its façade was completed in 1616.

Two rooms of the palace have been given over to the modest **Museu Diocesà** (Diocese Museum). The little museum has on display items from various churches in Mallorca as well as a selection of majolica tiles. Particularly noteworthy are: a picture of St George slaying the dragon in front of Palma's city gate, painted in 1468–70 by Pere Nisart; Bishop Galiana's panel depicting the life of St Paul (who is portrayed holding a sword); the Gothic pulpit in a Mudéjar (Spanish-Moorish) style; and the jasper sarcophagus of Jaume II, which stood in the cathedral until 1904.

⚜ City Walls
The Renaissance city walls were built on the site of earlier medieval walls. This recently restored section once included a gallery running along the top, from where the city's defenders could fire at besieging enemies. Progress in artillery design meant that the fortifications became lower and thicker. Work on remodelling the walls began in the mid-16th century, but the bastions were only completed in the early 19th century. Today, Palma's city walls feature a walkway that provides a wide view over Badia de Palma, the cathedral and the old town.

Restored city walls in Palma's old town

Painting by Pérez Villata from Museu d'Art Espanyol Contemporani

Further Afield

If you want to relax away from the hubbub of the crowded streets in Palma's old town, take a trip to the outskirts of the city. A stroll along the **harbour front**, or a trip to **Castell de Bellver**, with its lovely view of the city, is always a treat.

🚩 Carrer Sant Miquel

A narrow street that runs north from Plaça Major to Plaça Conquista, Carrer Sant Miquel is closed to traffic and is one of Palma's main shopping streets. Here, you can buy almost anything, though souvenir shops are a rarity. Here, too, you will find the Spanish Museum of Modern Art (*see below*) and, a little further on, the church of Sant Miquel. Nearby, in Plaça Olivar, stands the large iron structure of the market hall that was built in the early 20th century.

🏛 Museu d'Art Espanyol Contemporani

Carrer Sant Miquel 11. 🄲 971 713 515. ◯ 10am–6:30pm Mon–Fri, 10am–1:30pm Sat. 📷

The museum occupies a Renaissance building that was remodelled in the early 20th century by Guillem Reynes i Font in the *Modernista* style. Purchased in 1916 by Juan March, the building was the first headquarters of Banca March.

The museum's exhibition occupies the first and second floors and features works by contemporary Spanish artists including Pablo Picasso, Joan Miró and Salvador Dali.

Most of the 50 or so exhibited works are paintings and sculptures by less well known artists, who nevertheless played an important role in the shaping of Spanish modern art. The museum, which also stages temporary exhibitions, is part of Fundación Juan March, a major cultural foundation.

Rose window on the façade of Sant Miquel

🔒 Sant Miquel

Carrer de Sant Miquel 21. 🄲 971 715 455. ◯ 8am–1:30pm & 5–7:30pm Mon–Sat, 10am–noon & 6–7:30pm Sun.

This 16th-century church is one of the most popular in town. It was built on the site of a mosque in which the first victory mass was said after the conquest of Mallorca by Jaume I. The Baroque altarpiece with a picture of St Michael is the work of the Spanish religious painter, Francesc Herrera.

La Rambla

Palma's biggest flower market can be found in this shadowy avenue, lined with plane trees. Towards the lower section of the boulevard are two statues of Roman emperors, erected by the Francoists in honour of Mussolini. At La Rambla's northern end stands the vast building of **La Misericordia** remodelled in the mid-19th century in a Neo-Classical style. It houses, among other things, a conservatoire. Next to it is a botanical garden.

🚩 Plaça d'Espanya

This vast square, containing an equestrian statue of Jaume I, is Palma's main transport hub. The railway stations run services to Sóller and Inca. Most of the town's buses stop here or in the local side streets and many link up with Palma's suburbs and the nearby tourist resorts.

🏛 Poble Espanyol

Poble Espanyol, s/n. 🄲 971 737 075. ▦ ◯ Dec–Mar: 9am–6pm daily; Apr–Oct: 9am–7pm daily. 📷

"Miniature Spain" is located a short way west of Palma's old town. It was built in the 1960s on the orders of the Spanish dictator General Franco. Here you can see 20 or so mini-versions of outstanding examples of Spanish architecture. They include Granada's Alhambra Palace, El Greco's house in Toledo and Barcelona's Palau de la Generalitat. There's also a craft workshop, restaurant, bar and a souvenir shop.

Copy of Alhambra in Poble Espanyol

Arcades surrounding Castell de Bellver's courtyard

Opposite the entrance to Poble Espanyol stands the monumental **Palau de Congressos**. The congress centre features, among other things, the Roman Theatre and the Imperial Hall.

🏛 **Castell de Bellver**
C/Camilo José Cela s/n. 📞 971 730 657. 🚌 to Plaça Gomila. ⏰ Apr–Oct: 8am–8:30pm Mon–Sat, 10am–6:30pm; Nov–Mar: 8am–7:15pm Mon–Sat, 10am–4:30pm Sun
⬤ public holidays. 📷
About 2 km (1 mile) west of Palma's cathedral, on a pine-clad hill, near the entrance to the harbour, stands one of Europe's most beautiful Gothic castles. Though it has, alas, been over-restored, the Castell de Bellver affords spectacular views of the city and bay. Built as a summer residence for Jaume II by Pere Selvà in the early 14th century when Mallorca was an independent kingdom, it was later turned into a prison and remained as such until 1915.
    The castle, circular in shape, has an inner courtyard that is surrounded by two-tier arcades. Three cylindrical

towers are partly sunk into the wall. The free-standing Torre de Homenaje is joined to the main building by an arch and was designed to be the final stronghold. The castle's flat roof was built to collect rainwater into an underground cistern. The entire complex is surrounded by a moat and ground fortifications.

Fishing boats in Palma harbour

A part of the castle has been turned into a museum. It has an exhibition of archaeological finds and Roman sculpture collected in the 18th century by Antonio Despuig – a historian and cardinal who left his collection to the city.

🏛 **Museu Krekovič**
Carrer de Ciutat de Querétaro 3.
📞 971 249 409. ⏰ mid-Jan–mid-Dec: 9:30am–1pm & 3–6pm Mon–Fri, 9:30am–1pm Sat.
⬤ mid-Dec–mid-Jan.
The museum of the Croatian painter Kristian Krekovič (1901–85) opened in 1981. It includes not only works by the artist but also paintings and handicrafts from Spain and Latin America.

⚓ **Harbour Front**
Palma's harbour, overlooked by the cathedral, bustles with life, as magnificent yachts come and go. Here, at the wharf, you can see fishermen at work. The nearby **Reial Club Nautic** has an excellent restaurant that often plays host to Spanish royalty.
    Further on, opposite the **Auditorio** in Passeig Marítim, is a jetty for pleasure boats from where you can take a trip around the harbour. Beyond **Club del Mar**, to the south, is the ferry terminal providing regular services to the other islands of the archipelago and mainland Spain. Nearby, is a naval base. You can see most of the harbour on foot. Alternatively, hire a bicycle or horse-drawn cab. Routes end at the 15th-century **Torre Paraires** or by the lighthouse in **Potro Pi**.

ENVIRONS: Five km (3 miles) to the north lies the district of **Establiments**. Its historic sights include an old windmill that now houses a restaurant. Music lovers may be interested to know that it was here, in villa "Son Vent", on the outskirts of town, that Frédéric Chopin and George Sand stopped while on their way to Valldemossa.

Rough waters of the Badia de Palma

Badia de Palma ➋

THE BAY OF PALMA is bounded by Cap de Cala Figuera to the west and Cap Enderrocat to the east. During the tourist boom, in the 1960–70s, the bay became surrounded by miles of high-rise hotels and hemmed in by hundreds of restaurants, bars, nightclubs and shops. Today, the eastern part of this beautiful bay is popular with German visitors, while the British tend to congregate to the west.

Platja de Palma, stretching from S'Arenal to C'an Pastilla, is one of the best beaches on the islands if you can ignore the sprawl fringing the shore. The western side is more varied, featuring pine-clad hills, sloping down to the water's edge. The beaches are smaller here, situated in picturesque coves. Along the coast are the popular resorts of Bendinat, Portals Nous, Palma Nova and Magaluf.

Cala Major ➌

ℹ️ *Carretera Andrax 33, Illetes.*

THE RESORT AREA, situated to the west of Palma, is known for its **Fundació Pilar i Joan Miró**. Miró lived and worked on the island for 40 years. After his death in 1983, the artist's wife converted the house and former studio into an art centre. This modern edifice, nicknamed the "Alabaster Fortress" by the Spanish press, is the work of Rafael Moneo, a leading Spanish architect. The new building houses a permanent exhibition of Miró's paintings, drawings and sculptures, as well as a library, auditorium and a shop where you can buy items decorated with the artist's colourful designs. The Foundation owns some 140 paintings, 300

A sculpture by Miró

graphics and over 100 drawings by Miró. Standing nearby is the **Marivent Palace**, a carefully guarded holiday residence of the Spanish royal family. The main street is lined with *Modernista* villas, which remain from the days when this was a smart resort, visited by the rich and powerful. The **Nixe Hotel** is a throwback to those days.

🏛 **Fundació Pilar i Joan Miró**
C/ Joan de Seridakis 29.
📞 971 701 420.
🕐 10am–7pm Tue–Sat (summer); 10am–6pm Tue–Sat, 10am–3pm Sun (winter). ♿

ENVIRONS: Some 8 km (5 miles) west of Palma stands the 13th-century **Castell de Bendinat**. Remodelled in the 18th century, the castle is surrounded by pine woods and its imposing walls and towers are decorated with a Baroque frieze. Today, the castle houses a conference centre and is not open to the public. Five kilometres (3 miles) northwest of Palma are the **Coves de Genova**. These caves were discovered in 1906 and have some fine formations of stalactites and stalagmites.

Palma Nova is famous for its picturesque, though crowded, beaches and lively nightlife. Nearby **Magaluf** is a busy resort with a variety of high-rise hotels and numerous restaurants and English-style pubs where you can order a full English breakfast or fish and chips.

🐚 **Coves de Genova**
Carrer de Barranc 45. 📞 971 402 387.
🕐 10am–1pm & 4–7pm. ⬤ Mon. ♿

JOAN MIRÓ (1893–1983)

One of the best known artists of the 20th century, Miró was a Catalan through and through. Initially influenced by Fauvism, and later by Dadaism and Surrealism, he developed his own unique style, marked by lyricism and lively colouring. After arriving in Mallorca he became interested in graphics, ceramics and sculpture, scoring significant successes in every art form. His works can be seen in his studio on the outskirts of Palma, where he lived and worked from 1956. He died in Palma in 1983.

Joan Miró, famous for his life-long sunny disposition

Marineland ❹

MARINELAND IS THE ONLY amusement park in the Balearic Islands where you can see performing dolphins and sea lions. This mini-zoo also houses a number of aquaria containing sharks and exotic fish. As well as the sea life, there is a good aviary and you can also see exotic animals such as crocodiles and snakes. This is great fun for families with young children.

VISITORS' CHECKLIST

C/Gracillaso de la Vega 9,
Costa d'en Blanes. 🚌
☎ 971 675 125. ◯ Jul–Aug:
9:30am–6:45pm; Sep–Jun:
9:30am–5:15pm. (Note: no
food or drink can be taken in).
🍴 ☐ ♿

★ **Sea Lions**
The performing sea lions are well cared for at this fun park.

Entrance
Even on cloudy days there is always a queue at the front gates, with people eager to see the trained animal shows.

★ **Dolphins**
The dolphin shows always attract large crowds of appreciative spectators.

Parrots
Parrots can be seen in several places in the park, but shows are staged at a single location.

0 m   25
0 yards   25

STAR ATTRACTIONS

★ **Dolphins**

★ **Sea Lions**

KEY

Entrance ①
Sea lions ②
Playground ③
Tropical fish aquarium ④
Parrot shows ⑤
Mediterranean fish
  aquarium ⑥
Dolphins ⑦
Terrarium ⑧
Ray fish ⑨

Calvià ❺

🚌 ℹ️ C/Julià Bujosa Sans, batle 1,
971 139 109. 🌐 www.calvia.net
📅 Sant Jaume (24 Jun). 🔶 Mon.

THIS QUIET LITTLE town, west of Palma, is situated in the foothills of the Serra de Tramuntana mountains, and is the administrative centre of Calvià Province, which includes the resorts from Ses Illetes to Santa Ponça.

Standing on a hill in the centre of Calvià is the church of **Sant Joan Baptista**; its forecourt provides a fine view over the surrounding farms and olive groves. The original church was built here in 1245; the present structure dates from the late 19th century. The ceramic tiles lining the walls of the neighbouring public library provide a crash course in the town's history.

Few tourists make it to Calvià, where life proceeds quietly, according to a long established rhythm. Bars and restaurants serve authentic Mallorcan cuisine.

ENVIRONS: Santa Ponça is a small port, situated 7 km (4 miles) southwest of Calvià. Nearby are golf courses, good beaches and opulent residences. It was here that Jaume I landed in 1229, freeing Mallorca from Arab domination. The event is marked by the Creu de la Conquesta.

Neo-Gothic façade of Calvià's church

Typical Mallorcan fishing boats in Port d'Andratx

Andratx ❻

🚌 📅 Sant Pere (29 Jun), La Virgen del Carmen (16 Aug). 🔶 Wed.

ANDRATX HAS ANCIENT origins and was known as Andrachium by the Romans. It lies in a valley of olive and almond groves, at the foot of the Puig de Galatzó (1,028 m/3,400 ft). The local architecture is typical of the inland settlements that used to defend the island against raids by pirates. Old ochre-colour houses with colourful shutters blend well with the narrow cobblestone streets. The main historic sight is the fortified church of **Santa María**, towering over the town. It was built in the 13th century and remodelled in the early 18th century. The main tourist attraction, however, is the local market, which is held on Wednesday mornings.

Church tympanum in Andratx

ENVIRONS: Some 5 km (3 miles) southwest of Andratx is **Port d'Andratx**. The sheltered bay provides a mooring ground for exclusive yachts. As recently as the 1960s, this was just a small fishing village, which later transformed itself into a swanky resort with luxurious residences built within the woodland setting on the slopes of the La Mola cape, and affording beautiful views of the harbour. The coastal boulevard offers the best place for viewing the magnificent sunsets.

About 5 km (3 miles) east of Port d'Andratx, in **Camp de Mar**, is a vast beach and lovely bathing spot with large hotels situated close to the sea. Neighbouring **Peguera** has many inexpensive hotels. Its pleasant and safe beach is particularly favoured by families with small children and by older visitors. **Cap Andritxol**, between Peguera and Camp de Mar, is a small peninsula with an observation tower at its tip dating back to 1580. It is an excellent destination for walks and offers hikers the chance to see some rare animals and many species of native flora. **Cala Fornells**, a short way from Peguera, is a small, picturesque village and beautiful cove. Surrounded by pine trees, there are great views of the bay. It is also a good place for swimming.

A particularly scenic road runs northwards, from Andratx to Estellencs. The **Mirador de Ricardo Roca viewpoint** and Es Grau restaurant provide good stopping points for a rest en route (see pp62–3).

The delightful hillside village of **S'Arracó** lies 3 km (2 miles) west of Andratx, on the road leading to Sant Elm. The local church has a marble statue of Nostra Senyora de Sa Trapa, brought to the Trappist monastery near Sant Elm in the 18th century.

Sa Dragonera 7

A NARROW ROCKY ISLAND, Sa Dragonera lies at an angle to the coast, about one kilometre (half a mile) from Sant Elm. It has been a nature reserve since 1988 and is home to a wide variety of birdlife and wild flowers.

According to legend, the island is visited nightly by dragons. However, its name has more to do with its shape than its popularity with mythical beasts.

This wild island is just 4 km (2 miles) long and 700 m (765 yards) wide. A rocky path runs between its two headlands, both marked by lighthouses. Apart from the lighthouse keepers, the only inhabitants of the island are wild goats and birds – the island supports cormorants, Cory's shearwater and many birds of prey including the largest colony anywhere of Eleonora's falcon.

Sa Dragonera can be reached by a ferry from Sant Elm (May–Sep), which disembarks to allow you several hours to wander explore the island. Cruises around the island leave from Sant Elm and Port d'Andratx.

ENVIRONS: Sant Elm (San Telmo) is a quiet resort with a fine sandy beach, a wide selection of cafés and restaurants and beautiful scenery. About 4 km (2 miles) northeast of Sant Elm is an abandoned monastery. **Sa Trapa** has a mill displaying some preserved agricultural equipment. A commemorative stone stands as a warning

Bears in La Reserva Puig de Galatzó

against getting too close to the edge of the precipice, which affords a fantastic view over the island of Sa Dragonera.

Northwestern Coast of Mallorca 8

See pp62–3.

La Reserva Puig de Galatzó 9

18 km (11 miles) north of Palma, 4 km (2 miles) west of Puigpuñyent.
📞 971 616 622. Ⓦ
www.lareservaaventur.com
🕐 10am–7pm daily (summer), 10am–6pm daily (winter). 🐾

THIS PRIVATE nature reserve is situated on the eastern slope of the mighty Puig de Galatzó peak, in the southern region of the Serra de Tramuntana. Here, in an area of 250 sq km (100 sq miles), you can sample some of the splendours of nature, as the area features springs and

Sign of La Reserva Puig de Galatzó

streams, dozens of scenic waterfalls and caves, as well as a variety of interesting rock formations.

Specially designated pathways lead through the park. Notice boards explain the local flora, the origins of its unusually shaped rocks and the habits of local birds. There is much else of interest, too, including bears, a falcon show, a 1,000-year-old olive tree, *carboneros* (huts belonging to charcoal burners) and the Cova des Moro – Moor's Cave. Real adventures, such as rock climbing, abseiling and archery, are also on offer.

ENVIRONS: Set amid lemon groves, 2 km (1 mile) northeast, is the quiet little farming village of **Puigpuñyent**, which has a 17th-century church.

Galilea, situated a little way south of La Reserva, is a favourite haunt for artists from all over Europe. It affords a magnificent view of the southwestern coast of Mallorca. The founder of the local church of the Immaculate Conception was Captain Antonio Barceló, a man with a fierce reputation who, in the 18th century, defended Mallorca against pirates. In nearby El Capdella the same captain Barceló founded the church of Virgen del Carmen.

Sa Dragonera, Dragon Island, viewed from Sant Elm

Northwestern Coast of Mallorca ⑧

THE NORTHERN SLOPES of the Serra de Tramuntana provide some magnificent views and a wonderful sense of isolation. Andratx and Valldemossa have a number of interesting historic sights but it is the scenery of the rugged coastline, which manages to be both sinister and beautiful, that is most impressive. The route is dramatic, traversing tunnels and gorges, but it is not difficult, except for the approach to Port d'es Canonge and Port de Valldemossa. It can be covered in a single day. If you are fit, you could even cycle.

Mirador de Ses Ànimes ④
The former defence tower, standing on a steep rock, now serves as a viewpoint. The entrance to the tower is narrow and the top terrace is accessible only by stepladder.

Estellencs ③
A small town with old stone houses, an interesting, mostly 18th-century, church and a handful of souvenir shops. The route follows the main street.

Mirador de Ricardo Roca ②
This viewpoint is situated on the terrace of the Es Grau restaurant. It affords a spectacular view of the northwestern coastline.

Andratx ①
A charming little town with attractive houses and cobbled streets. The market is held on Wednesday and is a time when the usually empty streets teem with life.

SERRA DE TRAMUNTANA

C 710

CALVIÀ

C 719

C 719

PALMA

0 km   2

0 miles   2

Banyalbufar ⑤
Founded by the Arabs, this small town is surrounded by terraced fields descending to the sea. Until the late 19th century, the district was famous for its vineyards.

SÓLLER ◄

La Granja ⑦
Once a country estate, La Granja now houses one of the island's most interesting museums. It stages shows of regional dance, crafts and local wine-tastings.

PALMA ▲

Port d'es Canonge ⑥
The road leading to this small fishing port and beach is narrow and winding, but the beauty of the spot makes it worth the trouble. Fishermen's huts and a restaurant are by the beach.

PALMA ▼

Esporles ⑧
At the centre of this friendly town, far from the tourist haunts, is the shady Passeig del Rei, lined with numerous cafés and restaurants. The nearby church was built in the early 16th century.

Puigpunyent

Port de Valldemossa ⑨
A small, shingly beach and a few good fish restaurants are the main reasons to follow the winding road from Valldemossa to this pretty hamlet. It offers peace and idyllic scenery, and is visited by only a handful of holidaymakers.

TIPS FOR TOURISTS

Length: *50 km (30 miles).*
Stopping-off points: *Most places along the route have a bar or restaurant; the restaurant at Mirador de Ricardo Roca is superb. Accommodation can be found in Andratx and Valldemossa.*
Further information:
Valldemossa, Jardin de la Cartuja.
📞 *917 612 019.*

KEY

▬▬ Suggested route
═ Other road
▬▬ Scenic route
❋ Viewpoint

Valldemossa ⑩
Frédéric Chopin wintered here in 1838. It is worth taking a stroll through the town's narrow alleys, after visiting the monastery and the royal palace.

La Granja ⑩

THIS COUNTRY HOUSE *(finca)* lies in a wooded valley, near Esporles. From the 13th to the 15th centuries it belonged to an order of Cistercian monks, and after this to the Fortuny family. The estate has survived almost unchanged since the 18th century and is now a museum of folklore, full of antique furniture, ceramics and other artifacts. Mouth-watering hams hang in the antique kitchen, peacocks stroll around the beautiful garden and the local restaurant serves delicious Mallorcan cuisine. In the mornings it is quieter, and you can still see displays of folk dancing and local crafts.

Dye-house
This formed part of the domestic quarters, most of which were situated in basements and cellars.

Park
The estate, situated in a valley, is surrounded by a park to the south and west. Its landscaping includes streams and waterfalls; the house is almost completely hidden by a dense growth of trees.

Library
Situated next to the Renaissance bedroom, the library also served as the master's study.

Courtyard
The house is arranged around a courtyard. Don't miss the classic car that is parked in an open garage. The courtyard has a wide entrance gate to the east.

STAR ATTRACTIONS

★ **Garden**

★ **Salon**

VISITORS' CHECKLIST

2 km (1 mile) west from
Esporles. 971 610 032.
10am–7pm daily (summer),
10am–6pm (winter).
www.la granja.net.
Folklore shows: Wed & Fri
3:30–5:30pm.

★ Salon
*The formal rooms are situated on the north side.
Next to the salon are the games room and a small
theatre. From here, French windows open onto
the garden.*

Restaurant

★ Garden
*At the centre of
the garden is a
small fountain;
the escarpment
hides a grotto.*

**Gate to
the park**

Corridor
*Windows overlook
the courtyard. On its
east side is a row of
smaller rooms, where you
can see, among other
things, an exhibition of
model locomotives.*

Steam Engine
*Produced by Merlin & Co, the
engine is one of the items in
the extensive collection of
agricultural machinery,
exhibited in several indoor
rooms as well as outside.
The exhibition clearly
demonstrates changes in
soil cultivation methods.*

**Main
entrance**,
where the shop
and café are
located.

Enchanting little alleys of Valldemossa, beckoning strollers

Valldemossa ⓫

🏠 1,750. 🚌 ℹ Jardin de la Cartuja, 971 612 019.
🌐 www.valldemossa.com 🗓 Sun.
🎉 Santa Catalina Thomàs (28 Jul), Sant Bartomeu (24 Aug).

THE HISTORICAL RECORDS of Valldemossa go back to the 14th century, when the asthmatic King Sancho built this palace in the mountains to make the most of the clean air. In 1399, the palace was handed over to the Carthusian monks, who remodelled it as a monastery. The **Real Cartuja de Jesús de Nazaret** (Royal Carthusian Monastery of Jesus of Nazareth) was abandoned in 1835 when the monks were dispossessed.

The composer Frédéric Chopin rented a former monk's cell here in 1838 with his lover George Sand, the feminist French writer, and the monastery is now the town's main tourist attraction. In front of the entrance, in Plaça de la Cartuja de Valldemossa, is a monument to Chopin.

The monastery includes a chapel with a ceiling decorated with late-Baroque paintings by Miguel Bayeu, a relative of Goya's. Behind the chapel are rows of shady arcades. The prior's cell, despite its name, consists of several spacious rooms with access to a private garden offering a magnificent view of the valley below. The rooms house an exhibition of religious artifacts. The adjacent cells contain mementos of Chopin and George Sand.

The 17th-century monastery pharmacy contains a variety of ceramic and glass jars with wonderfully detailed descriptions of their contents (look out for the jar containing "powdered beasts' claws").

The monastery also houses the excellent **Museu Municipal Art Contemporani**, which has a small collection of works by distinguished Spanish artists including Antoni Tàpies, Joan Miró and Juli Ramis – a modernist painter and native of Mallorca. There is also a cycle of illustrations by Pablo Picasso, *Burial of Count Orgaz*, inspired by the famous El Greco painting.

On leaving the arcades you can proceed to the **Palau del Rei Sanç** – the Palace of King Sancho. This is the oldest fortified part of the monastery. The main point of interest is the wooden drawbridge connecting the two chambers over the palace's entrance. Once used as a political prison, the palace now serves as a venue for displays of folk dancing and recitals of Chopin's music.

Valldemossa itself is charming and always bustling. Most visitors are keen to see the places associated with Chopin, but a stroll along the town's narrow cobbled alleys is definitely worthwhile.

The modest house at c/Rectoría 5 is where the saintly nun Catalina Thomàs was born to a peasant family. The house has been converted into a richly decorated chapel, with the statue of the saint standing in front, holding a jug with flowing water. Nearby is the 15th-century church of Sant Bartomeu, now, unfortunately, partly destroyed.

🏛 Real Cartuja de Jesús de Nazaret

Plaça de Cartuja de Valldemossa.
📞 971 612 106. 🗓 Sun. 🏞 ♿

ENVIRONS: Port de Valldemossa lies some 6 km (4 miles) north of Valldemossa. This is a small fishing village scenically poised on the shores of a narrow bay and surrounded by rugged cliffs. It is reached by a narrow, hairpin road. The local beach, although small and pebbly, is enchanting and occupies a beautiful location. The demanding journey is rewarded by a number of local restaurants specializing in seafood.

SANTA CATALINA THOMÀS (1531–74)

Catalina Thomàs is the only Mallorcan saint. At the age of 23, she joined an Augustinian order. Known for her humility, she declined the position of Mother Superior, saying that she did not wish to govern but to serve God. She is buried in the chapel of Santa María Magdalena convent in Palma, where she spent many years of her life. She was canonized in 1930.

Tile with the image of the Saint, on one of Valldemossa's houses

Frédéric Chopin and George Sand

The great Polish composer Chopin spent four months in Valldemossa's 14th-century monastery *(see opposite)* during the winter of 1838–39. Chopin was accompanied by Aurora Dupin, better known as the French novelist George Sand, and her children. Their arrival here was partly to escape the prying eyes of Parisian society and partly on

Chopin monument in Valldemossa

account of the composer's health. Chopin suffered from tuberculosis though the weather was so bad during his stay that it made him worse. The short visit to the town by this unusual couple, described by Sand in *A Winter in Mallorca*, has contributed to the popularity of Valldemossa, despite the fact that Sand labelled the locals as "savages".

Garden in front of cell No. 2, *in which Chopin's scores and George Sand's manuscripts are held. To this day there is a dispute over which cell Chopin occupied (No. 2 or No. 4). The garden terrace affords a fine view.*

Portrait of George Sand – *Sand was a French writer and journalist. A highly unconventional figure, she was morally way ahead of her time – she wore trousers, smoked cigars and "lived in sin".*

Manuscript of Prelude No. 24, opus 28, *one of the many works composed by Chopin during his short visit to Mallorca, even though his piano only arrived three weeks before he left the island.*

A fresh red rose *is always placed on the upright piano in cell No. 2. The composer's favourite* Pleyel *piano was brought from Paris and now stands in cell No. 4.*

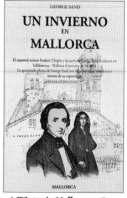

GEORGE SAND

UN INVIERNO EN MALLORCA

El inmortal músico Frédéric Chopin y la escritora George Sand tividieron en Valldemossa - Mallorca al invierno de 1838/39. La apasionada pluma de George Sand nos describe aquí relato intenso y intenso de su experiencia.

MALLORCA

A Winter in Mallorca – *George Sand's description of her visit to Mallorca with Chopin has enjoyed lasting popularity.*

Rotunda in the garden of Son Marroig

Son Marroig ⓬

3 km (2 miles) northeast of Deià
🕐 9:30am–8pm (summer);
9:30am–6pm (winter) ⬤ Sun. 🈂

THIS LATE-MEDIEVAL mansion, perched high above the seashore, was remodelled in the 19th century to become the residence of the Habsburg Archduke Ludwig Salvator. The Austrian aristocrat was fabulously rich and came to Mallorca hoping to escape from the strict morality of the Viennese court. He fell in love with the island, settled here and gave himself over to exploring and promoting the Balearic Islands.

The house is now a museum, dedicated to his life and work and including some of his pen drawings and manuscripts. It is surrounded by a terrace and graced by a rotunda of white marble. From here, the Archduke enjoyed fine views over the wooded shore to the narrow promontory of **Sa Foradada** where he used to moor his yacht *Nixe*. It takes less than an hour's walk to get there.

ENVIRONS: A short way southwest of Son Marroig is the **Monestír de Miramar**. The house was built in 1276 for Ramón Llull but was acquired by Ludwig Salvator in 1827. The Archduke entertained Princess Sisi here during her visit to Mallorca.

🏛 **Monestír de Miramar**
📞 971 616 073. 🕐 9:30am–2:30pm & 4:30–8pm Mon–Sat (summer); 9:30am–2:30pm & 4:30–6:30pm (winter). 🈂

Deià ⓭

🏃 700. 🚌 🏃 S/Joan Baptista (24 Jun).

THIS LOVELY, small mountain town lies at the spot where the mighty Puig d'es Teix meets the sea. Deià is mostly associated with the English novelist and poet Robert Graves *(see opposite)*. Graves settled here in 1929 and for the next 56 years lived and worked here, making the place popular with other artists including Picasso and the writer Anaïs Nin.

Towering over the town is the modest church of **Sant Joan Baptista** (1754–60). The adjacent building houses the **parish museum** with a collection of religious objects. Deià also has an interesting **Museu Arqueológic** founded by the American archaeologist William Waldren, displaying the prehistory of Mallorca.

Hotel La Residencia, in the grounds of a former estate, has attracted many famous guests including Princess Diana and Sir Bob Geldof.

LUDWIG SALVATOR

The Habsburg Archduke Ludwig Salvator was born in 1847. He first visited Mallorca at the age of 19 and became captivated by the island. He settled here permanently, learned the local dialect and created a scandal by marrying a local carpenter's daughter. He was tireless in exploring and promoting Mallorca, producing a seven-volume work devoted to the island's history, archaeology, folklore and topography. It is thanks to him that a 10-km (6-mile) long stretch of the coast that he owned has survived intact. In 1910, he was awarded honorary citizenship of Mallorca. He died in 1915.

🏛 **Museu Arqueológic**
Es Clo Deià 📞 971 639 001.
🕐 5–7pm Sun, Tue, Thu 🈂

ENVIRONS: A narrow winding road leads to **Cala de Deià**, with its shingle beach and clear water, situated in a picturesque cove surrounded by steep cliffs.

Hotel La Residencia viewed from the church hill

Modernista **building of Banco de Sóller, one of Sóller's landmarks**

ROBERT GRAVES (1895–1985)

Robert Graves was an English novelist, poet and classical scholar. Severely wounded on the Somme during World War I, his frank autobiography, *Goodbye to All That*, earned him enough money to move to Mallorca where he set up home, accompanied by his muse and mistress, the poet Laura Riding. Here, he wrote two tremendously successful historic novels: *I, Claudius* and *Claudius the God*, which made him world famous. The outbreak of the Spanish Civil War interrupted his stay but he returned to the island in 1946. He died in 1985 and is buried in the local church of Sant Joan Baptista beneath a simple gravestone.

Robert Graves' tombstone in Deià's cemetery

Sóller ⓮

🚌 🚏 ℹ️ *Plaça Constitució 1.* 📞 *971 630 200.* 🌐 *www.a-soller.es* 📅 *Sat.* 🎭 *Festes de Moros i Cristians (2nd Sun in May).*

SITUATED IN A valley, Sóller is sheltered by the Serra de Alfàbia mountain massif and overshadowed by the lofty Puig Major (1,445 m/4,740 ft). Its name reputedly derives from the Arabic word *suliar*, meaning "golden bowl" – the valley is famous for its many orange groves.

Arabs, who settled here in the late 8th century, built canals and irrigation ditches and the town grew rich thanks to its plentiful supply of oranges and the vineyards and olive groves, planted on the slopes of the Serra de Tramuntana. In exchange for its oranges and wine, it imported goods from France and links between the town and France remain strong.

Plaça Constitució is a lively square and the centre of Sóller. Mature trees, fountains and lively cafés give the place its unique atmosphere. Notable buildings include the *Modernista* castle-like **Banco de Sóller**, which is the work of Joan Rubió i Bellver, a disciple of Antoni Gaudí, and the Neo-Gothic church of **Sant Bartomeu**, also designed by Rubió. Particularly eye-catching is the vast rosette window on the church façade, carved in stone, and the Baroque sculptures contrasting with the dark interior.

To the north of the square stands **Museu Casa de Cultura**, occupying a renovated building in Calle Sa Mar. Here, you can recapture the atmosphere of old Sóller as you stroll through rooms decorated with antique furnishings, a courtyard and an old kitchen with amusing majolica plates.

Museu Balear de Ciències Naturals (Balearic Museum of Natural Science), on the outskirts of Sóller, was opened in 1992 in a late 19th-century mansion house. Its exhibits include a collection of Mallorcan fossils and rocks and specimens of the local flora. The adjacent **Jardí Botànic** contains plants native to the Balearic Islands. The town's **vintage electric train**, nicknamed the "Red Arrow", which runs between Palma and Sóller, provides a superb

Fountain in Plaça Constitució in Sóller

ride through the mountains. From the Sóller terminus you can hop aboard a **vintage tram**, which takes you on to Port de Sóller *(see p70)*.

🏛 **Museu Casa de Cultura**
C/ Sa Mar 9. 📞 *971 630 200.* ⭕ *11am–1pm & 5–8pm Tue–Fri.* 🖼
🏛 **Museu Balear de Ciències Naturals** and **Jardí Botànic**
Ctra. Palma–Port de Sóller 📞 *971 634 064.* ⭕ *Apr–Sep: 10am–8pm Tue–Sat, 10am–1pm Sun; Oct–Mar: 10am–5:30pm Tue–Sat, 10am–1pm Sun.* 🖼

ENVIRONS: Port de Sóller, situated 5km (3 miles) from Sóller, is a pleasant although crowded resort with numerous seafood restaurants next to the harbour and by the beach. Here, you can enjoy a boat trip along the coast, or go for a hike to the nearby lighthouse.

Punta Grosa lighthouse, near Port de Sóller

Train from Palma to Port de Sóller ⓯

THE MOST ENJOYABLE WAY to travel from Palma to Sóller is aboard the "Red Arrow", an electric narrow-gauge railway line, which opened in 1912. After passing through farmland, the 27-km (17-mile) route winds its way through the steep peaks and valleys of the Serra de Tramuntana. The line is justifiably regarded as one of the most attractive in Europe, and the narrow-gauge rolling stock, musty carriages and clanking engine only add to the experience.

Sóller ④
After a one-hour ride the train reaches Sóller. From here a vintage tram running through the busy town centre takes you to Port de Sóller.

Mirador Pujol d'en Banja ③
Two special tourist trains, leaving Palma daily at 10:50am and noon, stop briefly at this viewpoint to provide a splendid view of Sóller, the surrounding mountains and the coastline.

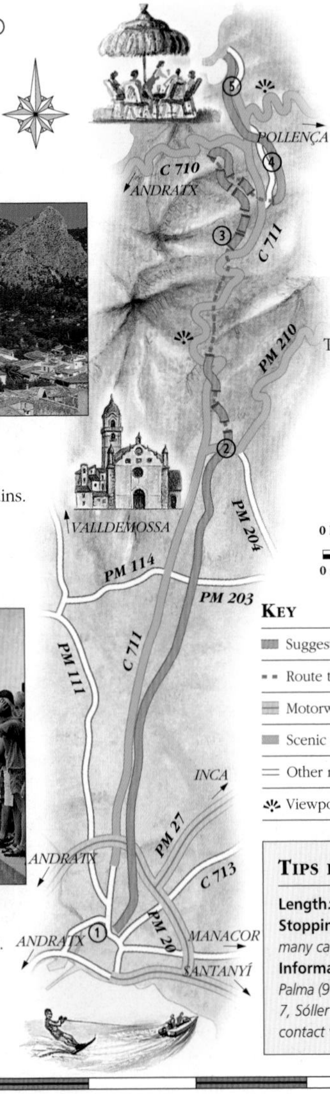

Port de Sóller ⑤
The journey from Sóller to Port de Sóller takes 15 minutes. The tram route runs along the beach and ends at the harbour. Trams run much more frequently than the train.

Bunyola ②
This is the last stop before passing through the dizzying Serra de Tramuntana mountains. This typical Mallorcan town, towered over by its church, enjoys an idyllic location in a beautiful verdant valley.

0 km 2
0 miles 2

KEY

- Suggested route
- Route through the tunnel
- Motorway
- Scenic route
- Other road
- Viewpoint

Palma ①
A trip aboard this vintage electric train is a real delight. The line was originally built to transport fruit to Palma from Sóller at a time when the journey by road took an entire day.

TIPS FOR TOURISTS

Length: *27 km (17 miles).*
Stopping-off points: *Sóller has many cafés and restaurants.*
Information: *Plaça d'Espanya 2, Palma (971 752 051); C/ Castanyer 7, Sóller (971 630 301); or contact* www.trendesoller.com

Jardines de Alfàbia 16

14 km (9 miles) north of Palma. 📠 🚍 *971 613 123.* ⏰ *Jun–Aug: 9:30am–6:30pm Mon–Fri, 9:30am–1pm Sat; Sep–May: 9:30am–5:30pm Mon–Fri, 9:30am–1pm Sat.* 🖼

MOST VISITORS COME to see the magnificent Moorish gardens of this old manor house, set amid lemon groves. Footpaths shaded by pergolas criss-cross streams and take you past murmuring fountains, ivy-clad walls and beds of splendid roses. The house is approached via a long stately avenue of plane trees.

Following the conquest of the island by Jaume I, the estate was given to the Moorish governor Benhabet. Benhabet had been the governor of Pollença but supported the king by provisioning the Catalan army during the invasion. For this help, Jaume I gave Benhabet this land and he set about planning an estate in the Moorish style. After his death the castle became the residence of the Mallorcan kings. The origin of the estate's name goes back to the days of Arab rule, when it was called *Al-Fabi* ("Jug of olives").

The house itself, with its courtyard surrounded by domestic buildings and shaded by a giant plane tree, is actually modest though attractive. Most notable is the 14th-century oak throne made for Jaume IV. The gatehouse features a lovely Mudéjar (Spanish-Moorish) style vault, with an inscription praising Allah.

Beach at the end of Torrent de Pareis canyon, near Sa Calobra

Sa Calobra 17

30 km (19 miles) NE of Fornalutx.

THIS TINY HAMLET occupies a beautiful cove surrounded by high cliffs. A busy tourist centre, its main attraction is the **Torrent de Pareis** (River of the Twins) canyon, which is reached by a coastal walkway, leading partly through a tunnel.

It is also possible to reach this impressive canyon from **Escorca**, a hamlet on the way from Sóller to Pollença. This route is extremely difficult, however, and requires rock-climbing skills, ropes and wetsuits! It takes about six hours to cover it. During the winter and spring or after heavy rainfall it is virtually impassable as the bottom of the canyon, known as the "Great Canyon of Mallorca", fills with torrential waters. Once upon a time Sa Calobra was accessible only by boat. Now there is a twisting road leading to it, which in view of its breakneck descents and bends has been nicknamed *Nus de la Corbeta* ("Knotted neck-tie"). Two kilometres (1 mile) before Sa Calobra you can take a left turn to the popular resort of **Cala Tuent**. Set against the northern slopes of Puig Major, the quiet village has a modest gravel and sand beach. The Es Vergeret restaurant has a large selection of fish dishes – its terrace affords a fine view of the rocky coast.

SERRA DE TRAMUNTANA

The northern coast of Mallorca is dominated by the Serra de Tramuntana (Mountains of the North Wind), which run from Sa Dragonera in the west to Formentor in the east. The highest peak of this 90-km (55-mile) stretch is Puig Major (1,445 m/4,740 ft), though part of this is used by the military and closed to visitors. The steep slopes are covered with sweet smelling wild rosemary and are home to goats, sheep and rare birds. The best way to enjoy this area is on foot and a number of maps are easily available that list walking routes through all or part of the mountain range. Alternatively, you can explore the mountains by car, although great care should be taken on the narrow and twisting roads and frequent hairpin bends that descend through steep cliffs to the sea.

Steep mountain slopes west of Monestír de Lluc

Sun shining through a pergola in Alfàbia gardens

Monestír de Lluc ®

THE MONASTERY AT LLUC is the spiritual centre of Mallorca and has been a place of pilgrimage for over 800 years. The main point of interest is the little statue of the Virgin (*La Moreneta*), which, so the story goes, was found in a cave by an Arab shepherd boy who had converted to Christianity. The image was initially moved to the church but it kept returning to the same spot. A chapel was built to house this miraculous object and this has since been decorated with precious stones. Thousands of pilgrims now arrive here every year to pay homage.

Statue of Joaquima Rosselló i Ferrá
Father Rosselló, who arrived at the Sanctuary in 1891, was the founder of the Sacred Heart Missionary Congregation and the spiritual reviver of the monastery.

Church
The original Renaissance-Baroque church was built during 1622–84 and was designed by Jaume Blanquer. Much of the complex dates from the 18th and 19th centuries.

Statue of Bishop Campins
Bishop Pere-Joan Campins, a great patron and promoter of the monastery, commissioned Antoni Gaudí to renovate the basilica and build its Way of the Cross.

STAR SIGHTS

★ **Els Porxerets**

★ **La Moreneta**

★ **Museu de Lluc**

★ **Museu de Lluc**
Opened in 1952, the museum houses local handicraft, such as siurells (whistles) and majolica, as well as works of art, paintings, coins and archaeological finds.

School Grounds
The buildings behind the church belong to the Los Blauets, a school choir founded in 1531. The name derives from the choir's blue cassocks.

VISITORS' CHECKLIST

From Palma. 9am, 11am, 12:30pm, 5pm & 7pm daily. **Museum** 971 871 525. @ info@ lluc.net 10am–1:30pm & 2:30–5:30pm daily. **Botanical Garden** 10am–1pm & 3–6pm daily. **La Fonda Restaurant** 971 517 022. 1–3:30pm Wed–Mon, 7:30– 9:30pm Wed–Sun. Cami dels Misteris del Rosari (Mar/Apr).

Dormitories

La Dormición de la Virgen
The last of the seven steles carved by Miguell Cosequell, once standing along the road between Caimari and the Sanctuary, now stands in Plaza de los Peregrinos.

★ Els Porxerets
The 16th-century building was extended in the early 18th century. It consists of pilgrim quarters on the first floor and stables on the ground floor.

★ La Moreneta
The tiny statue of La Moreneta ("the little dark one") is just 62 cm (24 inches) high. It stands in a niche inside the Royal Chapel, built during 1707–24, at the back of the main altar.

Plaza de los Peregrinos
The drive leading to the monastery is surrounded by greenery and lined with bars, cafés and souvenir shops. It provides a magnificent view of the Serra de Tramuntana.

Inca ⑲

🏃 23,000. 🚗 🚆 🚌 Thu.
📷 Dijous Bó (3rd Thu in Nov).

INCA, THE LAST STOP on the train journey from Palma, is the third largest town on the island. A modern industrial place, visitors come here nevertheless, attracted by the cheap leather goods in Avinguda General Luque and Gran Via de Colon. Thursday, market day, is Inca's busiest time. The stalls lining the streets and squares stretch over several districts of town. Here you can buy almost anything – souvenirs, household goods, flowers and food. Inca is also known for its traditional Mallorcan cuisine, including *caracoles* (snails) and for its wine cellars converted into restaurants (*cellers*).

ENVIRONS: About 2 km (1 mile) past the town, heading towards Alcúdia, is a right turn in the road that leads to the top of **Puig d'Inca** (296 m/970 ft), with a small sanctuary, **Ermita de Santa Magdalena**. For nearly 800 years on the first Sunday after Easter crowds of pilgrims have congregated here. There is a good view from the top over the surrounding fields and mountains. Near the road to Alcúdia are the **Coves de Campanet**, a complex of small but beautiful caves surrounded by tropical gardens. The neighbouring small town of **Sa Pobla** holds one of the best Sunday markets on the island.

🦇 Coves de Campanet
Ctra. Palma–Alcúdia, 39 km (24 miles). 📞 971 516 130.
🕙 from 10am daily. 🖼 📷 ∅

Steps of the Way of the Cross, leading to El Calvari, in Pollença

Pollença ⑳

🚌 ℹ Claustro de Santo Domingo, 971 535 077. 🚆 Sun. 📷 Sant Antoni (17 Jan), Los Moros y los Cristianos (2 Aug).

FOUNDED BY THE ROMANS in the foothills of the Serra de Tramuntana, Pollença has retained much of its old-world charm with narrow, twisting streets, some good restaurants and a lively Sunday market. The remains left by the town's founders include **Ponte Romà**, a bridge spanning the banks of the Torrente de Sant Jordi river, at the north end of town.

After 1229, the Knights Templar began the building of the parish church of **Nostra Senyora dels Angels**. Remodelled in the 17th century, the church façade has a fine rosette window, while its dark interior is decorated with paintings and a vast altar that is several storeys high.

The pride of the town is the beautiful **Via Crucis** (Way of the Cross). It leads to the **El Calvari chapel** standing on top of the hills and housing a Gothic statue of Christ. Climbing the seemingly endless set of steps (365 in all), you pass the Stations of the Cross. The chapel may also be reached by walking along the streets. The statue of Christ is carried down to the parish church in a moving torchlight procession every Good Friday, during the *Davallament* (the Crucifixion).

The building of the former **Convent de Santo Domingo** (Dominican monastery) now houses the **Museu Municipal** with its collection of Gothic sacred art, archaeological

Colourful stall with souvenirs at Inca's Thursday market

finds and a small collection of modern paintings.

To soak up the sleepy atmosphere of Pollença, head for **Plaça Major**, where the locals gather in the cafés and bars.

🏛 Museu Municipal
Carrer Santo Domingo. 📞 971 530 437. ⭕ Tue, Thu & Sun. 🈺

ENVIRONS: The family friendly resort of **Port de Pollença**, situated 6km (4 miles) to the east beside a pleasant bay, is an attractive place with a long, sandy beach. Just southeast of Pollença a steep narrow road, then a footpath, climbs 330 m (1,000 ft) to **Puig de Maria**, where a 17th-century hermitage has a rustic restaurant and bar, and simple rooms to let with wonderful views.

Cap de Formentor 🈯

6 km (4 miles) from Port de Pollença.

THE FORMENTOR PENINSULA, at the northern end of the Serra de Tramuntana, is a 20-km (12-mile) long headland of steep cliffs, that is in some places 400 m (1,300 ft) high. The footpath from the road leads to the **Mirador des Colomer** from which you can enjoy spectacular views of the sea and the **El Colomer** rock. There is also a beautiful view of the 16th-century watch tower, **Talaia de Albercutx**, standing much higher than the viewpoint. Further on, the road passes through the Mont Fumat tunnel and runs among rocky hills, covered with vegetation, up to the **lighthouse** rising to 260 m (850 ft). On a clear day you can see Menorca and its capital, Ciutadella. The rugged cliffs provide nesting sites for thrushes and rock doves, also falcons, swallows and martins.

A spur from the main road leads to the lovely public beach of **Cala Pi de la Posada**, which is served by bus from Port de Pollença and gets very crowded in summer. The road ends at one of the oldest, most luxurious resorts on the island – the Hotel Formentor. Opened in 1929, it is noted for its opulence and fashionable clientele *(see p146)*.

Inside the Gothic church of Sant Jaume in Alcúdia

Alcúdia 🈯

🚌 ℹ Ctra. d'Artà 68, 971 892 615. 🚆 Tue–Sun. 🎪 Romeria de la Victòria (2 Jul).

THE DELIGHTFUL TOWN of Alcúdia, surrounded by 14th-century walls, lies at the base of the peninsula separating Pollença Bay from Alcúdia Bay. Originally, this was a Phoenician settlement. Having conquered the island, the Romans built a town here, called Pollentia, which from the 2nd century was the capital of the island. In 456, it was destroyed by the Vandals. Around the year 800, Moors built their fortress here, naming it *Al-Kudia* (On the Hill). After the Reconquest, Alcúdia prospered as a trading centre well into the 19th century.

Town hall window in Alcúdia

The beautifully restored town is entered through the vast **Porta de Moll** gate. The Gothic church of **Sant Jaume** at the centre is 13th-century. Near the church are a few **remains of Roman houses**. Adjacent to these is **Museu Monogràfic**, which displays objects from Roman times.

On the outskirts of town, along the road to Port d'Alcúdia, is the **Oratori de Santa Anna**. Built in the early 13th century, it is one of the oldest Mallorcan sanctuaries. Nearby are the remains of a first-century BC **Roman theatre** – this is the smallest Roman theatre to have survived in Spain.

🏛 Museu Monogràfic
Carrer de Sant Jaume, 30. 📞 971 547 004. ⭕ 10am–1:30pm & 3:30–5:30pm Mon–Fri, 10:30am–1pm Sat & Sun. 🈺

ENVIRONS: Port d'Alcúdia, 2 km (1 mile) south of the town, is the most popular tourist destination on Mallorca's northeast shores. It has a lovely sandy beach, a marina and a harbour as well as hotels, restaurants and clubs. The road to Es Mal Pas brings you to **Cap des Pinar** where, in 1599, Philip II erected a watchtower, Torre Major. A branch road leads to the **Ermita de la Victòria**. It has a revered 15th-century wooden statue of Victoria, Alcúdia's patron saint.

Lighthouse on Cap de Formentor

The marshes of Parc Natural de S'Albufera, crisscrossed with canals

Parc Natural de S'Albufera ㉓

◯ 9am–7pm daily.

THE WETLAND SOUTH of Port d'Alcúdia, occupying the shores of Lake Grande up to C'an Picafort, was once a swamp. Most of it was drained in the 1860s, but a portion remains, which in 1985 become the Parc Natural de S'Albufera. The marshes, overgrown with reeds, can be explored on foot, following the marked trails. A major conservation project, this is an excellent place for observing over 200 species of birds including grey and purple herons, summer osprey and Eleonora's falcon. The park reception is in **Sa Roca** where you can obtain a free map and a list of some of the park's birds that you are likely to see.

Muro ㉔

13km (8 miles) east of Inca ▣
ⓦ www.ajmuro.net ▤ Sun.
▩ Revelta de Sant Antoni Abat (18 Jan).

THE agricultural town of Muro is a pleasant, sleepy place, situated at the centre of the plain, surrounded by cultivated fields. It is full of old mansions built by rich landowners, which give the town its unique charm. Each year on 18 January, Muro is the scene of the *Revelta i Beneides de Sant Antoni Abat* – a big fiesta on the eve of St

Antoni's day. The town's inhabitants and visitors gather around bonfires, drinking wine and eating sausages and *espinagades* – delicious pies made with eels caught in the S'Albufera marshes.

The town is dominated by the church of **Sant Joan Baptista**, remodelled around 1530. This large structure, built in the Catalan Gothic style, features colourful stained glass windows and a beautiful rosette on the façade. The interior includes Baroque furnishings and a vast main altarpiece. Adjacent to the church is a huge, seven-storey belfry that once served as a watchtower. The view from the top can be stunning and encompasses all of the surrounding area.

The **Convent des Minims** and the church of **Santa Ana** are in Plaça de José Antonio Primo de Rivera, once the venue for bullfights. Nearby is the **Museu de Mallorca, Seccio Etnològico**, which is situated in an old mansion house. Here, you can see a collection of local furniture, folk costumes, agricultural tools and a series of workshops including a blacksmith's and a cobbler's. The museum also has a collection of *siurells* – whistles.

Baroque cartouche from the museum in Muro

🏛 Museu de Mallorca, Seccio Etnològico
Carrer Major 15.
☎ 971 717 540. ◯ 10am–3pm &
2–5:20pm Tue–Sun, 10am–3pm &
5–8pm Thu. 🎦

ENVIRONS: Some 11 km (7 miles) east of Muro, on Badia d'Alcúdia, adjacent to the Parc Natural de S'Albufera, is the sandy beach of **Playa de Muro** with its stone-pines growing amid the dunes. About 3 km (2 miles) north is **Sa Pobla**, which has a lovely 17th-century Baroque church and two museums: Museu d'Art Contemporani and Museu de la Jugeta, which has a collection of toys from the 19th and 20th centuries. The town's main square, Plaça Constitució, hosts a busy Sunday market, selling mainly agricultural produce. **Santa Margalida**, situated 5km (3 miles) southeast, has a history reaching back to Roman times. The views of the mountains and plain are outstanding from here.

Multi-storey altarpiece in Muro's Sant Joan Baptista

Sineu ㉕

30km (19 miles) northeast of Palma.
▩ 3,200. ▤ ▤ Wed. ▩ Fira Maig (24 Apr).

SINEU IS ONE OF the most interesting agricultural towns of the central Es Pla plain and has a rich history. Attracted by its strategic position, at the very heart of the island, Jaume II built his **palace** here. King Sancho came here to benefit from the fresh air and declared the town the centre of Mallorca. Later, Jaume III slept here the night before the battle of Llucmajor, in which he was killed fighting the army of Pedro of Aragón. Today, the palace is occupied by an order of nuns that is known as the *monges del palau* (sisters of the palace).

Adjacent to the former royal residence stands the biggest parish church on the island, **Nostra Senyora de los Angeles**. This Gothic structure was built in 1248 and remodelled in the 16th century. In front of the church, in Plaça de Sant Marcos, stands a statue of a winged angel – the symbol of St Mark the Apostle, the patron saint of the town.

In the neighbouring Sa Plaça square are two excellent restaurants serving traditional Mallorcan cuisine: the Celler Ca'n Font and the Celler Es Grop.

At one time, the Inca-Artà railway line passed through the town. Now, the former station building, dating from 1879, houses the **S'Estació Art Gallery**. Wednesday's market is one of the biggest agricultural fairs in Mallorca and sells local produce and livestock.

Stained glass church window in Sineu

🏛 **S'Estació Art Gallery**

📞 *971 520 750.* 🕐 *9:30am– 1:30pm & 4–7pm Mon–Fri.* 🌐 *Sat.*

ENVIRONS: About 4 km (2 miles) north, near the road leading to Llubia, are the ruins of a Talayotic structure.

Monumental church in Petra, towering over the neighbourhood

Petra ㉖

🚌 *50 km (31 miles) east of Palma.* 🚂 🌐 *www.ajpetra.net* 📅 *Wed.* 🎉 *Santa Pràxedes (21 Jul), Festa de Bunyols (30 Oct).*

THIS SMALL TOWN is the birthplace of Junipero Serra. Aged 54, the Franciscan monk travelled to America and Mexico and after a series of arduous journeys on foot, founded missions in California. The old houses lining the labyrinth of narrow alleys have changed little since Serra's time here. The town makes the most of its famous son and all places associated with Junipero Serra are well marked. These include **Casa Natal Fray Junipero Serra**, a humble building in Carrer Barracar Alt where Serra was born.

Next to this is a small but interesting **museum**, opened in 1955. The exhibition is devoted to his life and work and includes wooden models of the nine American missions established by Serra as well as a range of memorabilia. At the end of the street in which the Serra family house stands, on the outskirts of town, is the 17th-century monastery of **Sant Bernat**, which has a statue of Serra standing in front of it. The Majolica panels down a side street next to the monastery are a gift from grateful Californians and pay tribute to the famous monk's many achievements.

🏛 **Museu y Casa Natal Fray Junipero Serra**

C/ Barracar Alt 6–8. 📞 *971 561 149.* 🕐 *Visits by appointment only.*

ENVIRONS: Some 7 km (4 miles) west lies the small town of **Sant Joan**. Its 13th-century parish church, remodelled in the 15th and 18th centuries, acquired its present form in the 1930s. If there is time, head for the Santuari de la Mare de Déu de la Consolació, standing on the outskirts of town. Built during the Reconquest period and restored in 1966, it is now a place of pilgrimage.

Ariañy, 4 km (2 miles) to the north, is a small agricultural town. Famous during the days of Jaume I, it became the region's capital in 1982. Its houses are dwarfed by the high tower of the Neo-Romanesque church.

JUNIPERO SERRA

Junipero Serra was born in Petra in 1713 and played an important role in the history of the Spanish colonization of North America. In 1749, he left on a mission to Mexico, and later travelled to California, where he established nine missions and sought to convert the native Indians to Christianity. Some of Serra's missions prospered after his death and became the cities of San Diego, Santa Barbara, Los Angeles and San Francisco. He died in 1784 and was beatified in 1988.

Statue of Junipero Serra in Palma

The medieval fortress of Capdepera

Artà ❷

🚌 🏛 *Wed.* 🎭 *San Antonio (12, 13 Jun), Sa Fira (2nd Sun in Sep).*

THIS HILLTOP TOWN was built on the site of an Arab stronghold; its name is derived from the Arabic word *jertan* ("garden"). Much of its medieval walls and fortifications have survived to this day.

The town's most interesting structure is the hilltop **Santuari de Sant Salvador**. It can be reached from the mid 13th-century parish church of **Transfiguració del Senyour** via steps (actually a Way of the Cross) shaded by a line of cypresses.

The chapel and its surrounding walls were built during 1825–32. It contains a revered 17th-century statue of the Virgin with Child. The courtyard affords a lovely view of the town's rooftops.

ENVIRONS: Ses Païsses, a short way to the south, is a 3,000-year-old Bronze Age settlement. The remains include fragments of the defence walls and a huge watchtower. Some of the stone blocks weigh about eight tons. The archaeological findings from this site can be seen in Artà's regional museum. The **Ermita de Betlem**, about 7 km (4 miles) to the north, is built on a hill. Established in 1805, the tiny church has a number of primitive frescoes.

Capdepera ❷

🚌 🎭 *Fiesta Nostra Senyora d'Esperança (18 Dec).*

TOWERING ABOVE the town is a castle. It was built in the 14th century to defend the coast against pirates. At the highest point of the castle stands the Gothic church of **Nostra Senyora d'Esperança**. The outside stairs lead to a flat roof from which there is a nice view of the town's terracotta roofscape.

Madonna from the Artà chapel

♦ Castell de Capdepera

📞 *971 818 746.* 🕐 *Apr–Oct: 10am–8pm daily; Nov–Mar:10am–5pm daily.* 📷

ENVIRONS: The **Coves d'Artà**, regarded as one of Mallorca's wonders, are situated some 6 km (4 miles) to the south. Two thousand Arabs were found hiding here by Jaume I during the Reconquest. In the 19th century, the caves were studied by a French geologist and became popular with tourists – Jules Verne is said to have written *Journey to the Centre of the Earth* after visiting them *(see opposite)*.

🦇 Coves d'Artà

Canyamel k. Capdepery. 📞 *971 841 293.* 🕐 *Apr–Oct: 10am–6:30pm; Nov–Mar 10am–5pm.* ⬛ *1 Jan, 25 Dec.* 📷

Cala Rajada ❷

ℹ️ *Plaça dels Pins, 971 563 033*

A SMALL SEASIDE RESORT and bay, Cala Rajada is famous for its beautiful beach shaded by a stone-pine forest. The rocky coast surrounding it is regarded as one of the most attractive in this part of Mallorca. You would hardly guess it but until recently this was just a small fishing village – only the old jetty, which is now used by pleasure boats and sailing yachts, remains.

Above the Cala Gat bay stands **Palau Joan March**, the stately home of a rich tobacco merchant, banker and patron of the arts; its lovely gardens are open to the public and contain numerous sculptures, mainly by Spanish artists (you can also see works by Auguste Rodin and Henry Moore).

🏛 Palau Joan March

C/ Joan March. 📞 *971 563 033.* 🕐 *By appointment with Cala Rajada's Tourist Information Office.*

ENVIRONS: From Cala Rajada it is worth taking a 2-km (1-mile) walk to **Cap de Capdepera**, the easternmost headland of Mallorca. The nearby **Platja de Canyamel** is a new resort with lovely sandy beaches. There is also a local golf course and the former watchtower Torre de Canyamel now houses a restaurant specializing in tasty Mallorcan cuisine.

Fishing boat leaving Cala Rajada's harbour

Mallorca's Caves

MALLORCA IS FAMOUS for its caves, which are carved out of the island's limestone rocks. Many were known by the locals for hundreds of years and they once provided shelter for the early settlers, or served as hiding places from marauding pirates, dens for smugglers and religious sanctuaries. In the 19th century Archduke Ludwig Salvator began to take an interest in them and recruited a French geologist, Edouard Martel, to study them. In 1896 Martel rediscovered the Coves d'Artà. He was amazed by their size (some are the size of a cathedral) and the large number of stalactites and stalagmites.

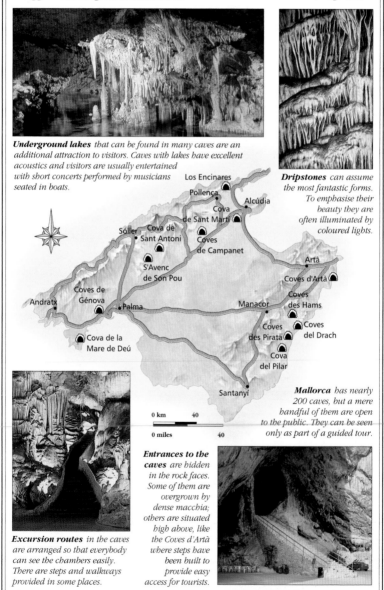

Underground lakes *that can be found in many caves are an additional attraction to visitors. Caves with lakes have excellent acoustics and visitors are usually entertained with short concerts performed by musicians seated in boats.*

Dripstones *can assume the most fantastic forms. To emphasise their beauty they are often illuminated by coloured lights.*

Los Encinares
Pollença
Alcúdia
Cova de Sant Martí
Sóller
Cova de Sant Antoni
Coves de Campanet
S'Avenc de Son Pou
Artà
Coves d'Artà
Coves de Génova
Andratx
Palma
Manacor
Coves des Hams
Cova de la Mare de Deú
Coves des Pirata
Coves del Drach
Cova del Pilar
Santanyí

0 km 40

0 miles 40

Mallorca *has nearly 200 caves, but a mere handful of them are open to the public. They can be seen only as part of a guided tour.*

Excursion routes *in the caves are arranged so that everybody can see the chambers easily. There are steps and walkways provided in some places.*

Entrances to the caves *are hidden in the rock faces. Some of them are overgrown by dense macchia; others are situated high above, like the Coves d'Artà where steps have been built to provide easy access for tourists.*

Sandy beach of Cala Millor, one of Mallorca's most popular spots

Cala Millor 🐦

📧 📍 *Avenida Joan Servera Camps, s/n, 971 585 864.*

CALA MILLOR is one of the most popular resorts on the east coast of Mallorca. The first hotels began to appear here as early as the 1930s, but the real tourist invasion did not start until the 1980s. Similar to neighbouring Cala Bona and Sa Coma, Cala Millor has many beautiful beaches; the main one is 1.8 km (1 mile) long and is quite magnificent. As you would expect, the resort has plenty of bars, restaurants and clubs.

ENVIRONS: At the **Safari-Zoo**, a wildlife park 2 km (1 mile) to the south, you can explore by car, miniature road train or as part of a guided coach tour. Some 4 km (2 miles) northwest is **Son Servera**. Not the prettiest of Mallorcan agricultural towns, its prime feature is the church, which was begun in 1905 by Joan Rubió, a disciple of Antoni Gaudí, and which remains unfinished to this day.

Porto Cristo 🐦

📧 📍 *C/ Bordils 53A, 971 815 103.*

THE ANCIENT FISHING port of Porto Cristo is situated at the end of a long bay, where the El Rivet flows into the sea. Today it is a pleasant family resort but as early as the 13th century this was a seaport for the inland town of Manacor. As the best sheltered harbour on the eastern coast of Mallorca it was also an important naval base. During the Spanish Civil War, Republicans landed here with the intention of taking over the island from General Franco's forces.

Aquarium decoration in Porto Cristo

Despite initial successes, the attack was repelled.

Porto Cristo is one of the few places on the eastern coast of Mallorca where you can find last-minute hotel accommodation during the high season. Among its attractions are the sandy beach and an **aquarium** with fish from all over the world.

ENVIRONS: Some 2 km (1 mile) south of Porto Cristo are the **Coves del Drac**. The "Dragon's Caves" are one of Mallorca's treasures. Although they have been known for centuries, they were unexplored until 1896. They feature an attractive array of dripstones, as well as one of the world's largest underground lakes, 177 m (580 ft) long, 40 m (131 ft) wide and over 30 m (98 ft) deep. A ride by boat under the stalactite vault is an unforgettable experience.

The **Coves d'es Hams**, 2 km (1 mile) to the east, derive their name from the hook-shaped stalactites *(hams)* found here. Boatloads of floating musicians on the underground lake produce an unusual musical ambience.

🦞 **Coves del Drac**
📞 *971 820 753.* @ cuevasdrach @portocristo.com ⏰ *Apr–Oct: 10am–5pm daily; Nov–Mar: 10:45am–noon & 2–3:30pm.* ♿

🦞 **Coves d'es Hams**
📞 *971 820 988.* 🌐 www.cuevas-hams.com ⏰ *daily.*

Yachting harbour at the end of Porto Cristo bay

Manacor 🈲

📷 🏛 *Pl. Ramon Llull s/n, 971 847 241.* ⏰ *8am–3pm Mon–Fri.*

MANACOR IS Mallorca's second largest town and boasts a centuries-long tradition of handicraft. It produces furniture and ceramics, including the famous Mallorcan black porcelain, but it is most famous for its simulated pearls. The town is also known for the local speciality – *sobrasada de cerdo negro* – spicy sausage, and sweets called *sospiros* (sighs).

Places worth visiting in Manacor include the church of **Nostra Senyora dels Dolors** in Plaça del Rector Rubi, built in the late 19th century on the site of a former mosque. Its lofty clock tower, resembling a minaret, is a town landmark. The most notable features of the church's interior are the vast wooden door and a figure of the crucified Christ, dressed in white robes, with long flowing hair.

Numerous shops in town sell simulated pearls, which have been produced here since 1890. In order to see them being made, you can visit **Perlas Majórica**, a factory offering free tours. Here, glass beads are covered with consecutive layers of a compound made of fish scale mixed with resin, dried, polished to a high shine and set in silver or gold.

Perlas Majórica
Avinguda Majórica, 48.
⏰ *9am–1pm & 2:30–7pm Mon–Fri, 10am–1pm Sat & Sun.* 🈳

Opulent interior of the Gothic church in Manacor

Music room in the stately home of Els Calderers

ENVIRONS: Sant Llorenç des Cardassar is 9 km (6 miles) to the northeast. The local church has two figures of the Madonna. The first is a wooden statue dating from the 12th or 13th century. The second, carved in stone, was made in the 15th century, probably in France.

Colourful fruit and vegetable stall in Vilafranca de Bonany

Vilafranca de Bonany 🈳

📷 🏠 *Wed.* 🎪 *Festa de Meló (Sep).*

THE AGRICULTURAL TOWN of Vilafranca de Bonany lies on the road to Manacor. It is known for its colourful market stalls set along the highway. These sell peppers, sun-dried tomatoes and garlic, as well as fruit and vegetables grown in the local gardens. Also on offer are tiny doughnuts called *bunyelos*. The only historic building in town is the **Santa Barbara church** (1731–38).

ENVIRONS: About 2 km (1 mile) northeast, on top of Puig de Bonany (317 m/1,040 ft) is the **Ermita de Bonany** sanctuary. The monastery's stone cross was erected for Juinipero Serra who left from here in 1749 on a mission to California *(see p77).* The sanctuary is 17th-century and was built as an act of thanksgiving for a good harvest – *bon any* or "good year". The modern church dates from 1925 and is entered via an imposing gate, decorated on top with ceramic tiles featuring portraits of St Paul and St Anthony. From the church forecourt you can see a splendid panorama of the central plains of Es Pla.

One kilometre (half a mile) northwest of Vilafranca de Bonany is **Els Calderers** – a landed estate established in the 17th century by the Veri family. The stately home is surrounded by fields and farm buildings. Today, parts of the estate are open to the public; these include the private chapel, the granary and the large kitchen. The rooms contain original furniture and are decorated with paintings, family photographs and *objets d'art*, all of which maintain the atmosphere of the former residence. The fire burning in the fireplace and the open piano give visitors the impression that the owners have only just stepped out.

🏛 **Els Calderers**
📞 *971 526 069.*
🌐 *www.todoesp.ws/els-calderers*
⏰ *10am–6pm daily.* 🈳

Felanitx ❸

ℹ️ *Avinguda Cala Marsals 15, Porto Colom, 971 826 084.* 🚌 *Sun.* 🎉 *Fiesta San Joan Pelós (24 Jun).*

FROM A DISTANCE, the busy little town of Felanitx looks as though it is surrounded by a wall with many turrets. As you approach, it becomes apparent that these are windmills built on the outskirts of town. Felanitx is the birthplace of the outstanding medieval architect Guillem Sagrera (1380–1456) and the highly original 20th-century painter Miquel Barceló.

This small agricultural town has a fine **13th-century church**. Sant Miquel's magnificent Renaissance-Baroque façade, approached by steep stairs, hides a building erected in 1248. It is also worth visiting Felanitx to taste the locally produced *sobrasada de porc negra* – spicy pork sausage, and to buy some of the ceramics that are made here.

ENVIRONS: About 5 km (3 miles) southeast, on top of the 400-m (1,312-ft) high hill, are the ruins of **Castell de Santueri**, an Arab castle remodelled in the 14th century by the kings of Aragón. The view from the ruins is a magnificent panorama of the surrounding area. The **Santuari de Sant Salvador** stands 4 km (2 miles) east of Felanitx, on top of Puig Sant Salvador, the highest mountain of the Serres de Llevant.

Giant cactus in the Botanicactus garden, near Santanyí

Founded in the 14th century, and remodelled in the 18th century, the sanctuary is an important place of pilgrimage. The view includes the south-eastern coast of Mallorca.

Santanyí ❸

ℹ️ *Avda. Cala Llonga, 971 657 463.*

THIS OLD TOWN is full of stone houses built from the local honey-coloured sandstone. The same sandstone was used in the building of the cathedral in Palma and Castell Bellver.

One of the old town gates, **Sa Porta**, in Plaça Port is a reminder of medieval times when the town was an important fortress defending southeastern Mallorca, and surrounded by several walls. Towering over the town is the vast church of **Sant Andreu**. The interior of this 18th-century church features a huge Rococo organ brought here from a Dominican monastery in Palma.

ENVIRONS: North of town, on top of the Puig Gros hill stands a 16th-century chapel with a beautiful picture of the Madonna. The **Santuari de Consolació** is accessed via stone steps, which have been climbed for centuries by footsore and weary pilgrims. Some 5 km (3 miles) east of Santanyí is **Cala Figuera**, with an unspoilt fishing harbour situated in a bay that resembles a fjord. The adjacent

Huge façade of Felanitx's main church

and equally picturesque **Cala Santanyí** bay is situated at the end of a rocky canyon with steep banks, overgrown with trees. Here, rising from the sea, is the **Es Pontas rock**. Six kilometres (4 miles) east is the **Botanicactus**, a garden which has nearly 400 species of cacti.

Rocky coastline in the Parc Natural Mondragó

Parc Natural Mondragó ❸

8 km (5 miles) east of Santanyí. ☎ *971 181 022.*

THIS RELATIVELY small, unspoilt area has wonderful footpaths and pretty country lanes and is an ideal destination for walking trips. The routes are marked and are generally easy going. The coastline itself is rugged, but it is still possible to find small, sandy coves, the best of which are Mondragó, S'Amarador and Caló des Burgit. In the pine forest, which covers most of the park, there are small ponds and dunes.

Ses Salines 🟤

📧 *Dr Barraquer 5, 971 656 073.*

SES SALINES IS a modest little town that is sometimes overlooked by visitors. It owes its origin, wealth and name to the nearby salt works. The **Salines de Llevant** are large salt lakes and marshes. This area is inhabited by numerous species of birds such as the spotted crane, marsh harrier, kestrel, warbler and hoopoe. During the migration season the marshes are visited by flocks of plover, avocet, tattler, godwit and osprey. There are many paths through the marshes, making them an excellent area for walking and cycling trips, particularly for bird-watchers.

ENVIRONS: Cap de Ses Salines is 3 km (2 miles) south of Ses Salines. This is the southernmost promontory of Mallorca. The view from the lighthouse is magnificent and encompasses the entire south coast of the island as well as Cabrera Island. **Banys de Sant Joan de sa Font Santa** lies 4 km (2 miles) northeast of Ses Salines. The local hot springs, with water temperatures rising as high as 38°C (100°F), have been known since the 15th century when they were used to treat a variety of conditions, including leprosy. The local chapel dates from this period. The present bathhouse was built in 1845. Today, the waters are still believed to be beneficial and are used to treat rheumatism and a variety of respiratory ailments. **Campos**, probably founded by the Romans, is situated

12 km (7 miles) from Ses Salines. The town, rarely visited by tourists, is full of historic remains. The Neo-Classical church of Sant Julià (1858–73) features a painting, *Sant Crist de la Paciència*, by the 17th-century Spanish master Bartolomé Esteban Murillo; the Gothic retable is the work of Gabriel Mògera. The church has a small parish museum. The former Torre de Can Cos, which once guarded the town against pirate attacks, became incorporated into the present town hall in 1649. Markets are held here every Thursday and Saturday. Some 10 km (6 miles) to the north is **Ermita de Sant Blas**, which has a recently restored 13th-century chapel.

Lighthouse at the Cap de Ses Salines headland

Colònia de Sant Jordi 🟤

52 km (32 miles) east of Palma.
📧 *Dr Barraquer 5, Ses Salines, 971 656 073.*

THE TOWN LIES on the southern end of the island. It has a handful of modest hotels, a few restaurants, a pretty beach and an interesting harbour.

Sa Ràpita beach, a favourite with windsurfers

Many people come here with the sole purpose of catching a boat to nearby Cabrera Island *(see pp84–5)*, which, according to Pliny, was the birthplace of the famous Carthaginian leader, Hannibal. The pleasure boats to Cabrera sail daily from May until mid-October.

The town's other main attraction is the nearby salt lake, *Salines de S'Avall*, from which huge quantities of salt were once extracted – the main source of the town's wealth.

🚢 **Excursions to Cabrera**
C/ Explanada del Port. 🎫 *971 649 034.*

ENVIRONS: One of Mallorca's most beautiful beaches is 7 km (4 miles) to the north, in **Es Trenc**, which can also be reached via a shorter route along the coast. This small but constantly developing resort is very popular with visitors to the southern coast of Mallorca. The 4-km (2-mile) stretch of beach can easily accommodate the large numbers of holidaymakers, and is not generally too busy. **Sa Ràpita** is a small place near S'Estanyol de Migjorn. The local beach provides good conditions for windsurfing. During the summer, the marina is also a popular place. The only historic remains are of the defence tower, which once guarded the coast against pirates. Equally beautiful beaches can be found to the south of Colònia de Sant Jordi. When they get too busy you can also try **Platja des ses Roquetes**.

Beach and harbour in Sa Ràpita, near Colònia de Sant Jordi

Cabrera Island National Park ③⑨

Native species of peony

CABRERA ("goat island") lies just 18 km (11 miles) from mainland Mallorca. A rocky, bare place and virtually uninhabited, it nevertheless has a rich history. It served as a prison camp during the Napoleonic War and was used as a base by Barbary pirates. Since 1991, Cabrera, together with an archipelago of 157 sq km (60 sq miles), has been designated a national park. This protection extends not only to rare species of plants, but also includes the surrounding marine life.

Es Castell
The 14th-century castle is one of the few reminders of the island's past. A small museum close to the jetty includes a history of the island.

Cala Santa Maria
In the course of a few hours, you can see the shore areas surrounding the bay. Exploring the interior requires permission from the park staff.

Asteriscus aquaticus
Though this plant is found on all the islands of the archipelago, Cabrera is home to some rare native plant species.

A memorial was built for the French soldiers abandoned on Cabrera by the Spanish during the Napoleonic Wars. Of the 9,000 prisoners, only 4,000 survived.

Es Port

Caserio Cabrera

Can Feliu

Cap de N'Ensiola
At the island's southwest tip is a lighthouse that can be reached via a winding road. Permission for this must be obtained from the park's office in Palma.

0 km   1

0 miles   1

Na Pobre

Illa Plana

Illa Conejera

VISITORS' CHECKLIST

Oficina del Parque Nacional Marítimo Terrestre del Archipiélago de Cabrera, Plaza de España, 8, 1°, Palma. ☎ 971 725 010.
@ cabrera@mma.es. *Boat trips leave from Mallorca's Colònia de Sant Jordi jetty: May–early Oct, daily. Journey time: 50 minutes.*
☎ 971 649 034.

Eleonora's Falcon
This rare species is strictly protected. In 1974, there were only nine nesting pairs, now there are about 30.

On Foradada
The northernmost rocky island of the archipelago has a lone lighthouse and a lighthouse keeper's cottage.

Illa Cabrera   *Illa Redona*

Sa Cova Blava
The 20-m (66-ft) high "Blue Grotto" owes its name to the colour of light that is reflected from the water, which illuminates the cave's walls. The grotto can be seen as part of a boat trip.

L'Olla
In an effort to protect the landscape and surrounding waters, this area is closed to the public.

Cas Garriuer

KEY

═	Other road
⋯	Footpath
🛈	Tourist information
⚓	Harbour
🏖	Beach
♦	Castle
✲	Viewpoint

Sunday market in Llucmajor

Llucmajor **40**

🚌 ℹ️ *Plaça Reina Mª Cristina, s/n, 971 440 414.* 🚌 *Tue, Fri.*

L LUCMAJOR HAS LONG been associated with Mallorca's shoemaking industry and had a thriving market in medieval times. Formerly the main town of the southern region, it was just outside Llucmajor's walls, in 1349, that Pedro IV of Aragón killed the last king of Mallorca, Jaume III. The monument standing at the end of Passeig de Jaume III commemorates the event.

The **town hall**, built in 1882, is in the main square. A short way from this, the 18th-century church of **San Miquel** has been built over a 14th-century church. The most prized historic building in town is the Franciscan **Església Conventual de Sant Bonaventura**. This 17th-century church contains many precious historic objects, including an impressive altarpiece (1597) painted by Gaspar Oms.

Capocorb Vell **41**

🚌 📞 *971 180 155.* ⭕ *10am–5pm Fri–Wed.* 📷

M ALLORCA HAS fewer prehistoric remains than Menorca, but this Talayotic settlement on a rocky plateau on the southern coast of the island is well worth visiting.

The settlement was probably established around 1000 BC. Originally, it consisted of five *talayots* (stone structures resembling towers, covered with a wooden roof) and 28 smaller dwellings. It is worth taking a closer look at the remains of the Cyclopean walls, reaching 4 m (13 ft) in places, which would have served as protection for this ancient village. Not much is known about the inhabitants of the settlement and the function of some of the rooms is unclear. The narrow underground chamber, for instance, is too small to be used for living quarters and may have served as a ritual site. A free leaflet, in English, is available at the site entrance, which provides more information on these fascinating remains.

The megaliths scattered through this quiet area, amid fields and fruit trees, were declared a cultural heritage site as early as 1931. Apart from a restaurant and a small bar, there are few other traces of modern civilization here.

ENVIRONS: Some 5 km (3 miles) southeast of Capocorb Vell, lies **Cala Pi**. This is a small cove with an enticing sand beach. Several luxurious villas have sprung up around here, well hidden behind pine

Ruins of the prehistoric settlement in Capocorb Vell

trees. During the high season, many yachts drop anchor here. The area is dominated by a watchtower (1659), which provides views of the entire Badia de Palma. About 7 km (4 miles) to the south is **Cap de Blanc**, which has a lighthouse. From here there is also a splendid view over the coast towards Cabrera Island. A large section of the peninsula is used for military purposes and it is therefore important not to stray from the route that leads to the lighthouse.

Tree-shaded courtyard of the church at Puig de Randa

Puig de Randa **42**

8 km (5 miles) northeast of Llucmajor. 📞 *971 660 994.*

I N THE MIDDLE OF the fertile plains of Es Pla rises the distinctive Puig de Randa hill (549 m/1,800 ft), which provides stunning views of the whole of Mallorca. Ramón Llull *(see opposite)* founded a hermitage on top of this hill in the 13th century and it was here that he trained missionaries bound for Africa and Asia. Nothing remains of the original building but Llull's legacy has ensured that the site is an important place for Catholics.

The monastery (the oldest part of which dates from 1668) is a popular destination for pilgrimages, particularly those associated with the blessing of the crops – *Benedición de los Frutos* – on the 4th Sunday after Easter.

Tucked under a steep cliff face, **Santuari de Nostra**

Senyora de Gràcia is the first of the religious buildings you come to. The interior of the chapel is decorated with beautiful majolica tiles. A little further up the hill is the 16th-century **Santuari de Sant Honorat**. This hermitage houses a courtyard that is filled with ancient trees. The passage to the church is decorated with tiles depicting the sanctuary's history.

The culmination of the pilgrimage is the **Santuari de Nostra Senyora de Cura**, which is on the site where Llull once lived. The gate in the wall surrounding the monastery is 17th-century and opens onto a courtyard built of typical golden Mallorcan sandstone. The monastery, much of which is fairly modern, houses a library and a study centre. The stained-glass windows of the church depict the most important moments of Llull's life.

Algaida 🚩

🚌 🅿 Fri. 🎏 Sant Honorat (16 Jan), Sant Jaume (25 Jul).

MOST PEOPLE PASS through the outskirts of this small town on their way to Puig de Randa. If you like churches, however, it is worth stopping here in order to visit the Gothic church of **Sant Pere i Sant Pau**, with its interesting doorway and ornamental gargoyles.

ENVIRONS: The odd-looking castle on the road from Palma to Manacor dates from the 1960s and houses **Ca'n**

Ceramic sign of Can Gordiola, advertised outside a Palma shop

Gordiola, a glassworks, museum and shop. Here, you can see skilled glass-blowers producing the pale blue and green glass that has been produced on the island for hundreds of years. On the first floor is a museum exhibiting items collected by several generations of the Gordiola family.

Some 9 km (6 miles) to the east is **Montuïri**. The town, built on a hill, is famous for its agricultural produce. Nineteen of the original 24 windmills still stand as testimony to the town's former glory. Just outside Montuïri, on the road that leads to Pina, is one of the best preserved Mallorcan Talayotic remains – **Son Fornés**. This prehistoric settlement has two *talayots* and includes nine dwellings, which were used up until Roman times.

S'Arenal 🚩

🚌

A LITTLE TO THE EAST of Palma, S'Arenal is a typical resort with several kilometres of sandy beaches. A tree-lined boulevard runs along the shore, with bars, restaurants, nightclubs and shops. A series of stainless steel beach bars stretch along the coast. These *balnearios* are numbered: No. 1 is near the harbour, No. 15 is by the Ca'n Pastilla marina (alternatively, you can take a miniature "tourist train" to the marina). At the height of the holiday season the narrow alleys of the resort throb with life, day and night.

One of several water slides in Aquacity near S'Arenal

S'Arenal's harbour provides mooring places for yachts. On the outskirts of town is **Aquacity**, a children's paradise of pools, water slides and playgrounds.

🏊 **Aquacity**
📞 971 440 000. ⏰ Jul–Aug: 10am–6pm daily; Sep–Jun 10am–5pm daily. 🎫

RAMÓN LLULL

This prominent Mallorcan was born in Palma to a noble family around 1232. During his youth he lived life to excess. Quite why he changed his ways is not known though legends abound. One story has it that he abandoned court life after seeing a vision of the crucified Christ. At the age of 30 he became a monk and devoted the rest of his days to the Catholic faith. He became a religious scholar, founded a missionary school and wrote over 260 works of theology, philosophy, physics, chemistry and warfare. During the final 30 years of his life he travelled around the world. He is believed to have been stoned to death in Algeria in 1315.

Statue of Ramón Llull in Palma

Mallorca's Beaches

Mallorca has nearly 80 beaches. The best are around Badia de Palma and to the north and northeast of the island. These are great for swimming and sunbathing and are very popular during the peak season. Some of the island's best beaches have been incorporated into larger resorts and include restaurants, fun parks, watersports and beachside bars. It is still possible to find more secluded beaches and coves, however, though these tend to have fewer facilities and may be difficult to reach.

Ses Illetes ⑥

This small beach, barely 120 m (390 ft) long, is off the beaten track. Despite that, and the lack of facilities, it remains popular.

Palma Nova ④

This is one of the best beaches on the Badia de Palma. The neighbouring houses and hotels are hidden among dense greenery; the Serra de Tramuntana hills can be seen in the distance. It is a good base for family holidays.

Portals Nous ⑤

This beach, typical of the Balearic Islands, is on a long narrow cove. The thrills and spills of Marineland are nearby *(see p59)*.

Magaluf ③

Magaluf's beach has long been popular with visitors and the town is one of the oldest resorts in Mallorca. The beach can often be busy and the town itself is full of nightclubs, restaurants and bars. The main attraction, apart from the beach, is the nearby Aquapark *(shown)*.

Costa d´en • Blanes

PM 1

Cala Portals Vells ②

Civilization has not as yet touched this small beach. The bay attracts those who seek peace, but at peak times it can be crowded even here.

C 119

El Mago ①

This small beach on the bay is favoured by nudists. This is one of three nudist beaches in this part of the bay.

Key

▬	Motorway
▬	Major road
▬	Scenic route
▬	Other road

Cala Major ⑦
🚍 🍴 🏖️

This small bay is lined with houses and hotels. The golden beach is hardly secluded but it is one of the nicest in this area.

Palma ⑧
🚍 🚐 ⊕ 🍴 🏖️ 🛏️

Inhabitants of the Balearic Islands' capital make the most of C'an Pere Antoni beach, or other beaches along the Badia de Palma.

Ca'n Pastilla ⑨
🚍 🚐 ⊕ 🍴 🏖️ 🛏️

A mini-tourist train runs from here to S'Arenal. The local beach is similar to Platja de Palma, with umbrellas and deckchairs for hire. It also has a playground for children.

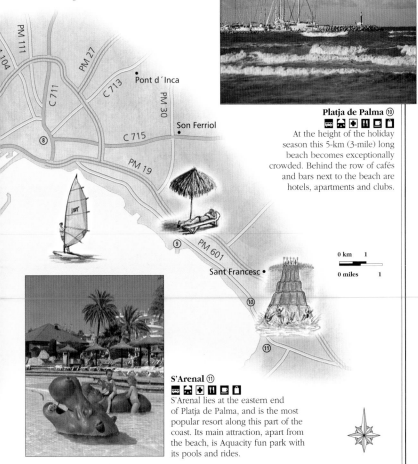

Platja de Palma ⑩
🚍 🚐 ⊕ 🍴 🏖️ 🛏️

At the height of the holiday season this 5-km (3-mile) long beach becomes exceptionally crowded. Behind the row of cafés and bars next to the beach are hotels, apartments and clubs.

0 km   1

0 miles   1

S'Arenal ⑪
🚍 🚐 ⊕ 🍴 🏖️ 🛏️

S'Arenal lies at the eastern end of Platja de Palma, and is the most popular resort along this part of the coast. Its main attraction, apart from the beach, is Aquacity fun park with its pools and rides.

MENORCA

ENORCA IS THE *second largest of the Balearic Islands and has low-key, family-friendly resorts and nearly as many beaches as Mallorca and Ibiza combined. Situated furthest from the mainland, it is one of the quieter islands and has escaped most of the side-effects of package holidays. Its small towns and villages appear to be havens of tranquillity, even at the peak of the season.*

Travelling across Menorca, the variations in landscape are perhaps less obvious those of Mallorca. The changes are more gradual, as red-soil and sandstone farmlands become pine-clad ravines, and small, sheltered coves alternate with steep, rocky shores.

Most of the Balearic Islands' megalithic monuments from the Talayotic period are found on this island, including a good number of the cone-shaped towers *(talayots)* which give the period its name. As with the other islands, Menorca has had its share of visiting conquerors including the Greeks, the Romans and, during medieval times, the Arabs who defended the island until 1287. During the 18th century, the island was ruled by the English and

Locally-bred black horse in Ciutadella

French in turn, before becoming a Republican stronghold during the Spanish Civil War.

The two oldest and largest towns in Menorca are Maó and Ciutadella; both are full of historic buildings. The island's capital, Maó (often referred to by its Spanish name of Mahón), is the best natural harbour in this part of the Mediterranean. Ciutadella, Menorca's former capital, is situated on the northwestern end of the island and also has a natural harbour. When travelling around Menorca you can appreciate the charm of the island's unhurried lifestyle. Its inhabitants are attached to their traditions and customs – for instance, unlike the rest of Spain, they prefer local gin to wine. Fiesta celebrations are particularly lively.

Colourful traditional folk dancers in Maó accompanied by live music

◁ **A narrow alley in Poblat de Pescadors in Binibeca**

Exploring Menorca

MENORCA IS SOMETIMES REFERRED to by the locals, jokingly, as "the bit between Maó and Ciutadella". The island mainly attracts those looking for peace and relaxation such as older visitors and families with young children, who wish to avoid the late-night clubs and bars found elsewhere. The island, proclaimed a biosphere reserve by UNESCO, is also a favourite with nature lovers. King Juan Carlos drops anchor in Fornells harbour from time to time, when he gets tired of the busy Mallorcan scene. In Fornells you can savour *caldereta de llagosta* – a delicious lobster stew for which the island is famous. Those who enjoy historic monuments can also find much of interest. The vast numbers of Talayotic structures, and the palaces and churches of Ciutadella and Maó are all worth visiting. One way to explore the island is on horseback.

LOCATOR MAP

CALA MORELL

16 CIUTADELLA

C 721

15 WESTERN COAST OF MENORCA

FERRERIES **13**

PMV 721-2

PM 714

SANTA GALDANA

14

ARTRUTX

Lighthouse at Cap d'Artrutx

GETTING THERE

The best way to travel to Menorca is by air. During the high season there are flights from many European countries and other regions of Spain. The most reliable way to travel out of season is via Palma. The airport is near Maó and has good transport links with major towns on the island. You can also travel to Menorca by ferry from Palma or Barcelona. The main road on the island connects Maó with Ciutadella. Minor roads branch from it, running towards the northern and southern coasts. There are no problems reaching large towns and resorts, but some small, attractive places maybe difficult to get to. It is best to travel around the island by hire car, as some of the smaller towns and villages have no bus service.

SIGHTS AT A GLANCE

Alaior **8**
Binibeca Vell **5**
Cala en Porter **7**
Cales Coves **6**
Cap de Cavalleria **11**
Ciutadella pp108–11 **16**
Es Castell **3**
Es Grau **2**
Es Mercadal **9**
Es Migjorn Gran **12**
Ferreries **13**
Fornells **10**
Maó pp94–7 **1**
Sant Lluís **4**
Santa Galdana **14**

Tours

Western Coast of Menorca **15**

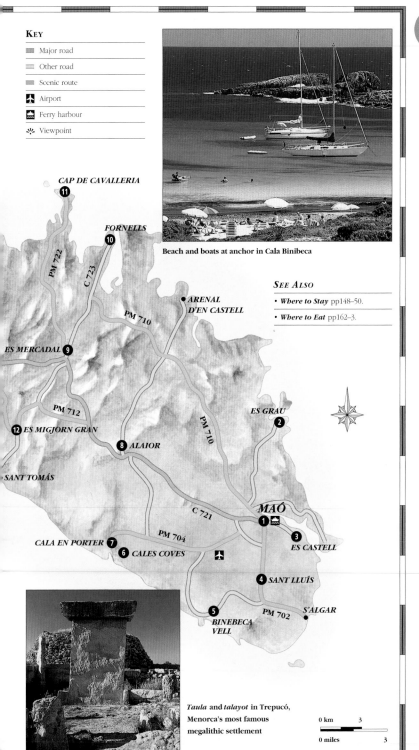

KEY

- ▪ Major road
- ▭ Other road
- ▪ Scenic route
- ✈ Airport
- ⛴ Ferry harbour
- ✻ Viewpoint

CAP DE CAVALLERIA ⑪

FORNELLS ⑩

PM 722

C 723

● ARENAL D'EN CASTELL

PM 710

ES MERCADAL ⑨

PM 712

⑫ ES MIGJORN GRAN

PM 710

● ES GRAU ②

⑧ ALAIOR

SANT TOMÁS

C 721

MAÓ ①⛴

③ ES CASTELL

CALA EN PORTER ⑦

PM 704

⑥ CALES COVES

✈

④ SANT LLUÍS

⑤

BINEBECA VELL

PM 702

S'ALGAR

Beach and boats at anchor in Cala Binibeca

SEE ALSO

- **Where to Stay** pp148–50.
- **Where to Eat** pp162–3.

Taula and *talayot* in Trepucó,
Menorca's most famous
megalithic settlement

0 km   3

0 miles   3

Maó ❶

I<small>N SOME RESPECTS</small>, Maó (or Mahón in Catalan) is like a small, provincial town. A pretty place, it has a population of 20,000 and lies on the steep, southern shore of a bay that is one of the best natural harbours in the world. The remains of the old city walls, several beautiful churches, colourful Spanish mansions and Georgian town houses make it a fascinating place to explore. At the same time, it is the island's capital and is a city of culture – its Teatre Principal was the first opera house in Spain when it opened in 1829.

Muse in front of Teatre Principal

Exploring Maó

When exploring Maó, it is best to start from Plaça d'Espanya. Here, and around the neighbouring squares, are the town's main historic buildings. The whole district is dominated by the vast Baroque church of **Santa Maria**. For most people, however, the real pleasure is in strolling along the narrow alleys of old Maó and soaking up its unique atmosphere. Some of Maó's streets have restricted car access, turning them into virtual pedestrian precincts. Stopping for a rest in one of the numerous cafés is an experience to savour.

🔒 Església del Carme

Plaça Carme

This imposing Baroque church began life as a Carmelite convent in 1751. In 1835, the convent was confiscated by the state and the building was substantially restored in 1941 after being damaged during the Spanish Civil War. The vast interior of the former church, one of the biggest in Maó, is preserved in a Rococo style,

Colourful houses built on the high escarpment in Plaça Espanya

but despite its opulence it gives an impression of emptiness.

The complex, mostly closed to visitors, occupies the vast quarter between Plaça Carme and Plaça de la Miranda. The square behind the monastery offers a beautiful view over Cala Sergo.

🏛 Mercat

Plaça Carme. ◯ 9am–9pm Mon–Sat.

Maó's famous town market (Mercat) takes place in a series of renovated monastery buildings next to Església del

Carme. The cool cloister has been turned into a picturesque fruit and vegetable market, where *queso Mahón*, one of Spain's most delicious cheeses, is much in evidence. Here, you can also buy meat and other food products, as well as souvenirs. The rows of market stalls set under the figures of the saints and other religious symbols provide a strange contrast.

🏛 Collecció Hernández Mora

Claustre del Carme, Plaça de la Miranda. (971 350 597.

The Menorcan historian Hernández Mora (1888–1975) donated his collection of antique furniture, sea charts, paintings, engravings and other works of art to the town. The exhibits provide a slice of Menorcan history during the 18th and 19th centuries, when the French and English ruled the island in turn.

🏛 Plaça Espanya

Plaça Espanya is the central square of old Maó. A busy **fish market** occupies a circular bastion on the north side of the square and offers countless varieties of fish, squid, shellfish and other seafood. From here steps lead down to Maó's waterfront.

🎭 Teatre Principal

Costa Deià, 40. (971 355 603, 971 355 776.

Maó's theatre opened in 1829, and beats the Liceu in Barcelona and Teatro Real in Madrid, to be Spain's first opera house. Built by the Italian singer and architect, Giovanni Palagi, it was often chosen by the big Spanish opera companies to premiere their Spanish tours. Today, it is used mainly as a cinema but it also hosts some concerts and cultural events including an annual musical festival at the end of March.

🔒 Santa Maria

Plaça Constitució. ⬛ 7:30 pm Mon–Sat, 8am,10.30am, noon, 8.30pm Sun.

This church standing near the town hall was begun in 1287 on the site of a mosque, after the defeat of the Moors by Alfonso III. It was later rebuilt

Narrow alleys leading away from Maó's old centre

Façade of the town hall opposite Església de Santa Maria

🏛 Ajuntament
Plaça Constitució.

The town hall was built in 1613 and its façade *(left)* was remodelled in 1789, giving it a typically Spanish appearance. It features an ornamental clock, presented to the town by Richard Kane, the first British governor of Menorca. Inside, the walls are lined with portraits of local notables, French and Spanish governors and, still hanging to this day, portraits of the British monarch George III alongside Queen Charlotte.

difficult to imagine a time when this was once a vast British naval base. Tours of the harbour in a glass-bottomed boat leave regularly from Maó and Es Castell.

⚓ Harbour
The best way to arrive in Maó is by sea so that you catch your first sight of its magnificent natural harbour from the prow of a ship. Several centuries ago the famous Genoese admiral, Andrea Doria concluded that June, July, August and Mahón were the best ports in the Mediterranean, by which he meant that outside the safe sailing season of the summer months, it was prudent to seek shelter here.

Today, the tranquil atmosphere of the harbour makes it

in a Neo-Classical style in the 18th century and subsequently remodelled several times after that, although the large, gloomy interior has retained much of its Catalan Gothic austerity and is almost devoid of any ornamentation, with only the transept and the vaults featuring rich Baroque decorations. The most striking features of the interior are the Rococo main altarpiece and the vast organ, built in 1806 by the Swiss maker Johann Kyburz and imported from Barcelona with the help of the British. It is a mighty piece with four keyboards and 3,120 pipes. Look out for the figures of trumpet-blowing angels.

Maó, perched on steep slopes, seen from the harbour

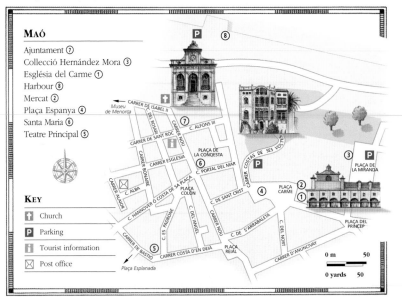

MAÓ

Ajuntament ⑦
Collecció Hernández Mora ③
Església del Carme ①
Harbour ⑧
Mercat ②
Plaça Espanya ④
Santa Maria ⑥
Teatre Principal ⑤

KEY

🛈 Church

🅿 Parking

🛈 Tourist information

⊠ Post office

0 m   50
0 yards   50

Further Afield

Venturing outside Maó's centre involves a pleasant stroll along narrow avenues lined with quaint houses, and passing all the main historic sights of the town. The most interesting include the magnificent chapel of the Immaculate Conception in the church of **Sant Francesc**, built in an ornamental Spanish Baroque style. The **Museo de Menorca** is also well worth a visit if only for its extensive range of items from the Talayotic period. Another interesting place to see is the **gin distillery**.

For a longer hike, Maó is a good starting point for a walk along the coast – head north to **Cala Llonga**, or south right up to **Port de Malborough**.

Some of the Xoriguer distillery's ancient gin-making equipment

🍷 Xoriguer Distillery

Andén de Poniente 91.
📞 971 362 197

Gin production on the island is a legacy of the British occupation, although its local brands taste rather different to the ones currently produced in Britain. You can acquaint yourself with the gin distillation process by visiting the Xoriguer distillery, close to the harbour steps, which was founded in the 18th century.

As well as juniper, which is imported from the Pyrenees, gin contains a number of other aromatic herbs. Menorcan gin is sold only in Menorca and in a handful of restaurants in Mallorca.

The distillery also produces various liqueurs, including the *hierbas* that are believed

Gobierno Militar, one of the most magnificent buildings in Maó

by some to have therapeutic properties. All these drinks can be tasted on site, and of course bought in the shop.

🏰 Sant Francesc

Plaça de Monestir. 🔼 6:30pm daily, 10am, 7:30pm Sun.

The church of Sant Francesc with its light-coloured Baroque façade (1719–92), stands at the end of **Carrer Isabel II**.

The church's imposing interior has a vast, dark nave with a soaring Gothic altar at the end of it.

The church's most outstanding feature is its octagonal chapel of the Immaculate Conception built in a fanciful Spanish Baroque style and decorated with stucco garlands of vine and roses. This is the most beautiful example of Baroque ornamentation in Menorca. Its creator is believed to be the famous painter, sculptor and architect, Francesco Herrara.

Ornament from Sant Francesc

Adjoining the south side of Sant Francesc is the monumental structure of the monastery, with an arcaded courtyard. Currently it houses the Museu de Menorca.

🏛 Museu de Menorca

Avda. Dr. Guàrdia s/n. 📞 971 350 955. 🕐 10am–2pm, 5–8pm Tue–Sat, 10am–2pm Sun. ⬤ Mon, public holidays. 📷

The Museu de Menorca occupies the former cloisters of a Franciscan monastery. The collection includes works of art and archaeological relics. Many of the exhibits date from prehistoric times and there is an extensive selection from the Talayotic period, as well as Roman, Byzantine and Arabic artifacts. Among the most interesting exhibits are a bronze statuette of a bull, Punic jewellery and some huge amphorae.

🏰 Gobierno Militar

Carrer Isabel II. 📷

The Military Governor's House and army headquarters are housed in one of Maó's most beautiful buildings. The palace was built in 1768, during the second British occupation. The building is still used by the army and can therefore be seen only from the outside, though the arcaded courtyard is well worth a peek.

Courtyard of the former Franciscan monastery

🏰 Plaça Bastió

This small, irregular-shaped square has limited vehicle access, and serves as a good place for children to let off steam. Visitors who are fatigued by sightseeing often stop here for a rest.

At the north corner of the square stands

the medieval **Portal de Sant Roc** that is named after Saint Roch, a 14th-century hermit who was believed to be able to ward off the plague. Flanked by bulky twin turrets and a connecting arch, it is one of the few remaining fragments of Maó's medieval walls and was once the exit point from the city onto the road leading to Alaior. The fortifications did not stop Barbarossa from plundering the town, which he took in 1535, destroying most of the city's defences.

Portal de Sant Roc, viewed from the street leading to the town hall

Plaça Esplanada
Plaça Esplanada, with its flower beds shaded by pine trees, is the biggest square in the city and was once used as a military parade ground. Now, it provides a popular meeting place for the locals, especially at the weekends. The ice-cream sellers and swings make it equally popular with local children. There is a market on Tuesday and Saturday mornings.

The square is flanked on three sides by low buildings, many of them housing bars, cafés and restaurants. The western section of the square features a huge Civil War memorial erected during the days of Franco. At the back of the square are army barracks built during the first British occupation of the island and now used by the Spanish Army.

Buses on their way to other island towns stop near here.

MAYONNAISE

Following his victory over the British, Louis-François-Armand du de Vignerot du Plessis, a cousin of Cardinal Richelieu, stopped at a local inn where he was served a tasty sauce. On his return to Paris, he introduced the sauce to the royal court, where the new garnish was an instant hit. Already known on the islands as "salsa mahonesa", it became known in France as "mayonnaise".

Ateneu Científic Literari i Artístic de Maó
Rovellada de Dalt 25.
971 360 553.
Menorca's Centre of Culture and Science can be visited by appointment only. It has a collection of local ceramics, natural history exhibits (shells, birds etc.), maps and charts, a library and permanent exhibitions of works by Spanish artists Pasqual Calbó, Màrius Verdaguer and Juan Vives Llull.

Sant Antoni
Carrer de Vassollo. 8pm Mon–Sat; 10:30am Sun.
The 17th-century church of St Anthony was closed after it was pillaged during the Civil War. Following its restoration, it is once again used as a place of worship and provides a venue for cultural events.

Es Freginal
The park is a green oasis in the middle of town. During high season is serves as a venue for nightly cultural events. It also provides a stage for musicians taking part in the annual jazz festival.

ENVIRONS: About 2 km (1 mile) east of Maó, on the opposite side of the bay, are two swanky suburbs – **Sant Antoni** and **Cala Llonga**. A short distance further, at the end of the headland, stands the vast **La Mola** fortress, guarding the entrance to the harbour. During the days of Franco it was used as a jail for political prisoners.

Near Sant Antoni is the stately home of **Golden Farm** – a beautiful example of Menorcan Palladian architecture. Admiral Nelson is reputed to have first met his mistress Lady Hamilton here, although this is unlikely. Inside is a collection of mementos associated with the couple and an extensive library. The house is not open to the public.

Es Mutar, 9 km (6 miles) to the northeast, is a charming village of white houses standing at the foot of a rocky crag, on the shores of a bay. Neighbouring **Sa Mesquida** lies further along this rocky shoreline. The village is dominated by a well-preserved watchtower.

Plaça Esplanada, where locals come to relax

Lush shores of S'Albufera's Es Grau

Es Grau ❷

6 km (4 miles) north of Maó.

THIS SMALL FISHING village, fringed by dunes and pine forests, lies on the bay with a wide, sandy, horseshoe-shaped beach. Its safe shallow water is perfect for families with young children. At the weekend, the place becomes busier with day-trippers from Maó. From here you can take a cruise boat to nearby **Illa d'En Colom**, which has some nice beaches, the best of them being S'Arsenal des Moro.

West of Es Grau is the fresh water lagoon, S'Albufera, the largest stretch of marshland on the island. The **Parc Natural S'Albufera**, where hunting and fishing are prohibited, is a UNESCO biosphere reserve and a magnificent area for hiking or bird watching.

Es Castell ❸

2 km (1 mile) southeast of Maó.

ES CASTELL, once known as Villa Carlos, is a former military outpost. Originally called Georgetown, it was established in 1771 by the British and named for George III. The Georgian houses surrounding Plaça d'Esplanada serve as reminders of the British presence. One of the barrack buildings, **Cuartel de la Cala Corp**, houses a small museum with a collection of weapons and uniforms. Another sight is the parish church of **Nostra Senyora del Roser**.

🏛 **Museo Militar de Menorca**
Plaça Esplanada, 19.
📞 971 362 100. ⬛
11am–1pm Mon & Thu.

ENVIRONS: Illa Pinto was the site of the main British Navy base on the island, built in the 18th century. The local chapel is dedicated to Virgen del Camen, the patron saint of fishermen and the Spanish Navy.
    Illa del Rei is where Alfonso III landed in 1287 during the Reconquest. **Illa Plana**, the smallest island on the bay, has the remains of a quarantine centre built in 1490 for those arriving at the island. **Illa Llazaret**, the largest of the islands, situated at the entrance to the bay, was once a peninsula, until it was cut-off from the mainland by the St George Canal at the beginning of the 20th century. On the nearby headland are the remains of **Fort San Felip**, a 16th-century fortress which once guarded the southern entrance to Maó's harbour. In its day, the fortress was one of the most highly advanced systems of defence in Europe and could house an entire garrison of soldiers underground. It was destroyed by the Spanish in 1782 and now only its ruins remain. On the opposite side of the bay, near the village of Sant Esteve, is **Fort Malborough**. Built by the British to back up Fort San

French honeysuckle

Felip, it has since been restored and now houses a museum and has a number of displays (some with loud sound effects) on Menorca's military history.

Sant Lluís ❹

5 km (3 miles) south of Maó.

THIS QUAINT LITTLE town, consisting of a square, a church and a few dozen whitewashed houses, was built by the French during the Seven Years War (1756–63), as a quarters for Breton sailors. The French coat of arms on the church façade stands as a reminder of those days.

A windmill, **Moli de Dalt**, at the town's entrance was built in 1762. Today, this is the only working windmill on the island and serves as the town's symbol. Next to it is a small museum with a collection of farm implements. The road into town bypasses the centre and heads towards the resorts of S'Algar, Cala d'Alcaufar, Punta Prima, Biniancolla, Binibeca Vell and Cap d'en Font.

ENVIRONS: Trepucó is a prehistoric site with a well-preserved *taula*. In the seaside villages of **S'Algar** and **Cala d'Alcaufar**, hotels stand side by side with fishermen's cottages. **Punta Prima** is the largest local resort. From here you have the view of the uninhabited island of **Illa de l'Aire**, with its lighthouse. West of town is a guard tower built by the Spaniards in the 18th century.

Colourful houses and apartments in Es Castell

Prehistoric Menorca

MENORCA IS EXCEPTIONALLY rich in megalithic structures. Most of the remains date from the Talayotic period – a civilization that flourished between 2000 and 1000 BC. The period derives its name from the *talayots* (from *atalaya*, the arabic word for a watch-tower), the stone structures that are dotted around the island, mostly in former settlements. There are various theories as to what their original purpose was – they may have been used as defensive towers, burial sites or storehouses. Nobody really knows.

Huge *talayot* in the Trepucó settlement

TYPES OF STRUCTURES

The ancient stone structures scattered throughout Menorca (and to a lesser extent found in Mallorca) fall into three main categories: *taulas, talayots* and *navetas*.

Taulas *(table) consists of two slabs of rock, one placed on top of the other in a "T" formation. Some are up to 4.5 m (15 ft) high. Suggestions as to their original function range from a sacrificial altar to a roof support.*

Talayots *are circular or square buildings. Their purpose is a mystery – they may have been tombs, guard-houses, meeting places or even dwellings.*

Navetas, *shaped like an upturned boat or a pyramid, were probably built as a sepulchre or a dwelling. At least 10 of them remain in Menorca.*

Spectacular 3-m (10-ft) high *taula* at Talati de Dalt settlement

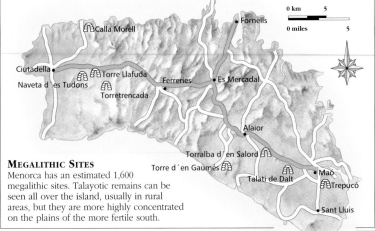

MEGALITHIC SITES

Menorca has an estimated 1,600 megalithic sites. Talayotic remains can be seen all over the island, usually in rural areas, but they are more highly concentrated on the plains of the more fertile south.

White houses and steeple in Binibeca Vell

Binibeca Vell ❺

9 km (6 miles) south of Maó.

B INIBECA STANDS OUT amid the similarity of many of Menorca's southern seaside resorts. Also known as *Poblat de Pescadors* ("Fishermen's Village"), it was built as a resort in 1972 to resemble a traditional Menorcan coastal fishing village. It has whitewashed, two-storey houses, wooden balconies and a maze of streets that are so narrow you can touch the buildings on both sides with outstretched arms. The blaze of white walls, small patios and lush gardens enhance the Mediterranean atmosphere with a touch of eastern influence. The "village" even has a church steeple, though no church.

Nearby are a number of pleasant coves and beaches, including **Cala Binibeca**, **Cala Binisafúller** and the smallest beach in Menorca – **Es Caló Blanc**.

ENVIRONS: The nearby resorts lack any distinguishing features, apart from the beaches and their associated attractions, so it is worth taking a trip to the village of **Sant Climent**, which has a small market and lovely 19th-century church. Sant Climent also has a venue, the Restaurant-bar Casino, which puts on jazz concerts twice a week. These concerts are popular, as long as you can hear the music above the noise from the nearby international airport. Nearby **Torelló**, right on the edge of the airport, has a *talayot* with aircraft warning lights!

Cales Coves ❻

11 km (7 miles) west of Maó.
🚌 Sant Clement.

T HIS COMPLEX OF prehistoric caves is best seen from the sea. Carved in the cliffs above a picturesque bay, the caves date from the Neolithic era. During the Talayotic period, the caves were used solely as burial chambers. Later they became the site of pagan rituals. On the shore are the remains of a Roman harbour

(some of the "newest" caves have Roman inscriptions). Nearby is a small beach.

Cala en Porter ❼

15 km (9 miles) west of Maó.

T HE SEASIDE RESORT of Cala en Porter is one of Menorca's oldest holiday towns and is a sprawl of virtually identical holiday villas. Nevertheless, it provides good tourist facilities, including one of the loveliest beaches on the island, which is accessible via winding stairs and suitable for children. Its most unusual attraction is **Cova d'en Xoroi**, a huge cave, situated halfway down a steep cliff, which consists of several large chambers and tunnels. It has now been turned into a nightclub.

🎵 **Cova d'en Xoroi**
☎ 971 377 236.
🕐 Apr-May: 11am–9pm daily; Jun-Oct: 11am–11pm daily. 🏖

ENVIRONS: About 15 km (9 miles) northwest is the resort of **Son Bou** with the ruins of an early Christian basilica (5th–6th century AD). The cliffs hide a number of caves that have been cut into them.

Alaior ❽

🚌 Ⓦ www.alaior.org 🎪 Sant Llorenç (2nd Sat & Sun in Aug).

T HIS MARKET TOWN, situated on a hill along the road from Maó to Ciutadella, is famous for its production of exquisite Menorcan cheeses.

Cala en Porter, one of the loveliest beaches in Menorca

Restaurant set in an old windmill in Es Mercadal

This is the dairy capital of Menorca (the island is also famous for its ice cream), with the biggest factories producing the famous *queso Mahón*, a white, half-fat cheese made of pasteurised cow's milk with added sheep's milk that gives it its distinctive flavour.

Besides buying cheese, you could also visit the fortified Baroque parish church of **Santa Eulàlia** (1674–90). The Munt de l'Angel **watchtower** stands on a hill behind the church and provides a beautiful view of the area. The huge fiesta celebrated on the day of St Lawrence includes riding shows, parades and horse races through the streets of the town.

ENVIRONS: Torralba d'en Salord, one of the biggest Talayotic settlements on the island, is situated along the road to Cala en Porter, about 3 km (2 miles) from Alaior. The local *taula* is one of the best-preserved and the tallest on the island. The rectangular temple has also survived in good condition. A bronze statuette of a bull discovered on this site can now be seen in the Museu de Menorca, in Maó *(see p96)*.

Some 5 km (3 miles) to the south is **Torre d'en Gaumés**, another settlement dating from the Talayotic period, which has a range of buildings including three *talayots*.

Es Mercadal ❾

🚆 🅿 *Sun.* 🎭 *Sant Martí (3rd Sun in Jul).*

Detail from the façade of Alaior church

Es MERCADAL LIES at the very heart of Menorca, along the Maó–Ciutadella road. Founded in the 14th century, the town has been largely overlooked by tourism and earns its keep through farming and a number of local industries. The town itself is charming, with trailing bougainvillea and the pretty 18th-century parish church of **Sant Martí**. Es Mercadel is known for its excellent Menorcan cuisine and you may like to stop for a snack or meal in one of its pleasant small cafés or in Can Aguedet, at c/Lepanto 3, a restaurant that is very popular with the locals.

ENVIRONS: Some 3 km (2 miles) east, the convent of **Santuarii de Toro** was built in 1670 on the steep hill of Monte Toro, which at 350 m (1,148 ft) is the highest point in Menorca. Occupied by the nuns of a Franciscan order, it is regarded as the spiritual centre of Menorca and an ancient centre of pilgrimage.

Inside this 17th-century church is a statue of the Black Madonna – Verge del Toro – set within the main altarpiece, which depicts the Virgin Mary in a golden crown, holding the infant Jesus in her arms.

According to local tradition, the statue of the Virgin Mary has been worshipped here since the 13th century. These days, pilgrims visit Monte Toro, particularly on the first Sunday in May, to participate in the *Festa de la Verge del Toro*. Following mass in the church, the pilgrims then descend the stairs leading to Es Mercadal on their knees.

The old fortress has a military surveillance station. Nearby stands a huge stone statue of Christ, commemorating the Spaniards killed during the colonial war in Morocco.

Some 6 km (4 miles) northeast, are **Hort de Llucaitx** – an amusement park where you can go horseriding, and **Son Parc** – the only golf course on the island.

CALDERETA DE LLAGOSTA

This delicious lobster stew is the speciality of the northern regions on Menorca. Fresh lobsters are brought in every morning by local fishermen. The best stews are served in Fornells, which is famous for its seafood. The dish is extremely expensive but absolutely delicious. One popular way to enjoy it is to eat the gravy with bread, treating it as a soup, and have the lobster with mayonnaise as a main course.

Tempting lobster stew

Harbour and yacht marina in Fornells

Fornells ⑩

🚌 🎏 *Fiesta de San Diego de Alcalá (13 Nov).*

A PICTURESQUE FISHING village, Fornells is situated 10 km (6 miles) north of Es Mercadal. During the summer season luxury yachts moor side by side with the fishing boats. The place has some excellent seafood restaurants. The local speciality is *caldereta de llagosta (see p101)* and it is thought to be so good here that King Juan Carlos frequently sails over in his yacht from Mallorca just to eat in one of the waterfront restaurants. Once Fornells was a major port and you can still see the remains of fortifications built as a defence against Arab and Turkish pirates. At the entrance to the harbour is a huge round watchtower. The village has no beach, but offers excellent facilities for diving, sailing and windsurfing.

In high season there are cruises to the small island of **Illa Ravells**, with its ruins of an old English fort. Boat trips can also be taken to **Illa dels Porros** and to the cape of **Na Guillemassa**, which has some interesting caves.

ENVIRONS: West of Fornells is **Cala Tirant** with a red sand beach. On the east coast of the bay are luxury villas surrounded by masses of colourful flowers, shrubs and cacti. The view from here extends to Cap de Cavalleria.

Cap de Cavalleria lighthouse rising above the rocks

Cap de Cavalleria ⑪

CAP DE CAVALLERIA is situated 13 km (8 miles) north of Es Mercadal. This is the northernmost point of

---

Menorca's Beaches

MENORCA HAS FEWER easily accessible beaches than Mallorca or Ibiza. The best ones are to be found at the eastern end of the south coast. These are small, sandy beaches, tucked away in coves. There is an increasing number of beaches being developed west of Santa Galdana, and the local resorts of Son Xoriguer and Cala en Bosch are gaining popularity. Beaches on the northeastern coast are also popular.

Els Canutells ②
A golden beach lies at the end of a narrow bay that cuts deep into the land. Small beaches on the eastern part of the bay are also good places for swimming.

• Es Migjorn Gran

PM 713

PM 711

• Sant Tomás

① • Son Bou

Son Bou ①
Some 3 km (2 miles) long, Son Bou is the longest beach in Menorca. At its eastern end are the ruins of an early-Christian basilica.

Cala Binisafúller ③
This 40-m (130-ft) long beach is situated next to the road between Cap d'En Font and Punta Prima. It is mainly used by holidaymakers staying at the nearby apartments and bungalows.

◁ **Marina and the old town of Ciutadella, illuminated by the rising sun**

Menorca and of all the Balearic islands: a tall, rocky headland swept by the northern wind – the "tramontana" – and washed over by the rolling waves of the sea. The steep cliffs provide nesting grounds for peregrine, sea eagle and kite. The road leading to it runs through lovely picturesque areas, but you will have to stop several times on the way to open and shut the numerous farm gates.

At the western end of the peninsula are the remains of **Sanitja**, a Phoenician settlement mentioned by Pliny, which you can visit on a boat trip from Fornells. The Romans built a port on this site, called Sanisera. Nearby is a museum with a modest exhibition of Talayotic and Roman relics. More worthwhile is a trip to the **Torre de Sanitja**, a watchtower built by the British in the late 18th century in order to guard the entrance to this natural harbour.

Magnificent beach in Sant Tomàs near Es Migjorn Gran

Further west is a stretch of barely accessible, unspoilt beaches. The most beautiful of these are **Cala del Pilar**, **La Vall d'Alagiarens** and **Cala Pregonda**.

Es Migjorn Gran ⑫

11 km (7 miles) south of Es Mercadal. 🚌 Wed. 🎊 San Cristobal de Ses Corregudes (Jul–Aug).

A SMALL, TRANQUIL village set among fertile fields, Es Migjorn Gran has a sleepy, provincial flavour. From here you can take a 5-km (3-mile) walk to the sea shore. The road leads through the **Barranc de Binigaus** canyon filled with fragrant wild herbs and flowers. You could stop on the way to see the limestone walls and caves, including the biggest of them – **Cova des Coloms**.

ENVIRONS: Some 11 km (7 miles) south of Es Migjorn Gran is the resort of **Sant Tomàs**. A dozen or so hotels line its main street, but there are no all-night clubs, and few restaurants. However, the place does have a great beach.

Cala Binibeca ④
This wide beach is near Binibeca Vell. The beach and the surrounding area have hardly been developed. A restaurant is by the car park.

Cala Alcaufar ⑥
The beach runs along the bay, on the southeast coast. The northern shore of the bay is densely built up.

Punta Prima ⑤
This southernmost beach of Menorca is one of the most popular on the island. The beach overlooks the rocky island of Illa de l'Aire.

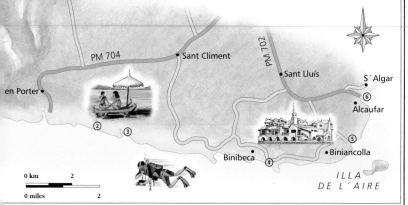

PM 704 • Sant Climent

PM 702

• Sant Lluís

S´Algar

en Porter •

② ③

Binibeca ④

• Biniancolla

Alcaufar ⑥

⑤

0 km 2

0 miles 2

ILLA DE L´AIRE

Beach on Santa Galdana bay

Ferreries ⓭

C/ Sant. Bartomeu. 971 373 003. W www.ferreries.org
10am–1pm & 6–9pm Sat.
Sant Bartomeu (23–25 Aug).

FERRERIES IS SITUATED at the foot of the S'Enclusa hill. At 142 m (466 ft) above sea level, this picturesque little town is the highest settlement in Menorca. Its name derives from the many blacksmiths *(ferreries)* who once worked around here. At the heart of the village is the **Plaça d'Espanya**. Here, at a weekly Saturday market, you can buy leather goods as well as produce brought in by local farmers, including vegetables, fruit, cheese and honey. In Plaça l'Església is the parish church of **Sant Bartomeu** (1705) and the town hall. It is also worth stepping into the **Museu de la Natura de Menorca**, to see a selection of the island's natural wonders.

🏛 Museu de la Natura de Menorca
C/ Mallorca 2. 971 350 762. @ museu.natura@ gobmenorca.com
10am–1pm & 6–9pm Tue–Sat; 10am–1pm Sun.

ENVIRONS: About 6 km (4 miles) north of Ferreries are the ruins of **Santa Agueda** castle. Not much remains of this Moorish stronghold, but the view from the top of the second highest mountain in Menorca justifies the effort of the 260-m (853-ft) climb.
The strategic advantages of the hill were well known to the Romans who, in the 2nd century, chose it as the site for their first fortress. The Moors adapted the site to build a summer residence for the Menorcan governor and improved the surrounding fortifications. The fort was the

Festa de los Roselles in Ferreries

last stronghold to surrender during the Reconquest.
Ferreries is the centre of the leather industry. Along the road to Maó are several shops selling Menorcan sandals.

Santa Galdana ⓮

5 km (3 miles) south of Ferreries.

THE ONLY WAY TO get to Santa Galdana is by car from Ferreries or on foot, along the d'Algendar canyon. Situated on a beautiful bay, the town's popularity is growing, and a number of high-rise hotels have begun to pop up. Most of the other buildings are villas, set among the trees. The main tourist attraction is the beach with its white sand and turquoise water, sheltered from the wind by high cliffs and a pine forest.
It is worth taking a walk west from here to the charming **Marcella cove**. The adjacent **Macarelleta cove** has a nudist beach. Both beaches are well established and can be accessed by steps carved into the rock.
Further west is **Cala'n Turqueta**, probably the most beautiful bay on this part of the coast. Another beach, situated in a charming cove east of Santa Galdana, is **Cala Mitjana**, which is a lovely spot although it can get busy in the summer.

Carrer Fred, close to the main square in Ferreries

GIN IN MENORCA

One legacy of the 100-year rule of Menorca by the British is the tradition of producing and drinking gin, which was a popular drink with the many British sailors stationed here. Unlike the rest of Spain where wine is the most popular tipple, Menorcans have taken to gin in a big way. The production process can be seen in the 18th-century Xoriguer distillery, next to the landing stage in Maó *(see p96)*. The gin produced by the Xoriguer distillery is the most popular brand on the island and is sold in *canecas* – ceramic bottles reminiscent of the clay jugs that were once used by British sailors.

Gin from the distillery in Maó

Western Coast of Menorca ⑮

T HE REGION BETWEEN Ciutadella and Cap d'Artutx is excellent for exploring. Whether walking, cycling or driving, you can enjoy the best of the island, including a nature reserve near Son Xoriguer, the Son Olivaret megalithic remains and the churches and museums of Ciutadella, the former capital of Menorca. Parts of this unspoilt region can even be explored on horseback.

CALA MORELL

CALA EN BLANES ⑦

C 721 MAÓ

Sa Caleta ⑤
Near the beach, at the entrance of Cala Santadria bay is a former defence tower, Es Castellar.

TORRE-SAURA

Cala Blanca ④
This small beach is tucked away between bungalows, villas and a cluster of narrow streets. Visited mainly by locals, it is uncrowded and has safe swimming.

•Santandria

Son Olivaret ③
The two sets of megalithic structures – Son Olivaret Nou and Son Olivaret Vell – include both *talayots* and *taulas*.

PMV 721-2

Son Oleo ⑥
On the outskirts of Ciutadella is a small beach, lying at the end of a long narrow bay. It is fairly quiet and used mainly by the locals.

Ciutadella ⑦
Take at least one day to explore the former capital of Menorca. From here you can make trips north to Cala en Blanes or to Cala Morell.

Cala en Bosch ②
This harbour, situated in a sheltered bay, has a landing stage for pleasure boats. Next to the harbour there is a shopping centre.

Son Xoriguer ①
Son Xoriguer is also the starting point for trips on horseback to the neighbouring reserve. The route leads past two beaches and then along the seashore.

TIPS FOR TOURISTS

Length: *16 km (10 miles).*
Stopping-off points: *Stop off for refreshments at one of the restaurants in Cala en Bosch or Ciutadella. A good place for swimming is Cala Blanca, halfway along the route.*

KEY

▦ Suggested route

═ Other road

☆ Viewpoint

0 km   1
0 miles   1

Ciutadella ⑯

A PICTURESQUE TOWN WITH narrow, winding streets, handsome palaces and a busy harbour, Ciutadella has always competed with Maó. In the days of Arab rule it was the island's capital and in 1558 it was invaded by the Turks who killed many of its inhabitants and carted off some 3,500 more to slave markets in Istanbul. Of its buildings, only the cathedral remained. Those who survived were determined to rebuild Ciutadella. Most of the Menorcan aristocracy continued to make it their home, even after Maó became the capital.

Cross from Santa Clara's façade

Neo-Gothic canopy above the cathedral altar

Plaça d'es Born, the town's principal square

Exploring Ciutadella

Though there are few traces of Arab rule, Ciutadella has much to offer in the way of architecture. Numerous opulent palaces and Gothic and Baroque churches reveal just how successful the restoration of Ciutadella in the 17th and 18th centuries was. The main square in town is Plaça d'es Born, a characterful area close to the Gothic cathedral. The Museo Diocesà, housing sacred art objects that document the cultural and religious life of the island, is well worth a visit.

🕎 Plaça d'es Born

This is a former Arab military drill ground and was rebuilt in a Neo-Renaissance style in the 19th century. It is considered to be one of Spain's most beautiful squares. At its centre stands an **obelisk** marking *Any de la Desgràcia* – the "Year of Calamity", when Turkish corsairs invaded Ciutadella. The square is lined with historic buildings, including the **town hall**, a former palace of the Moorish governor, as well as the late 19th-century **Teatre Municipal d'es Born** and 19th-century palaces with Italian-style façades. The most imposing of these is the early 19th-century **Palau de Torre-Saura**. The adjacent **Palau Salort**, dating from the same period, is Ciutadella's only aristocratic residence that is open to visitors. The opulent Hall of Mirrors and the majestic painted ceiling in the ballroom make this handsome house well worth visiting. The square is also worth seeking out for its restaurants and open-air cafés and bars.

🔒 Cathedral
Plaça de la Catedral.
Work on the cathedral began towards the end of the 13th century on the site of a mosque. Although it suffered fire damage, it escaped much of the destruction during the Turkish raid but was heavily remodelled after 1558. During the Civil War the workers' militia destroyed most of its furnishings.

One of the oldest parts of the cathedral is the Gothic south entrance that bears stone carvings of weird creatures and the heraldic crests of the Menorcan knights and nobility. The main Neo-Classic entrance dates from the early 19th century. The dominant feature of the interior is the Neo-Gothic canopy hanging over the main altar.

🕎 Capella del Roser
C/del Roser.
The façade of this small church includes a beautiful 17th-century Spanish Baroque-style doorway. Destroyed during the Civil War, the church was rebuilt and is now used as a municipal exhibition hall.

Cafés spilling onto the pavements at Plaça Nova

🏛 Can Saura and Palau Martorell
C/de Santissim.
These two adjacent palaces were built in the 17th century. Their distinctive façades reflect the character of the town's noble mansions built during that period.

🏛 Museo Diocesà de Menorca
C/ Seminari 7. 📞 971 481 297.
🕐 10:30am–1:30pm Tue–Sat.
The Diocese Museum occupies a former Augustinian convent and cloister. Its collection of prehistoric and modern artifacts includes a miniature statuette of a bull and a bronze casting of a mermaid. It also has a collection of Catalonian paintings, and som sacred objects made of precious metals, including chalices and communion cups. Next to the monastery is the Baroque **Església de Socors**.

Ses Voltes' arches line the walkway leading to the cathedral

🔒 Sant Crist
Near the bank building that was formerly the house of Menorcan aristocrat, Joan Miquel Saura, stands the Baroque Capella del Sant Crist, built in 1667. Its fanciful façade is decorated with stone carvings of fruit

VISITORS' CHECKLIST
🏙 23,500. 🚌 🏢 Plaça de la Catedral 5. 📞 971 382 693.
🌐 www.ciutadella.org
📅 Fri & Sat. 🎉 Festa Sant Joan (23 Jun).

garlands and masks. The statue of Christ above the high altar is said to have dripped with sweat in 1661 and became the object of a folk cult. Standing near the chapel is a column topped with a bronze figure of the Lamb of God, the work of local artist Matias Quetglas.

🏛 Plaça Nova
This small square is the site of the town's most popular cafés and bars. Ses Voltes, an arcarded walkway which runs from here to the cathedral, is one of the main streets of the old town. The Moorish vaulted arches that line the street hide a good selection of patisseries and souvenir shops.

🏛 Plaça Llibertat
This charming square situated at the rear of the former Augustinian monastery is well known to all who shop for food. Its two covered markets, selling fresh meat, fish, fruit and vegetables, are popular with the locals.

Arcades of the covered market in Plaça Llibertat

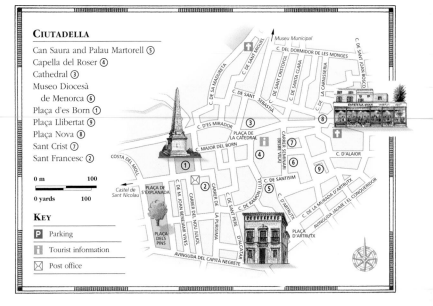

CIUTADELLA
Can Saura and Palau Martorell ⑤
Capella del Roser ④
Cathedral ③
Museo Diocesà de Menorca ⑥
Plaça d'es Born ①
Plaça Llibertat ⑨
Plaça Nova ⑧
Sant Crist ⑦
Sant Francesc ②

0 m   100
0 yards   100

KEY
🅿 Parking
ℹ Tourist information
✉ Post office

Further Afield

The old town boundaries are defined by the wide avenues of Avda. del Capità Negrete, Avda. del Jaume I and Avda. de la Constitució. Outside these limits there are a few interesting sights, including the **Castell de Sant Nicolau**, the remains of the city fortifications and the harbour. A stroll along the north coast of the bay will take you to **Punta na Mari**. Ciutadella, situated on Menorca's west coast, makes a good base from which to explore the area. From here you can get to **Cala Morell** in the north, or **Cap d'Artrutx** 10 km (6 miles) to the south.

Statue of a horse, the star of the Festa Sant Joan

🛈 Santa Clara

C/ Santa Clara. 🕂 10:15am Sun.
The original church and convent of Santa Clara was founded in 1287 by Alfonso III. Destroyed during the Turkish raid in 1558, it was rebuilt in the 17th century only to be destroyed again during the Spanish Civil War. A community of nuns still lives here. The wood carving depicting the *Adoration of Shepherds*, seen in the convent, was stolen by the Turks and taken to Istanbul but subsequently recovered.

🏛 Museu Municipal de Ciutadella, Bastió de sa Font

Plaça de sa Font s/n. ☏ 971 380 297.
Ⓦ www.museuciutadella.cjb.net
⏲ 10am–2pm Tue–Sat. 🎫
The museum occupies the bastion of the former town fortifications built in 1677. This is the only preserved fragment of the town's fortifications. Founded in 1995, the Museo Municipal has a good collection of Talayotic, Roman and Muslim artifacts, most of which are kept in a large, vaulted room. There are crafted beakers and tumblers, ceramic bowls and jugs, bronze weapons and jewellery (with a distinct Phoenician influence). There is also an odd collection of human skulls, showing the damage caused by the practice of trepanning.

🚇 Plaça Alfons III

This modest square is on the outskirts of the old town, by Avda. de la Constitució. Several cafés and restaurants shelter under the trees. The square can be seen from some distance and you can't miss the old windmill, now housing the tourist office. This is a good place to sit or pick up a souvenir.

🚇 Plaça de s'Esplanada and Plaça dels Pins

These two adjacent green squares are the lungs amid the historic buildings of Ciutadella. The many bars and restaurants provide pleasant places in which to relax and the peace is broken only by the screech of brakes from the nearby bus garage. In the evening there are jazz concerts here.

An alley leading to Santa Clara

Windmill and tourist office in Plaça Alfons III

🛈 La Ermita de Sant Joan de Missa

Carrer de Comte Cifuentes
The chapel situated southeast of the town centre is an important venue for the Festa Sant Joan celebrations. Vespers are sung here on the evening of 23 June. The nearby road, which leads to Marcarella, Marcarelleta and Cala'n Turqueta beaches, is transformed into a racecourse during the two days of celebrations *(see box)*.

⚓ Harbour

Moll Comercial.
Ciutadella's shallow harbour was the main reason the British moved the island's capital to Maó. Today, the harbour has been dredged and can accommodate large ferries linking Ciutadella to Barcelona, as well as the many yachts and fishing boats that moor here. Having descended from Plaça d'es Born to the ferry terminal, it is worth taking a walk along the bay to soak up some of the harbourside activity. Early in the morning you can see fishermen returning with their catch, the first bars opening and the town waking up to a new day.

From **Punta na Mari**, at the entrance to the bay, you can see Castell de Sant Nicolau. On the other side of the harbour bay, about 500 m (1,640 ft) further on, is **Cala des Degollador**'s tiny beach. The beaches of **Platja Petita** and **Sa Platja Gran** are several hundred metres further on.

A phenomenon peculiar to Ciutadella bay is the mysterious *rissaga* wave. No-one is able to predict when this event will take place, but it can cause flooding of the port to a height of several metres. The last big *rissaga* occurred in 1984 and left the harbour under 2 m (7 ft) of water.

Fishermen in the harbour preparing their nets

♣ Castell de Sant Nicolau
Plaça Almirall Farragut.

The 17th-century Castell de Sant Nicolau was built as a watchtower to protect the harbour. You can still enter the stronghold via a drawbridge and in the evening the castle remains open to provide a vantage point for the spectacular sunsets over the harbour. It also serves as a venue for temporary exhibitions.

Standing near the castle is the statue of a four-star admiral of the United States Navy, David Farragut, hero of the American Civil War and son of an immigrant from Menorca. The admiral is depicted in his uniform with epaulettes, holding a telescope. When he returned to Menorca in 1867, he was awarded honorary citizenship and a huge crowd turned out to greet him.

ENVIRONS: Naveta d'es Tudons, 5 km (3 miles) east of town, is Menorca's best preserved prehistoric ruin.

FESTA SANT JOAN

This midsummer festival (23–24 June) has provided the citizens of Ciutedella with an opportunity to go wild since the 14th century. St John's Day begins with mass in the cathedral but fireworks, jousting and the carrying of a live sheep through the streets are also part of the fun. For most, the highlight of the day is the *caixers* (horsemen). Representing the medieval social classes, they ride among the noisy crowds.

Prancing horse in the streets of Ciutadella

The Bronze Age structure, built of stone blocks, is 7 m (23 ft) high and 14 m (46 ft) long and was used as a burial chamber. When it was excavated in the 1950s more than 50 bodies were discovered. In **Torre Llafuda**, about 3 km (2 miles) away, amid the shade of olive groves, stands one cracked *taula* and a well-preserved *talayot*. The pleasant setting and the surrounding fertile farmland make this a good place to stop and relax. Travel southeast of Ciutadella and you find a number of beautiful beaches hidden in small coves. These include **Cala des Talader**, dominated by a stone watchtower. Along the road leading to **Son Saura** is Son Catlar, Menorca's biggest prehistoric settlement. Its wall is several metres high and built of enormous stone blocks. Inside, amid the sea of ruins you can distinguish one *taula* and five *talayots*.

A short way to the north are two large resorts – **Cala en Blanes** and **Los Delfines** (which has a small aquapark). Eight kilometres (5 miles) northeast is the tourist village of **Cala Morell**. These man-made prehistoric caves are dug into rocks and were used for burials in the late Bronze and Iron Ages. They are now open to the public.

🌊 Aquapark
Urb. los Delfines.
📞 971 388 251. ☐ May–Aug: 10:30am–6:30pm daily.

Castell de Sant Nicolau guarding the entrance to the harbour

IBIZA

····················

DESPITE ITS REPUTATION *as a party island, Ibiza has maintained much of its rural charm. Fields of almonds and figs, olive groves, the relentless munching of the flocks of sheep – all are part of modern-day Ibiza. Yet there is no denying that the island is a magnet for clubbers, who flock here every summer attracted by the music, lovely beaches, lively nightlife and extraordinary tolerance of the locals.*

The closest of the Balearic Islands to mainland Spain, Ibiza is intersected by a modest range of mountains and surrounded by scores of islets and protruding rocks. Its 200-km (125-mile) long coastline is extremely varied with small coves hiding beautiful beaches and mysterious caves.

Together with Formentera and a number of outlying islets, Ibiza belongs to the group of islands dubbed by the Greeks as the Pitiusas or "pine tree islands". Besides the Greeks, Ibiza's visitors included the Phoenicians, the Carthaginians and the Romans. The last big invasion took place in the 1960s when the island was "discovered" by hippies, and subsequently began to appear in all the European holiday brochures. Tourism took a firm and rapid hold on the economy and

Peasant woman in traditional costume

during the 1990s Ibiza gained entry into the *Guinness Book of Records* as the entertainment island of the world. Thousands of visitors fill the resorts, and big-name nightclubs offer a wealth of drum-heavy entertainment. Ibiza sets the new trends in fashion – what is worn here will subsequently become a "must" in the rest of Europe.

Away from the clubs, the north of the island is a rural patchwork of almond, olive and fig groves. The most distinctive features of the southern region are the vast salt lakes where sea salt is extracted to this day. Dalt Vila, the old part of Eivissa, is one of the best preserved medieval towns in Europe, despite its influx of pleasure seekers. For many locals time still moves at a gentle pace on the island.

An alley in Sa Penya, in the old district of Eivissa.

◁ **Sunset seen from the beach in Cala Benirràs**

Exploring Ibiza

IBIZA HAS MUCH to offer holidaymakers. It is the Mediterranean's club capital and the majority of visitors come here to enjoy the delights of over 50 local beaches in sheltered coves, as well as to revel in the nightclubs of Eivissa and Sant Antoni. Everyone should visit Dalt Vila, Eivissa's old town, for its Gothic cathedral and to see and be seen in one of the many swanky restaurants and chic bars. Those in search of tranquillity can head for the island's interior where the hilly countryside is peppered with old stone cottages. For the energetic, the rugged coastline to the northwest provides excellent walking.

LOCATOR MAP

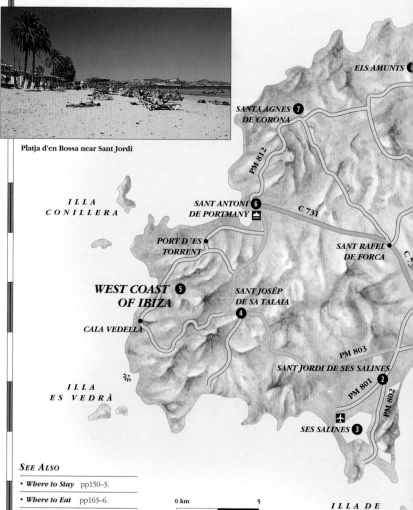

Platja d'en Bossa near Sant Jordi

ILLA CONILLERA

ELS AMUNTS

SANTA AGNES **7** DE CORONA

SANT ANTONI **6** DE PORTMANY

C 731

PORT D'ES TORRENT

SANT RAFEL DE FORCA

WEST COAST 5 OF IBIZA

SANT JOSÉP DE SA TALAIA **4**

CALA VEDELLA

ILLA ES VEDRÀ

PM 803

SANT JORDI DE SES SALINES **2**

PM 801

PM 802

SES SALINES **3**

SEE ALSO

- *Where to Stay* pp150–3.
- *Where to Eat* pp163–6.

0 km   5

0 miles   5

ILLA DE AHORCADOS

GETTING THERE

Ibiza has fewer scheduled fights than Mallorca. Most
visitors arrive by charter flight. During the holiday
weekends, Ibiza's airport becomes one of the busiest
on the planet. The planes landing here are mainly
from the UK, bringing tourists for a week or two of
partying. Barcelona and Madrid also have frequent
flights to the island. Ferries from Eivissa and Sant
Antoni de Portmany harbours sail for Mallorca and
Formentera, as well as to Barcelona and Dénia.

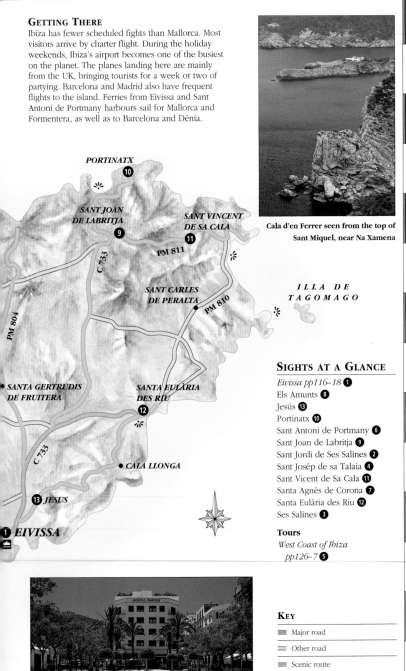

**Cala d'en Ferrer seen from the top of
Sant Miquel, near Na Xamena**

SIGHTS AT A GLANCE

Eivissa pp116–18 **1**
Els Amunts **8**
Jesús **13**
Portinatx **10**
Sant Antoni de Portmany **6**
Sant Joan de Labritja **9**
Sant Jordi de Ses Salines **2**
Sant Josép de sa Talaia **4**
Sant Vicent de Sa Cala **11**
Santa Agnès de Corona **7**
Santa Eulària des Riu **12**
Ses Salines **3**

Tours
*West Coast of Ibiza
  pp126–7* **5**

Plaça des Parque below Dalt Vila in Eivissa

KEY

▨	Major road
▭	Other road
▨	Scenic route
✈	Airport
⚓	Ferry harbour
☀	Viewpoint

Street by Street: Eivissa ❶

Eivissa's coat of arms

ATTRACTED BY THE hilltop site and sheltered harbour, the Phoenicians founded Eivissa in the mid-7th century BC. The Puig de Molins necropolis dates from those days. Dalt Vila (Upper Town) is the oldest remaining part of Eivissa and since 1999 has been a UNESCO World Heritage site. Strengthened by fortifications begun by the Emperor Charles V, it once guarded the entrance to the bay. Sa Penya, at the end of the harbour under Dalt Vila, was once the fishermen's quarter and is still one of the more colourful parts of town. La Marina, stretching out along the waterfront, is the place to go for night-time entertainment.

★ **Portal de ses Taules**
A broad paved drive leads from Sa Penya to Portal de ses Taules – the main town gate.

Museu d'Art Contemporani

Plaça del Sol's shady square looks out over the harbour and is full of shops and cafés.

ROSARI

SANT CARLES

SANT JOSEP

CONQUISTA

JOAN ROMAN

RONDA DE JOAN BAPTISTA CALVI

Capella de Sant Ciriac
A mass is celebrated here each year in August to mark the capture of the town by Jaume I in 1235.

Plaça de la Vila
The main square of Dalt Vila is lined with shops, restaurants and cafés to tempt passing visitors.

KEY

– – – Suggested route

Dalt Vila
The Upper Town, built on a hill, is best seen from the harbour shore where its strategic importance is obvious.

VISITORS' CHECKLIST

🏙 26,000. ✈ Es Codolar, 8 km (5 miles) to the southwest. ☎ 971 809 000. 🛈 C/ Antoni Riquer 2, 971 301 900. 🚢 Mon–Sat (summer). 🎉 Sant Cristòbal (10 Jul), Nostra Senyora de les Neus (5 Aug), Sant Salvador (6 Aug), Sant Ciriac (8 Aug).

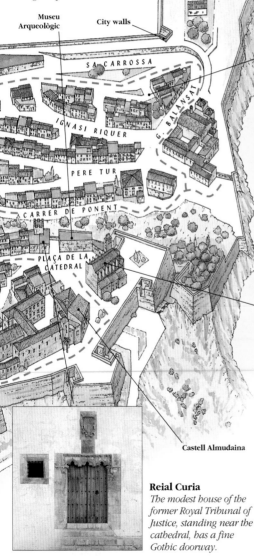

Museu Arqueològic

City walls

Sa Carrossa
Quiet by day, Sa Carrossa is popular with Eivissa's gay visitors and is a hip night-time hangout in the summer.

★ **Cathedral**
The cathedral, dedicated to Our Lady of the Snows, was completed in 1592. It is Dalt Vila's most impressive building.

Castell Almudaina

Reial Curia
The modest house of the former Royal Tribunal of Justice, standing near the cathedral, has a fine Gothic doorway.

STAR SIGHTS

★ **Cathedral**

★ **Portal de ses Taules**

Vast city walls surrounding Dalt Vila

Exploring Eivissa

Eivissa is the largest and most beautiful town on the island. To avoid the crowds, visit early in the morning. For a romantic stroll, visit after dark when it is a bit cooler. In Sa Penya and Sa Marina, the harbour district, you can take a break and see evidence of present-day Eivissa. The place is full of bars, restaurants, clubs and market stalls. As night falls, the streets outside Dalt Vila become one huge dance floor.

🔒 Cathedral

Plaça de la Catedral.
The cathedral church of Santa María de las Nieves (Our Lady of the Snows) stands at the highest point in Dalt Vila, near the severely dilapidated medieval castle (Castell).

Ibiza's consecutive rulers used this place as the site for their temples in Punic times. In AD 283, on the orders of the Roman Emperor Marcus Aurelius, a temple was built here and dedicated to the god Mercury. Following the conquest of the island by the Catalans, work began to build a Christian church, which was completed in 1592. The only remains of the original Gothic structure are the tower and the vestry portal. In the 18th century, the cathedral was remodelled in a heavy Baroque style. The vestry houses a small museum with a collection of beautifully embroidered chasubles (priestly garments), as well as Gothic and Baroque paintings. On the first floor is a collection of altar pieces in silver and gold plate.

⚓ Fortifications

The present city walls surrounding Dalt Vila were erected in the 16th century during the reign of Felipe II, according to plans by the Italian architect Giovanni Battista Calvi. In 1585, with the completion of the impressive Portal de ses Taules (decorated with the coat of arms of Felipe II and replicas of ancient Roman statues), the city's defences were in place.

The view from the northern bastion of Santa Llucia encompasses the new town, the harbour docks and the nearby island of Formentera.

🏛 Museu Arqueològic

Plaça de la Catedral 3. 📞 971 301 231. ⬜ Mar–Oct: 10am–2pm, 6–8pm Tue–Sat, 10am–2pm Sat–Sun; Nov–Apr: 9am–3pm Tue–Sat, 10am–2pm Sun. 🈲
The archaeological museum houses a major collection of prehistoric artifacts and relics dating from the times of the island's Carthaginian, Roman and Moorish rulers. On display are tombstones, statuettes and coins, as well as glass and ceramic objects. The museum building is itself impressive, and was the home of Ibiza's government for 300 years.

🏛 Museu d'Art Contemporani

C/ Ronda Narcis Puget.
📞 971 302 723.
The Modern Art Museum in Portal de ses Taules consists of two underground galleries of the former arsenal, built within the city walls. The museum was founded in 1969 and includes several hundred works by artists living in Ibiza. Some works are for sale, but prices can be rather steep.

🏛 Plaça de Espanya

The **Ajuntament** (town hall) dominates this square and occupies a building that was once a Dominican monastery and a school for the town's poor. Adjacent to it is the church of Santo Domingo (*see p119*) with its later Baroque façade (entrance from Carrer Balasant). The local *chiringuito* bar, open 24 hours, serves a variety of Balearic snacks and specialities. Caile Per Tur features several splendid 18th-century mansions. Among them is **Casa Riquer**, once home to Antonio Riquer, the most famous buccaneer in Ibiza.

Replica Roman statue at Portal de ses Taules

Fresh fruit at a stall in Es Mercat Vell

Sa Torre bastion guarding the harbour

🏰 Santo Domingo
Carrer Balasant.
Below the city walls is the late 16th-century church of Santo Domingo, commonly known as El Convent.

It is worth visiting this to see the lovely paintings covering the vaulted ceilings, and the ceramic tiles lining the walls and floors. The Capella del Roser has an interesting Baroque altar.

🏛 Es Mercat Vell
Plaça de la Constitució.
The old market building lies north of Portal de ses Taules. The hall, resembling an ancient Greek temple, was built in 1873. Every morning it is packed with vendors selling fresh fruit and vegetables. A short distance further on is the **Sa Peixateria** fish market.

🏛 Sa Penya
The Sa Penya district, situated between Dalt Vila and the harbour, was once inhabited mainly by fishermen and has always been a fairly "picturesque" part of town. Even today, it does not enjoy a good reputation and when venturing here you should take extra care of your wallet and any valuables you might have. During high season, the streets get very crowded. The place is full of cafés, bars and clubs. Life in Sa Penya only starts in earnest after dark.

🏛 Sa Marina
Like Sa Penya, Sa Marina was originally a working class district and sprang up as overcrowding in Dalt Vila forced many people to live outside the city walls. Now the area around the harbour provides ferry links to mainland Spain and is packed with restaurants, cafés, bars and shops. Its narrow alleys are full of stalls selling clothes and souvenirs. Many of these offer items reminiscent of the days when the island was a favourite with hippies.

⚓ Sa Torre
A small military defence tower stands at the end of Carrer Garijo. The bastion was restored in 1994 and is a relic of the fortifications that once guarded the entrance to the harbour. Today, it affords a view over the entire bay and the harbour and on to Formentera.

🏛 Monument als Corsaris
Passeig des Moll.
In the early 19th century, the inhabitants of Ibiza, tormented by constant pirate raids, enrolled the help of Antoni Riquer, a buccaneer who fought battles with the pirate ships that brazenly attacked the passing merchant vessels.

His struggles with Novelli, a buccaneer in the pay of the British who commanded the large brig *Felicity*, became the stuff of legend. Despite being hugely outgunned by Novelli, Riquer sank the enemy vessel after a fierce battle, for which the grateful Ibizans erected this monument. It is believed to be the world's only monument that is dedicated to a pirate.

📷 Teatro Pereyra
C/ Conde Rosselón, 3.
Built in 1898, this was the first theatre in Ibiza. Now this Neo-Classical building houses a cinema. It is worth dropping in to the adjacent café Teatro Pereyra one evening, when the live music only adds to the unique atmosphere of this place.

🏛 Passeig de Vara de Rey
Eivissa's main street is named after General Joachim Vara de Rey, a Spanish general who perished in Cuba during the Spanish–America war in 1898. The street's many bars and restaurants are very popular in the evenings.

🏛 Puig des Molins
Via Romana 31. ☎ 971 301 671.
⭘ 10am–1pm, 4–6pm Mon–Fri; 10am–2pm Sat–Sun
Many of the objects associated with Punic culture on display in the Museu Arqueològic were unearthed from this ancient burial site. The "Hill of the Windmills" was one of the Mediterranean's top burial sites and the remains of the nobility would have been brought here from all over the Carthaginian empire. Ibiza, being free of snakes and scorpions, was attractive to the Carthaginians whose religion despised a burial site free of poisonous creatures.

ENVIRONS: There are several beaches near Eivissa served by local buses. **Playa de Talamanca** is not large, but is nearest to the town. On the opposite side of the capital, at its southern end, is **Platja de ses Figueretes**. **Es Cavallet**, a short way down the coast, is very popular, especially with gay people. **Ses Salines'** beach, a little further on, is favoured by many people staying in Eivissa and has regular bus links to the city.

Neon sign of Teatro Pereyra café

Monument to General Vara de Rey

Nightlife in Ibiza

I N THE EARLY 1960s, Ibiza became a popular haunt of hippies who were drawn to this isolated Spanish outpost by the beauty of the scenery and the relaxed way of life. They brought with them valuable foreign cash and the local bars, shops and businesses started to prosper. At times, though, even the islanders' legendary tolerance was strained and in 1968 the loud music, drugs and sex on the beach led to the deportation of 41 people. Where hippies led, however, the rest have followed and Ibiza is today the club capital of the world.

Foam party, popular in the clubs of Ibiza

BIRTH OF CLUB CULTURE

T HE PIONEERS OF clubland were Pacha and Amnesia, which opened in the early 1970s. The Ku club, currently known as Privilege, joined the scene shortly afterwards. Banking on the popularity of the party scene at the time, they offered their own more stylish and restrained version. Gradually, word spread and the clubs became fashionable with the rich and the famous.

The 1980s and 1990s heralded the emergence of DJs who decamped to Ibiza for the summer and forged a new type of dance music. Some became stars in their own right, performing to crowds of 3,000 or more. From then on, the club scene in Ibiza gained its own momentum and it is now a major part of the island's economy.

CLUBS

T HERE ARE SEVEN MAJOR clubs on the island, each capable of accommodating several thousand people. The biggest of them, **Privilege**, can host parties for up to 10,000 guests.

Every night they offer new attractions, including parties in foam, Brazilian nights, ghost nights and "Flower Power" balls. In addition, the clubs make their premises available to other promoters that operate on the continent. The biggest and best known of these is Manumission. Admission charges are high and may be anything up to 50 euros. Drinks are also expensive.

Smaller clubs are cheaper. They do not offer such elaborate entertainment, but have their own unique charm. They tempt their guests in with free drinks and various fun gimmicks. In the Sa Penya and La Marina districts of Eivissa, revellers often end up partying on the streets. During high season, special night bus services run between Eivissa and Sant Antoni, where most of the clubs are concentrated.

Scantily clad podium dancer – a big feature of many Ibiza clubs

CLUBBERS

P EOPLE OF ALL AGES can be found in Ibiza's clubs because there are no age limits, although young people prevail. Many come to party, others are drawn by sheer curiosity. For some, the Ibiza club scene is simply a way of life. The clubs are most frenetic during summer weekends, when they are invaded by clubbers from all over Europe. The rule is to visit several clubs each night. As is usual at such hectic events, there may be an occasional petty theft or scuffle. You may also come across drug dealers and con artists offering various goods at bargain prices to drunken passers-by. Nevertheless, generally speaking, the clubs have tight security and are safe places.

Neon sign of a club in Eivissa

Coloured lights and laser beams at El Divino

MUSIC AND DANCING

DANCING IN THE LOCAL clubs is led by some of the world's top DJs. They include Fat Boy Slim, Paul van Dyk, Mark Spoon, Carl Cox and John Digweed, to mention but a few. These DJs dictate which music will later find its way into the clubs of London, Paris and Berlin. Each year they try to surprise their fans with something new. As the party season ends in Ibiza, most of the seven top clubs and their associated DJs go on worldwide tours, promoting their latest music. Individual clubs also produce CDs of last season's hits.

Although many kinds of music can be heard in Ibiza, the clubs have become famous for their summer anthems and for a unique Balearic Beat that is a fusion of electronic music with Latin and funk rhythms. Much of it is based on drum machines pounding out four beats to the bar but Ibiza is known for its eclectic tastes and has produced a more subtle sound often branded as "chillout".

Gaudy poster advertising Space

No one style of dancing prevails in the clubs and you will often see a free-form frenzy. Many people just copy the podium dancers.

CLOTHES

YOU DO NOT NEED any special clothes to be admitted to a club, the exception being theme parties, when you are expected to wear appropriate costume and come dressed as a "Flower Child" or astronaut for example.

Clubbers playing in foam or jets of water tend to be scantily dressed. Regular clubbers are usually fashionably dressed, with clothes that are often provocative and sexy. As with the music, club fashions change every year.

DJ Sonique at the decks in Es Paradis Terranal

BEFORE AND AFTER

MOST CLUBBERS DO NOT wait until midnight to begin partying. After a day spent relaxing on the beach, many people start their evening in cafés, bars and pubs. The first to open are the small clubs. By the time **El Divino** or **Amnesia** open their doors, the party on the island is already in full swing. Even at dawn, you can still see people dancing in the streets of Eivissa. Some beaches have daytime dance cafés and clubs, such as Bora-Bora opposite the flamboyant **Space** club on Platja d'en Bossa (Space hosts a party that begins at 8am!).

Dancing crowds at Amnesia enjoy a sudden deluge of foam

THE BEST CLUBS IN IBIZA

Amnesia, Sant Rafael.
971 314 136.
www.amnesia-ibiza.com

Angels, Passeig de Juan Carlos I, Eivissa. 971 341 612.

Blue Rose, C/ Navarra 27, Figueretas. 971 399 137.
bluerose@ibiza-online.com

Eden, c/Salvador Espriu s/n, Sant Antoni. 971 342 551.
www.edenibiza.com

El Divino, Puerto Eivissa Nueva s/n, Eivissa. 971 318 338.
www.eldivino-ibiza.com

Es Paradis Terrenal, c/Salvador Espriu s/n, Sant Antoni.
971 346 600.
www.esparadis.com

Inox, C/ Cervantes, Sant Antoni de Portmany.

KM5, Ctra. Sant Josep
971 396 349.
www.km5-lounge.com

Manumission
www.manumission.com

Pachá, Avinguda ocho de agost s/n, Eivissa.
971 313 612.
www.pacha.com

Privilege, Sant Rafael.
971 198 160

Pussycat, Passeo Marítimo I, Sant Antoni de Portmany.
971 346 167

Space, Platja d'en Bossa.
971 396 793.
www.space-ibiza.com

Summum, Edificio Cala Blanca, Sant Antoni de Portmany.
971 343 997.

Sant Jordi de Ses Salines ❷

4 km (2 miles) southwest of Eivissa.
🚌 *Sat.*

THE SMALL VILLAGE OF Sant Jordi de Ses Salines lies along the road leading from Eivissa to the airport. It was established in the 15th century, but there is not much evidence left of its ancient pedigree. The most important local sight is the modest white church of **Sant Jordi** that stands surrounded by a high wall. A quirky Saturday market takes place here from 8am and has a good mix of cheap jewellery, clothes and second-hand books.

ENVIRONS: A little further on is **Platja d'en Bossa**. The local beach is popular with young people, especially the southern end where a dynamic club scene has developed. Much of this is based around Space, a huge club that opened in 1988 (*see pp120–21*). Close to this is Bora-Bora, a club-bar where parties spill out onto the sand.

Children have not been forgotten here. Behind the beach is a large water park, Aguamar, with numerous pools and slides.

A short way south of Sant Jordi is a hippodrome where you can bet on trotting races, popular throughout the Balearic Islands.

🏊 **Aguamar**
Platja d'en Bossa. 📞 *971 396 790.*
🕐 *May–Oct: 10am–6pm daily.* 🅿

Slides in Aguamar, near Sant Jordi

Ses Salines, a haven for many species of bird

Ses Salines ❸

10 km (6 miles) southwest of Eivissa.

SITUATED AT THE southern end of Ibiza are the saline lowlands – Ses Salines. These natural salt pans are extremely important for the local wildlife and were known as the "Salt Gardens" in Phoenician times.

They are sheltered to the north by the Serra Grossa hills that rise up to 160 m (520 ft) in some places; to the south they are flanked by the wooded areas of Faló and Corbari. In 1992, the area was given special protection as a nature reserve.

For centuries, the revenue from the local salt production provided a large chunk of the island's income. Until quite recently, the place was served by a narrow-gauge railway carrying salt to La Canal – a small port at the southern end of the peninsula. Salt production still continues here, though not on such a grand scale – some 70,000 tonnes of the stuff are exported each year.

Built between the salt lakes is the village of **Sant Francesc de S'Estany**, where some salt workers still live. It has a small picturesque church. The asphalt road that passes the church leads to a 16th-century watchtower, **Torre de sa Salt Rossa**, 2 km (1 mile) away. From here there is a fine view over nearby Illa Sal Rossa island, the wide beaches of Figueretes lying to the south of the capital and Dalt Vila in Eivissa.

Ses Salines' beach, **Platja de Salines**, is one of the island's most fashionable spots. One section of this beautiful, long sandy beach has been set apart for nudists.

Sant Josép de sa Talaia ❹

🏘 *1,000.* 🚌 🛈 *C/ Pedro Escanellas 33–9, 971 343 363.* 🎉 *Sant Josép (19 Mar).*

THE SMALL TOWN OF Sant Josép de sa Talaia, 13 km (9 miles) west of Eivissa, is the municipal capital of the southwestern portion and is off the beaten track. Its pace of life is slow. It is worth visiting the local traditional tavern, Bernat Vinya, where men gather to play cards and chat over a glass of wine. The only historic relic to visit is the **church**, built in the typical island style.

ENVIRONS: The town lies at the foot of Ibiza's highest mountain, **Sa Talaiassa** (475 m/1,558 ft). Keen walkers can make the two-hour hike to the peak along a well-marked trail that starts in Sant Josép. From the top there is a magnificent panorama of the district, including the rocky islet of **Es Vedrà**. In order to take a closer look at Es Vedrà you need to drive along the coast up to the sandy bay of **Cala d'Hort**, with its pleasant sandy beach and several terraced restaurants.

According to legend, Es Vedrà was once the home of sirens that lured Odysseus. Sailors and divers experience a strange magnetic anomaly here and some believe the island to have been a landing site for aliens. This lofty rock, now inhabited only by birds and flocks of wild goats and sheep, makes an extraordinary impression. Occasionally, in calm weather, it even blows off a plume of steam.

Some 5 km (3 miles) from Sant Josép, situated to the right of the road that leads to Eivissa, is **Cova Santa**. The main attractions of this cave, which is the largest in Ibiza, are its huge stalactites, some of which are a dozen or so metres long.

West Coast of Ibiza 5

See pp126–7.

Sant Antoni de Portmany 6

🏠 16,500. 🚌 🚢 ℹ️ Passeig de Ses Font s/n, 971 343 363. 🎭 Sant Antoni (17 Jan), Sant Bartolome (24 Aug).

T HE SECOND LARGEST town in Ibiza was known as Portus Magnus by the Romans. The large bay that provided a natural harbour for ships now boasts yacht marinas and a ferry terminal. Once upon a time this was a small fishing village until it was transformed in the 1960s into a busy, commercialized summer resort with scores of hotels. Regular bus services run from here to Eivissa and Santa Eulària des Riu.

Fountain in Passeig de ses Fonts in Sant Antoni de Portmany

Amid the sea of high-rise hotel buildings stands the 14th-century church of **Sant Antoni Abat**. This fortified parish church, now standing in Plaça de Església, was built on a hill, away from the harbour, and served as a shelter for the local population during pirate raids. Originally, there were defensive guns positioned on the church roof.

Columbus' Egg
in Sant Antoni

The bustling fishing harbour is popular with visitors. A palm-fringed promenade runs along the bay. At one end is a large flower bed with sculptures made in Sant Rafael, including the ingenious *Columbus' Egg*. The famous entertainment district between Carrer de Mar and Carrer Ample comes to life

only after dark. The local clubs, including Es Paradis and Eden, are among the island's best *(see pp120–21)*.

Of the nearby beaches, **Cala Bassa** and the blue-flag **Cala Conta** are probably the best. **Port d'es Torrent** is also popular, especially with families *(see p127)*.

Santa Agnes de Corona 7

8 km (5 miles) northeast of Sant Antoni de Portmany. 🚌

S ANTA AGNES DE CORONA has maintained its old-world atmosphere. There is not much here apart from a small quaint church, a shop and a bar where you can quench your thirst and enjoy a plate of *tapas*. You can take a walk from here to the nearby summit of **Es Camp Vell** and on to the neighbouring village of **Sant Mateu d'Aubarca**.

ENVIRONS: Southwest of Santa Agnes de Corona is an original early-Christian chapel of **Santa Agnes**, discovered in 1907 in a grotto. Local legend says that a sailor was saved from drowning by St Agnes during a fierce storm, and built a chapel to her on the spot where he was washed up by the waves. On St Agnes's Day, local people make a pilgrimage to this site.

Village church in Santa Agnes de Corona

West Coast of Ibiza ❻

THE MAIN ATTRACTION OF Ibiza's west coast is its magnificent beaches, many of which are tucked away in small coves and offer family-friendly facilities and safe bathing. Some of the resorts have become built up in recent years but the west coast remains one of the island's most beautiful areas with a romantic coastline, pristine waters and remote mountains clad in pine trees. The mysterious islet of Es Vedrà *(see p123)*, just off the coast, is a remarkable sight and featured in the film *South Pacific* as Bali Hai. The route suggested here cuts across the Serra de Sant Josép in the south and bypasses the highest peak on the island, Sa Talaiassa (475 m/1,558 ft).

Illa Sa Conillera

Illa de s´Esparta

Cala Molí ⑥
This small resort is flanked by steep cliffs and consists of modest villas and pensions surrounded by green pine trees. Its beach *(right)* is regarded as one of the most beautiful on the island.

Cala Vedella ⑤
This little resort is slowly becoming fashionable. Situated at the mouth of a narrow inlet, there is a wonderful beach and plenty of low-rise hotels and apartments. The resort is unlikely to be spoilt as there is no room for large hotels.

Mirador des Savinar ③
The best way to reach nearby Torre de Pirata, a former watchtower and now a viewpoint, is on foot. A drive over the bumpy road may damage your car. The point provides the best view of Es Vedrà.

Cala d'Hort ④
This is the southernmost resort on the western coast. Many visitors come to this beach, far from the main resorts and towns, to admire the view of Es Vedrà, others to enjoy the exquisite local *paella*.

Illa Es Vedrà

Illa Vedranell

Cap Llentrisca ②
The rough track leading along the craggy cliffs is fairly difficult, but from here you can see the entire south coast of the island.

| 0 km | 2 |
| 0 miles | 2 |

◁ **Es Vedrà, a forbidding and mysterious rock rising from the sea**

Cala Tarida ⑦
Another beautiful cove, Cala Tarida has golden beaches and a number of family-friendly hotels. Until recently a quiet corner of the island, it is beginning to get busy, especially during high season.

SANT ANTONI
DE PORTMANY

SANT ANTONI
DE PORTMANY
PM 803

Port d'es Torrent ⑧
Here you can join an organized canoe trip to Illa Sa Conillera and Cala Bassa. Several of the nearby villas are owned by the rich and famous, including Claudia Schiffer.

• Sant Agustí des Vedrà

Sant Josép de sa Télaia
PM 803

EIVISSA

Cala Bassa ⑨
One of the most beautiful and popular beaches in the region of Sant Antoni de Portmany; it can be reached by bus. Numerous cruising boats visit the local harbour.

Es Cubells ①
This village has a beautifully simple church and a modest restaurant. It offers a magnificent view over Cala d'Es Cubells. On a clear day you can see Formentera from here.

Vista Alegre •

KEY

▬ Suggested route

═ Other road

▬ Scenic road

✼ Viewpoint

Animals grazing around St Mateu d'Aubarca

Els Amunts ❽

IBIZA'S SPECTACULAR mountain range is situated in the northern part of the island and stretches from Sant Antoni de Portmany in the west to Sant Vicent de Sa Cala in the northeast.

Rarely visited by tourists, the region has maintained its unspoiled charm. Pinewood hills are interspersed with fertile valleys full of olive, almond and fig groves, as well as the occasional vineyard. The shore rises steeply and the roads leading to the water's edge are narrow, unmade and rugged, presenting a challenge even to four-wheel-drive vehicles. The area is a hiker's paradise; walking around you are likely to meet only the local shepherds.

Except for the small resorts, such as Port de Sant Miquel, Portinatx or Cala Sant Vincent, the inland towns, including Sant Joan de Labritja and Santa Agnes de Corona (see p123), have maintained their traditional, rural character. A good example of this is the little village of **Sant Mateu d'Aubarca**, where you can see flocks of sheep and goats grazing in the orchards.

Near Sant Llorenç lies the fortified settlement of Balàfia. Believed to be the island's only surviving Moorish hamlet, the whitewashed interlocking houses with flat roofs and amber coloured watchtowers once acted as fortresses during pirate attacks.

Sant Joan de Labritja ❾

16 km (10 miles) north of Eivissa. 🚌 🚉 Sant Joan (24 Jun), Santa Maria (5 Aug).

THIS QUIET little town in the north of Ibiza lies in the shadow of the Es Fornás mountain (410 m/1,345 ft). The only buildings of note in town are the **Ajuntament** (town hall) and a small 18th-century **church**. The local cafés and restaurants are well worth visiting. Sant Joan was popular with hippies in the 1960s and you can stock up on beads, Roman sandals and magically endowed crystals at the New Age Bazaar.

ENVIRONS: About 7 km (4 miles) west of town is the small village of **Sant Miquel de Balansat**. It has an impressive 16th-century fortress-church that provided shelter during the frequent raids by pirates, who once ventured deep into the island's interior in search of loot and slaves. Every Thursday at 6pm, there is a music and dance show performed by a local folklore group in front of the church. Dressed in traditional costumes, they entertain people with lively dances to tunes played on traditional instruments including drums, local flutes *(xeremia)* and triangles *(espasi)*.

Hibiscus flower in full bloom

Port de Sant Miquel is 4 km (2 miles) north of Sant Miquel. It has a fishing harbour and a handful of hotels. The resort is popular with families and has facilities for water sports as well as a diving centre. Nearby, on top of a hill, stands one of the island's most exclusive hotels – Hacienda Na Xamena. The top of the 200-m (656-ft) high cliff provides a magnificent view over the surging waves below.

To the north of the town is the **Cova de Can Marça**. This cave, which was used by tobacco and liquor smugglers, is one of the most beautiful of its kind on the island, and is on a par with the caves found in Mallorca. There is an entrance fee which buys you a sound and light show and a 40-minute guided tour.

East of Port de Sant Miquel is **Cala de Benirràs**. It gets very busy in the evenings, when visitors arrive to admire one of the most beautiful sunsets on the island. At other times it is relatively quiet. On Thursday nights it becomes a venue for hippy concerts and dances.

🐾 **Cova de Can Marça**
Port de Sant Miquel. ⬜ Daily. 📷 ⌀

Portinatx ❿

8 km (5 miles) north of Sant Joan de Labritja. 🚌

THE NORTHERNMOST holiday village of Ibiza was built as a family resort. It consists solely of hotels, apartments,

Lighthouse on Punta des Galera, near Portinatx

Coastal boulevard in Cala de Sant Vincent

on the land using age-old methods and tools. They have neither telephones nor any other modern conveniences. The island authorities set up the **Camp d'Aprenatge** here, where pupils from local schools learn about the old ways of rural life and about Ibiza's natural environment.

ENVIRONS: About 3 km (2 miles) east of town is **Cala de Sant Vicent**. This beautiful cove has become a modern resort, with quiet hotels and good restaurants. Visitors love the beach with its clean water and rugged scenery, surrounded by green pine forests.

From here, signposts point towards the famous **Cova d'es Culleram,** discovered in 1907, which was a temple to the goddess Tanoit during the days of the Carthaginian rulers. The caves are closed but the finds unearthed here can be seen in the Museu Arqueològic at Dalt Vila, in Eivissa *(see p118)*.

Another interesting destination for a walk is **Punta Grossa** – a headland situated a little way to the east, which has a lighthouse. The view from here includes the Illa de Tagomago and the eastern cost of the island. **Tagomago** island lies 6 km (4 miles) southeast of Cala de Sant Vicent. It is uninhabited and has no regular ferry links with the main island but it is often visited by cruise boats and yachts. The clear waters around the island are popular with scuba divers.

souvenir shops, restaurants and numerous cafés.

It is an attractive, quiet place with four beaches – Sa Torre, S'Arenal Petit, S'Arenal Gran and Es Portitxol – separated from each other by rocky protusions. It can become busy during high season, but instead of baking on a beach you may prefer to go water skiing or take a trip in a glass-bottomed boat to admire the life lurking beneath the clear waters.

ENVIRONS: Nearby, just 4 km (2 miles) west of Portinatx, is **Cala Xarraca**, a beautiful beach with views along the north coast. The beach provided the setting for the film *South Pacific*.

Sant Vicent de Sa Cala ⓫

8 km (5 miles) east of Sant Joan de Labratija.

SANT VICENT DE SA CALA lies along the main road leading from Sant Joan de Labratija to the east coast of

Ibiza. Running to the south of it is the range of the Serra de Mala Costa mountains. The only local historic building is the modest 19th-century **parish church**, open only during service hours.

Sant Vicent de Sa Cala is nevertheless worth visiting for a different reason. The passage of time seems almost to have ground to a halt here. The locals live in old, whitewashed houses overgrown with flowering plants. They work

HIPPIES

Hippies began arriving in Ibiza in the 1960s, attracted by the beaches, the people and the unhurried lifestyle. It soon became the "in" place and tour operators were quick to catch on. Most of the hippies moved on long ago but the hippy style has found its way into the island's culture. A small number of hippy families still live on the island; one community is near Balàfia.

Hippy stall selling jewellery

Fortified church at the top of Puig de Missa in Santa Eulària

Santa Eulària des Riu ⑫

🏠 5,300. 🚌 🛈 C/ Riquer Wallis s/n, 971 330 728. 🎉 Santa Eulària (12 Feb).

IBIZA'S THIRD LARGEST town stands on the banks of the island's only river, the Riu de Santa Eulària. The town's main shopping street is Passeig Generalíssim. This **Ramblas** connects the main street with the coastal promenade. During the day, the palm trees provide welcome shade. At night there are many lively clubs, restaurants and cafés to enjoy.

You can escape the town by by walking up nearby **Puig de Missa** (67 m/219 ft). At the top is a 16th-century **fortified church**, regarded by many as the loveliest and best-preserved example of its kind in Ibiza. This whitewashed building, once used by the town's inhabitants as a shelter from pirates, is surrounded by a handful of picturesque local houses and a small cemetery. The adjacent flat-roofed building houses the modest **Museu Etnològic**. Just a short walk away is the **Museu Barrau**, which has a collection of paintings, furniture and drawings by the Spanish Impressionist, Laureá Barrau.

🏛 **Museu Etnològic**
Puig de Missa. 📞 971 332 845. 🕐 10am–1pm & 4–6pm Tue–Sat, 4–6pm Mon.
🏛 **Museu Barrau**
Puig de Missa.
📞 971 339 411.

ENVIRONS: Es Canar, a popular resort 4 km (2 miles) north of Santa Eulària des Riu, lies on the shore of a pine-fringed bay with a beautiful beach. The local hippy market (May–Oct: Wed) is the best known and biggest in Ibiza. Held in the grounds of the Punta Arabí club, it attracts large crowds. Here, you can buy jewellery and unusual clothes and T-shirts though much of the stuff on sale is not made locally. Nearby are two large camp sites and a couple of beaches – **Cala Nova** and **Cala Llenya**. During the summer there is a daily boat trip to Formentera.

Anita's Bar in **Sant Carles de Peralta**, a little town 8 km (5 miles) northeast of Santa Eulària, was the cradle of the island's hippy culture and still remains popular. Two kilometres (1 mile) south of Sant Carles is a hippy bazaar, Las Dalias. On Saturdays and Sundays, the colourful stalls display everything from beads and bangles to bongos and

Town hall in Plaça de Espanya

intricate water pipes. There is also a café-bar here.

About 5 km (3 miles) south of Santa Eulària is **Cala Llonga**. This is one of the most popular resorts on the southeastern shores of the island. Its beautiful sandy beach makes it an ideal place for families with young children.

Arcaded entrance to a church garden in Jesús

Jesús ⑬

2 km (1 mile) north of Eivissa. 🚌

THIS MODEST village is situated near Eivissa, on the road to Santa Eulària. The church of **Nostra Mare de Déu de Jesús** has a unique early 16th-century Gothic-Renaissance altar of the Virgen de los Angeles. Painted by the Valencian artists Pere de Cabanes and Rodrigo de Osona, it illustrates scenes from the life of the Virgin Mary, Christ and the Apostles. A couple of cafés are opposite the church.

ENVIRONS: A short way to the south and within walking distance of Eivissa is **Talamanca**. Its main attractions, beside the 2-km (1-mile) sandy beach, are the Aqualandia water park and some good fish restaurants.

Ibiza's Beaches

APART FROM THE clubs, Ibiza's main attraction is its beaches. There are over 50 of them, adding up to over 50 km (30 miles) of stunning coastline. Many of the most popular ones are on the southeast coast, between Santa Eulària des Riu and Cala de Sant Vicent, and have excellent facilities. It is still possible to find a quieter spot. The delightful Cala d'en Serra, for instance, near Portinatx, has a *chiringuito* ("refreshment shack") and little else.

Cala es Figueral ①
A long, sandy beach with small, rocky islets near the shore. The northern portion is used as a nudist beach.

Es Figueral •

Sant Carles de Peralta

La Joya

Cala de Boix ②
Surrounded by green hills, this beach remains relatively deserted even during high season. It is situated near Punta Prima, offering a view of Illa de Tagomago.

PM 810

• s'Argamassa

Santa Eulària del Riu

PM 810

PMV 810-1

Platja des Canar ③
This popular resort has a small beach, situated near the pleasure boat harbour. The surrounding area is full of shops, bars and restaurants.

Platja des Niu Blau ④
This pine-fringed beach in a cove with shallow water is a particular favourite of families.

0 km   1
0 miles   1

Cala Llonga ⑥
Situated between Puig de ses Torretes and Punta Roja, on a 300-m (1,000-ft) wide bay, Cala Llonga is a friendly resort and attracts hundreds of holidaymakers.

Platja del Pinos ⑤
The beach, close to Santa Eulària, is situated at the mouth of the seasonal Riu de Santa Eulària that dries up in the summer.

FORMENTERA

THE TINY ISLAND OF FORMENTERA, *4 km (2 miles) south of Ibiza, is just 85 sq km (32 sq miles) in area and that includes its two satellite islets, Espardell and Espalmador. A sense of peace and tranquillity pervades the island. The beaches are secluded, the grassy farmland is serene and the tiny clusters of whitewashed houses that make up the island's villages are positively slumberous.*

It is the very lack of high-profile tourist facilities that attracts visitors. Its beaches are some of the emptiest and cleanest to be found anywhere in Spain, high-rise hotels are nowhere to be seen and the main means of transport on the island are bicycles and scooters – the tourist office will encourage you to cycle rather than hire a car.

Scooter – the basic means of transport on the island

The Greeks called it Snake Island (although snakes are rarely seen), but never settled here. The more practical Romans left settlers on the island to grow cereals and other crops, and named it *Frumenteria* (Wheat Island), giving rise to its present name.

Following the fall of the Roman Empire, the island became a refuge for outlaws and pirates. For two centuries it was ruled by the Arabs. Throughout the Middle Ages, Formentera remained practically deserted. The second major wave of settlers arrived in the late 17th century. It was at that time that several defensive watchtowers were built, although only a handful of them survive today.

Ever since that time, Formentera has managed to maintain its unique character as a virgin island. The quiet farmsteads and villages appear to have remained unaffected by modern living and the loveliest corners of the island are only reached by rough, unpaved roads. For the peace-loving visitor, it is a tranquil idyll. Even so, the island's economy is entirely dependent upon its summer visitors, most of whom come for day trips. Each summer the island's population doubles but there are still plenty of quiet spots to be found.

A popular beach party in Es Pujols – a rare sight on Formentera

◁ **Northern coast of Formentera, seen from the Es Mirador restaurant**

Exploring Formentera

WITH FEW HOTELS AND plenty of seclusion on offer, Formentera is a paradise for those seeking a quiet holiday, free from distractions. The coastline is stunning, with crystal-clear turquoise waters and pristine beaches. The nightlife is calm and unhurried in the bars and restaurants of Sant Francesc – the island's tiny capital. Es Pujols is the main resort. It, too, is small scale but it is a lively, fun place to be with some good bars and a couple of laid-back clubs. For a little gentle sightseeing, the island has a handful of ancient defensive towers, pretty village churches and some prehistoric ruins in Ca Na Costa.

Lonely lighthouse at the end of the road on Cap de Barbària

SIGHTS AT A GLANCE

Catamarans with sails aloft on the beach in Es Pujols

ILLA ESPALMADOR **4**

5 SES SALINES

CA NA COSTA
Estan   **6**
LA SAVINA **3**
Puden   **7**
ES PUJOLS

SANT FRANCESC
1
SANT FERRAN

PLATJA MIGJORN **8**

2 CAP DE BARBÀRIA

0 km   3

0 miles   3

Illa Espardell

LOCATOR MAP

Platja Migjorn, the longest beach on Formentera

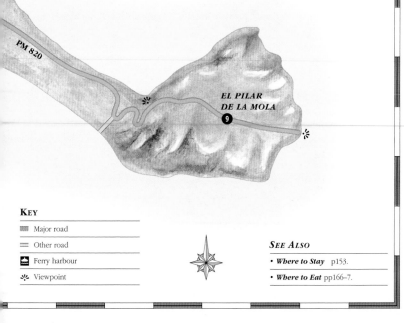

Quiet beach in Cala Saona, used by the guests of the only hotel

GETTING THERE

There is no airport on Formentera, but the island has good sea links with Ibiza. Most services run between La Savina and Eivissa. The voyage takes about one hour (fast ferries take 25 min) although journey times can vary. Sant Antoni and Santa Eulària des Riu also have ferry links with Formentera. Buses from La Savina harbour go to various parts of the island, but the best way to travel is by scooter or bicycle. The main road cuts across the island, connecting La Savina to Punta sa Ruda. There are also good roads leading to Es Pujols, Cala Saona and Cap de Barbària.

PM 820

EL PILAR DE LA MOLA

9

KEY

▦ Major road

▭ Other road

⚓ Ferry harbour

❊ Viewpoint

SEE ALSO

• *Where to Stay* p153.

• *Where to Eat* pp166–7.

Plaça de la Constitució in Sant Francesc

Sant Francesc ❶

🏛 *1,000.* ℹ *Port de la Savina, 971 302 057.* 🎉 *Sant Francesc Xavier (3 Dec).*

FORMENTERA'S TINY CAPITAL is situated a mere 3 km (2 miles) from La Savina harbour and contains most of the island's historic buildings. In Plaça de la Constitució is an imposing **fortified church** dating from 1729, which was used by the many of the island's inhabitants as a shelter from the frequent pirate raids that ravaged the island. Now it houses the local government offices and a post office. Nearby is the **Museo Etnòlogic**. Carrer de Jaume I and its adjacent streets are full of market stalls selling clothes and souvenirs. Among them, you can find hippy stalls offering jewellery.

The oldest building in town is the 14th-century **Capilla de sa Tanca Vell**, a stone structure with no windows and covered with a barrel roof, which was also often used as a refuge from pirates. Also worth visiting is the local restaurant, Es Pla, situated along the road to Cala Saona, which is famous for its Indian cuisine and large selection of beers.

ENVIRONS: Some 3 km (2 miles) to the east is **Sant Ferran**. This modest village with a lovely church was once the centre of alternative culture, taken over by large numbers of hippies. The legendary Fonda Pepe bar and the library, run by an American called Bob, were hippy meeting places in the 1960s. It is worth going there for a drink, just to savour the hazy atmosphere of "flower power" nostalgia.

Not far from Sant Ferran is **Cova d'en Xeroni**, a limestone cave, discovered by accident in 1975. The cave has been illuminated with 1970s disco lights, which only adds to the charm of the guided tour.

🎟 **Cova d'en Xeroni**
Ctra. Sant Ferran–La Mola, 6 km (4 miles). ⬜ *May–Oct: 10am– 1:30pm & 2:30–8pm Mon–Sun.* 🎟

Cap de Barbària ❷

8 km (5 miles) southwest of Sant Francesc.

A BUMPY ROAD LEADS from Sant Francesc southwards, across an area of wild desert, to the distant Barbària headland. This is the southernmost point of Formentera and features an 18th-century defence watchtower, **Torre des Garroveret**, and a lighthouse warning passing ships of the numerous rocks that jut from the sea at the island's tip. Nearby are the unearthed remains of a fortified megalithic settlement. The area is also rich in sculptures built of stones placed one

by one by passing visitors. The most typical features of this windswept desert are pine trees twisted into weird shapes by the wind, and rocks eroded by centuries of wind and water.

ENVIRONS: Travelling from Sant Francesc, you pass the little road leading to **Cala Saona**. Here, in a small cove, are a beautiful sandy beach, a handful of restaurants and a solitary hotel.

Moored boats in the Estany d'es Peix lake

La Savina ❸

3 km (2 miles) north of Sant Francesc.
⛴

THE ONLY HARBOUR in Formentera providing ferry links with Ibiza is situated in the northern part of the island. Apart from when visitors are spilling on or off the ferries, La Savina is a fairly sleepy, unassuming place. Nevertheless, you will find several shops and supermarkets here as well as car, scooter and bicycle hire. Buses to Sant Francesc, El Pujols and other villages depart from stops behind the ticket offices. There is also a taxi stand here. In view of the small distances involved, cab rides are not very expensive.

La Savina adjoins the protected salt water lagoons of **Estany Pudent** and **Estany d'es Peix**. The latter has a fishing harbour that is always full of boats seeking shelter in the shallow, calm waters of the lagoon; drying nets can be seen hanging along the shore.

Torre des Garroveret in Cap de Barbària

The southern coast of Illa Espalmador as seen from Formentera

Illa Espalmador **❹**

THIS SMALL, 3-km (2-mile) long, island is situated between Formentera and Ibiza. There is no regular ferry service but during high season it is visited by pleasure boats sailing from La Savina.

The tiny island is popular with day trippers from Ibiza who flock here for the chance to sunbathe on the shores of **s'Alga**, a large natural harbour situated at the southern end of the island. This is also a favourite spot for yachts cruising the archipelago. A short walk north of the beach is a **sulpherous mud pool** where you can indulge in a bath of warm, sticky ooze (get there early to avoid the rush). The island's only monument is the **Torre de sa Guardiola**, an 18th-century defence tower that has recently been restored.

At low tide, some people attempt to walk across the sound to Formentera, although this is prohibited by the notice boards displayed at the tip of the **Es Trucadors** peninsula – the only traces of man's presence on this spit of white sand are the fragments of boats, nets and buoys washed ashore by the sea.

Ses Salines **❺**

3 km (2 miles) north of Es Pujols.

THE FLAT, SALTY marshes along the road leading from La Savina to Es Pujols are famous for their birdlife. The most common species include the heron and the fen-duck. During the summer season, the grounds are also visited by flamingoes. Until recently it was commercially viable to produce salt here, but in 1955 the area was declared a listed zone in view of its ecological importance. Now the area including Ses Salines, Estany Pudent and the Punta de sa Pedera headland to the west of La Savina, form a nature reserve.

Situated to the north of Ses Salines are **Platja Illetes** and **Platja Llevant**, which are considered to be among the loveliest beaches the Balearic Islands have to offer. The adjacent 200-year-old salt-mill now houses a restaurant.

Salt was valued for centuries, not only as a condiment but also as legal tender. Even today it is still being produced in the traditional way in many places throughout the Balearic Islands. Sea water floods the shallow lagoons and evaporates when heated by the sun, leaving behind pure salt. This creates a specific environment on which salt-loving flora and fauna thrive. Salty shrimps are the favourite food of many birds, including the black-winged stilt.

Ca Na Costa **❻**

1.5 km (1 mile) north of Es Pujols.

SITUATED CLOSE TO Es Pujols is the megalithic burial chamber of Ca Na Costa (1800–1600 BC). A circle of seven vertical limestone blocks, the simplicity of the stone ring belies its historical importance as it is the only structure of its kind in the Balearic Islands and the most precious historic relic on Formentera. It is also the only evidence of prehistoric human habitation remaining on the island.

The excavations were begun in 1974 and unearthed a number of objects, including ceramic and bronze vessels and axes, which are now on display in Eivissa's Museu Arqueològic (see p118).

Ses Salines seen from the Es Moli de Sal restaurant

Popular beach in Es Pujols

Es Pujols ❼

7 km (4 miles) northeast of Sant Francesc. 🚌 🛥️ *Virgen del Carmen (16 Jul).*

THE SMALL RESORT of Es Pujols is the island's main holiday centre. It is a low-key, relaxed kind of place with a small marina at the eastern end of the town. Some of the island's best beaches are within easy walking distance and the nightlife in the bars, restaurants and clubs, for otherwise sleepy Formentera at least, is quite lively.

ENVIRONS: A short way east of Es Pujols, standing on a peninsula, is a 17th-century watch tower – **Torre de Punta Prima**; next to it is one of the best hotels on the island – the luxury Punta Prima Club. A little further along the coast, among the rocks, is **Cova de ses Fumades Negres.**

Platja Migjorn ❽

THIS LOVELY BEACH IS a 5-km (3-mile) long stretch of fine sand, with pale-turquoise waters. It is fringed by pine forests and is the longest beach on the island. At its eastern end is the **Torre d'es Català**; at its western end are the **Cova d'es Ram** caves. The holiday village of **Maryland** in the east and **Es Ca Marí** in the west have numerous hotels and apartments tucked away in the woods. The central section of the beach is the most

pleasant and secluded. A handful of bars and restaurants are set back from the beach and are more easily accessible by car. The most popular of them, the Blue Bar, doubles up as a low-key nightclub.

Platja Migjorn in the vicinity of Es Arenals

El Pilar de la Mola ❾

11 km (7 miles) southeast of Sant Ferran. 🚌

SITUATED AT THE heart of the La Mola plateau, El Pilar de la Mola is a fairly sleepy little place and makes a good stopping off point on a trip to Formentera's 19th-century lighthouse, **Faro de la Mola** *(see below).*

El Pilar de la Mola's most interesting historic building is the whitewashed church of **Nostra Senyora del Pilar**, built in 1784. The town is best known for its craftsmen, whose workshops are open to visitors. At the popular Sunday market you can buy jewellery, good quality leather goods and excellent local cheese (which goes perfectly with a glass of the local dry red wine).

ENVIRONS: Es Caló is a small fishing village on the north coast of the island. Unusually, it has no harbour and the boats have to be pulled ashore on special rails. When travelling from here towards La Mola it is essential to stop at the **El Mirador** bar, which offers a magnificent panoramic view of Formentera. Some 2 km (1 mile) north of El Pilar de la Mola, rises the 133-m (436-ft) high Ferrer hill. A little further on, to the west, is the **Cova d'es Fum**, a large cave where the locals hid their treasures during a Viking raid in 1118. Unfortunately for them, the Viking pirates discovered the hiding place and, having smoked them out, slaughtered the defenders and made off with the loot.

Travelling 3 km (2 miles) east, you arrive at **Punta de sa Ruda** – a rocky crag that drops steeply towards the crashing sea, over 100 m (320 ft) below. The views of the island from here are stunning. The Faro de la Mola lighthouse, built in 1861, is situated at the edge of the crag and was the inspiration for "the lighthouse at the end of the world" in Jules Verne's *Journey Around the Solar System.* A statue of the French writer stands close by.

The village church in El Pilar de la Mola

Formentera's Beaches

IN TERMS OF BEAUTY, the beaches of Formentera can easily rival those of Ibiza. The unspoiled natural environment, magnificent sand and clean waters attract an increasing number of visitors. Most have no hotels or clubs nearby and only a few feature bars or restaurants, which for many people only adds to their charm. The roads leading to some of the beaches (even the popular ones) can be quite rough and, as a consequence, they are never as busy as elsewhere on the Balearic Islands.

Platja de Illetes ①
The most popular beach in Formentera. Stretching to the north of it is the Es Trucadors peninsula.

Platja de Llevant ②
This beach, occupying the eastern side of the peninsula, is much quieter than Platja de Illetes. Its northern end is a favourite spot for nudists.

Platja de sa Roqueta ③
Situated next to the only hotel in this area, you can walk along the shore to Es Pujols or Platja de Llevant from here.

Platja de Tramuntana ④
A number of small beaches are tucked among the rocks. This spot is popular with nudists and anyone who wants to escape the bustling atmosphere of Illetes and Platja Migjorn.

Es Caló de Sant Augusti ⑤
Several beaches are situated to the west of town. They can be reached via the footbridges that cross the thicket covering the dunes.

La Savina
ESTANY PUDENT
Sant Francesc
Sant Ferran
PM 820
El Pilar de la Mola

0 km 2
0 miles 2

TRAVELLERS' NEEDS

WHERE TO STAY

THE BALEARIC ISLANDS are one of Europe's most popular holiday destinations. Their magnificent climate, fine beaches and close proximity to mainland Europe means that visitors arrive in their thousands between June and September. Unsurprisingly, a large number of hotels have been developed to cater for the demand. Until recently, this has meant that much of the

AMIC HOTELS

Logo of Amic Hotels chain

accommodation on offer has been fairly basic and it can be hard to find better accommodation at affordable prices. The hotels still include mostly two- and three-star places, but the local authorities are raising the standard of service. Many hotels close down during low season. Mallorca has the best-developed hotel facilities. Formentera has the fewest hotels.

The exclusive La Residencia in Deià, Mallorca

HOTELS

MOST HOTELS on the Balearic Islands are situated along the coast, around the old town centres and harbours, and are usually within easy reach of the beaches. There are more hotel beds in the Balearics than in the whole of Greece. Even so, at the height of the season it can be difficult to get a room unless you have booked with a tour operator, as most of the rooms are snapped up well in advance. The most popular resorts are so densely packed that finding a quiet hotel with a sea view is virtually impossible. As an alternative, some historic buildings such as palaces have been turned into luxury hotels. These offer a higher standard and bags of old-world charm but at a premium price.

Many hotel developments are located in remote spots. Most provide a range of attractions. These include evening entertainment as well

as recreation facilities such as tennis courts, swimming pools and gymnasiums. It is certainly advisable to check in advance to find out whether these facilities are included in the basic price.

FINCAS

AS ELSEWHERE, rural hotels and apartments are becoming popular on the Balearic Islands, especially with those seeking quiet, out-of-the-way places. This type of holiday is offered by *fincas*.

Ca'n Curreu bungalows on Ibiza

Fincas are hotels that occupy former country mansions or farmhouses, predominantly in the island's interior. Mostly found in Mallorca, they are not necessarily a cheap option but can provide a degree of authenticity not found elsewhere. Rooms are mostly furnished with period furniture, which accentuates the character of the place.

Some *fincas* are very high-class, and cater for the wealthy. Others are in ordinary country houses and may be surrounded by holiday bungalows and apartments. When choosing to stay in a *finca* you should bear in mind that they are typically far from the beaches and town nightlife. All tourist information offices have lists of organizations offering this type of service. Details can also be found on the Internet.

CAMP SITES

THOSE WHO ENJOY camping or caravanning will have difficulties in the Balearics. There are few camp sites and those that do exist are generally situated in unattractive locations. Before travelling, check the facilities on the island you intend to visit. Camping on unauthorised sites is allowed with some limitations. You are not allowed to pitch a tent in town, on military grounds, tourist sites or within 1 km (half a mile) of an official camp site.

◁ **Soaking up the sun on Cala Millor's beach, Mallorca**

Reception in Horizonte Hotel in Palma, Mallorca

CONVENTS AND MONASTERIES

THE BALEARIC ISLANDS do not have the equivalent of the state-run parador hotels that you find elsewhere in Spain but as well as the *fincas* it is also possible to find accommodation in convents and monasteries. This is mainly true of Mallorca, where the most popular hotel of this type is the Monestír de Lluc. These inexpensive rooms are intended for people who are prepared to put up with a certain lack of luxury (it is a monastery after all). However, they are very popular with visitors and you may have problems finding a room during the high season, despite the fact that they are away from the big resorts.

Handprints at the El Palacio Hotel

PRICES

THE PRICE YOU WILL have to pay for a hotel room depends on the season. Although the main holiday season coincides with the summer months, prices only peak during the month of August. This is a general rule that applies despite the fact that tariffs vary considerably from one island to the next. Out of the tour operators' peak season, rates are generally much lower. When enquiring about prices, you should remember that hotels can quote their tariffs in a variety of ways. Some are per room, others per person per night. Always check what is included in the price. In many cases breakfast has to be paid for separately.

Most of the Balearic Islands' hotels and apartments are block-booked in advance by travel agents and tour operators. Booking this way can prove much cheaper than trying to book directly with the hotel. You should also bear in mind that not all hotels accept credit cards. Many smaller places may insist that you pay in cash.

BOOKING

ACCOMMODATION may be booked in writing or via the Internet, as many hotels have their own websites. Obviously, you can also book over the telephone, but it is always preferable to have a piece of paper to confirm your reservation. It is relatively easy to find accommodation off-season, even at short notice. Problems can arise with the more popular hotels. If you are planning a visit during the peak season, you should book well in advance.

Some hotels may require a deposit or even full payment at the time of booking, in which case you should take your receipt with you. Despite the set price lists, it can be worthwhile to haggle over the price, particularly out of season.

Princesa Playa Hotel's pool, Menorca

DIRECTORY

GENERAL ACCOMMODATION

- w www.hotelsearch.com
- w www.ibiza-hotels.com
- w www.interhotel.com
- w www.mallorcahotelguide.com
- w www.tourspain.es
- w www.visitmenorca.com

HOTEL CHAINS

- w www.barcelo.com
- w www.iberostar.com
- w www.insotel.com
- w www.riu.com
- w www.solmelia.es

FINCAS

Asociación de Agroturismo Balear
Avda. Gabriel Alomar i Villalonga 8A, 2nd floor, Palma.
(971 721 508.
FAX 971 717 317.
- w www.agroturismo-balear.com
- w www.baleares.com/fincas
- w www.fincasmenorca.com
- w www.mallorcaonline.com
- w www.rusticrent.com
- w www.weeking.com

CAMP SITES

Federación Española de Empresarios de Campings
C/ San Bernardo, 97–98, 28015 Madrid.
(914 481 234.
FAX 914 481 267.
- w www.campingsonline.com
- w www.infocamping.com
- w www.fedcamping.com
- w www.interhike.com/spain/ baleares.html

Choosing a Hotel

HOTELS OF VARIOUS price categories have been chosen for their standard, their good value and their attractive location. They are listed separately for each island, in the order in which they appear in the guide. For each island they are listed in alphabetical order according to their location and price. For more information on hotels see page 142.

	NUMBER OF ROOMS	CREDIT CARDS	OPEN ALL YEAR	ROOM WITH A VIEW	SWIMMING POOL

MALLORCA

ALCÚDIA: *Ca'n Faveta* €€
Ctra. Palma–Alcúdia, 07400, 46 km (28 miles). 971 530 152
This small rustic-style hotel, set in a country house, makes an ideal holiday base for large families. TV 🏊

	4	●	■		■

BINISSALEM: *Scott's* €€€
Plaza de la Iglesia 12, 07350. 971 870 100. FAX 971 870 267.
W www.scottshotel.com @ enquiries@ scottshotel.com
This American-run hotel is one of the finest on the island. The 19th-century town house has been lovingly restored. The suites, with high ceilings, are individually furnished with period furniture. Other rooms are more modern. Highly recommended. 🍴 Y 🍴 P

	18	●	■		

BUNYOLA: *L'Hermitage* €€€
Ctra. Alaró–Bunyola, 07349. 971 180 303/011. W www.hermitage-hotel.com
Situated high up in picturesque mountains, this 17th-century country house was once the residence of the Mallorcan bishops. It is a perfect place for hikers and anyone wanting to relax in quiet, peaceful surroundings.
Y 🍴 🍴 🎵 🏊

	24	●			■

CALA D'OR: *Cala d'Or* €€
Avda. de Belgica 33, 07660. 971 657 249. FAX 971 659 351.
W www.hotelcalador.es @ reservas@hotelcalador.es
Built in 1932 and subsequently restored, the hotel has maintained its original 1930s ambience. It is situated near the beach and surrounded by a garden and forest. All rooms have balconies. TV 🍴 Y 🍴 🍴 🍴 P 🍴 🏊

	95	●		●	■

CALA RAJADA: *Bella Playa* €€
Adva. cala Agulla 125, 07597. 971 563 050. FAX 971 565 252.
W www.bellaplaya.com @ bellaplaya@bellaplaya.com
This modern hotel recently scooped the "Tourist Merit Prize". It is just yards from the beach, and is clean and comfortable. All the rooms have balconies.
TV 🍴 Y 🍴 🍴 🍴 🍴 🍴 🍴

	214	●		●	■

CALA SANTANYÍ: *Club Pinos Playa* €€
Costa de Noffre 15, 07659. 971 165 000. FAX 971 165 003.
W www.pinosplaya.com @ email@pinosplaya.com
Perched on a high escarpment, a short distance from the beach, the hotel consists of two buildings connected by a tunnel. All rooms have balconies. A variety of apartments is dotted throughout the gardens. TV 🍴 Y 🍴 🍴 🍴 🏊

	198	●		●	■

CALA SANT VICENÇ: *Cala Sant Vicenç Hotel* €€€
C/ Maressers 2, 07469. 971 530 250. FAX 971 532 084. W www.hotelcala.com
Run by the venerable Suau family, this luxurious hotel is situated near three attractive coves and offers traditional decor and two of the island's best restaurants. TV 🍴 Y 🍴 🍴

	38	●	■		

CAMP DE MAR: *Dorint Royal Golf Resort & Spa* €€€€€
Calle Taula 2, 07160. 971 136 565. FAX 971 136 070. W www.dorint.de
This hotel enjoys a magnificent location on the southwestern coast of Mallorca. Many of the luxurious rooms have sea views. It offers various themed holidays including stress-relief and slimming. The hotel overlooks the 18-hole Golf de Andratx golf course. TV 🍴 Y 🍴 🍴 🍴 P 🏊

	162	●	■		■

CAMPANET: *Monnaber Nou* €€€
Predio Monnaber Nou, 07310. 971 768 040. W www.monnaber.com
@ monnaber@ila-chateau.com
Situated in an area of forest at the foot of the Serra de Tramuntana, this hotel occupies a former country mansion. It represents an outstanding combination of old world charm and modern facilities and provides a tranquil atmosphere and an excellent rest. TV 🍴 🍴 🍴 🍴 🍴

	25	●	■		■

	NUMBER OF ROOMS	CREDIT CARDS	OPEN ALL YEAR	ROOM WITH A VIEW	SWIMMING POOL

Price categories for a standard double room per night including breakfast, service and tax.

€ below 75 euros
€€ 75–150 euros
€€€ 150–225 euros
€€€€ 225–300 euros
€€€€€ over 300 euros.

CREDIT CARDS
Accepted credit cards usually include American Express, MasterCard, Visa, Diners Club.

OPEN ALL YEAR
The hotel is open throughout the year.

ROOM WITH A VIEW
Hotel rooms have good views, including country vistas or sea views.

SWIMMING POOL
Hotel has a pool for the exclusive use of its guests.

	No.	CC	OAY	View	Pool
COLÒNIA DI SANT JORDI: *Hostal Playa* € C/ Major, 25, 07638 Colònia Sant Jordi. 971 655 256. W www.restauranteplaya.com @ info@restauranteplaya.com Adorably old-fashioned and just a little bit funky, this secret hideaway has a wonderful patio-terrace on its own practically private beach. Old ceramics decorate every room, enhancing the white-washed, red-tiled character of the place. ▤ Υ ⅱ	8	●		●	
COSTA D'EN BLANES: *Mardavall Hotel & Spa* €€€€€ Passeig Calvià s/n, 07181. 971 629 400. FAX 971 629 631. W www.mardavall-hotel.com @ sales@mardavall-hotel.com, guestservice@mardavall-hotel.com A swanky hotel, standing near the Puerto Portals harbour. As well as its luxurious ambience and excellent service, it offers a variety of health and beauty treatments. ▥ ▤ Υ ⅱ ⅗ ⅘ 24 P	133	●	▦	●	▦
COSTA DE CALVIÀ: *Son Caliu* €€ Urbanización Son Caliu, 07184. 971 682 200. @ soncaliu@baleares.com A large hotel positioned near the Palma Nova beach. There are good views from the rooms. The swimming pool is surrounded by lush vegetation. ▥ ▤ Υ ⅱ ≈ ⅗ ⅘	223	●	▦	●	▦
DEIÀ: *Hotel Es Molí* €€€ Ctra. de Valldemossa, 07179. 971 639 000. FAX 971 639 333. W www.ila-chateau.com/es_moli @ esmoli@ila-chateau.com A quiet hotel in a former mansion, the rooms here have been lavishly refurbished. Most of the larger rooms have balconies with sea views. The restaurant is excellent. ▤ Υ ⅱ ⅗ P	87	●		●	▦
DEIÀ: *La Residencia* €€€€€ Son Canals s/n, 07179. 971 639 011. FAX 971 639 370. W www.hotel-laresidencia.com @ reservas@hotel-laresidencia.com One of the most luxurious of Spain's rural hotels, La Residencia occupies two former *fincas*. All of the suites have four-poster beds and the quality carries through to the award-winning restaurant. The hotel is invariably listed among the top establishments recommended by *Condé Nast Traveller*. Now part of the Orient-Express group. Υ ⅱ ⅗ ⅘ ⅖	62	●	▦		▦
ESPORLES: *La Posada del Marqués* €€€ Urbanización Es Verger, 07190. 971 611 230. FAX 971 611 213. W www.posadamarques.com @ posada@posadamarques.com Situated in a 16th-century mansion, the hotel's terrace has a fine view over Palma. Each room is decorated in a unique way. ▥ ▤ ⅱ Υ	17	●	▦	●	▦
FELANITX: *Villa Hermosa* €€€€ Ctra. PM 401, 07200, 6 km (4 miles). 971 824 960. FAX 971 824 592. W www.hotel-villahermosa.com @ info@hotel-villahermosa.com The hotel occupies a palatial country mansion, high on a pine-covered hill with a view to the distant sea. Its stylish rooms are light and spacious and the restaurant is excellent. The Vall D'Or golf course is nearby. ▥ ▤ Υ ⅱ ⅗ ⅘ ⅖	10	●		●	▦
FORMENTOR: *Formentor* €€€€€ Playa Formentor s/n, 07470. 971 899 100 FAX 971 865 155. W www.hotelformentor.net @ reservas@hotelformentor.net Mallorca's first luxury hotel was built in 1929. Recently renovated, the rooms are extremely elegant. Peaceful gardens and five luxurious apartments make this one of the island's top hotels. Over the years the hotel has played host to many celebrities, including Charlie Chaplin, Audrey Hepburn, Peter Ustinov, Mikhail Gorbachov, Winston Churchill, Grace Kelly, Gary Cooper, Laurence Olivier and the Dalai Lama. ▥ ▤ ⅱ ⅗ ⅘ P	126	●	▦	●	▦

For key to symbols see back flap

Price categories for a standard double room per night including breakfast, service and tax. € below 75 euros €€ 75–150 euros €€€ 150–225 euros €€€€ 225–300 euros €€€€€ over 300 euros.	**CREDIT CARDS** Accepted credit cards usually include American Express, MasterCard, Visa, Diners Club. **OPEN ALL YEAR** The hotel is open throughout the year. **ROOM WITH A VIEW** Hotel rooms have good views, including country vistas or sea views. **SWIMMING POOL** Hotel has a pool for the exclusive use of its guests.	**NUMBER OF ROOMS**	**CREDIT CARDS**	**OPEN ALL YEAR**	**ROOM WITH A VIEW**	**SWIMMING POOL**

	Rooms	Credit Cards	Open All Year	Room With a View	Swimming Pool
FORNALUTX: *Balitx d'Avall* €€ Ctra. Sóller–Lluc, 07109, 15 km (9 miles). ☎ 971 768 040. This remote 16th-century mansion is situated at the heart of the Serra de Tramuntana and is reached via an unmade road. It is an ideal place for anyone looking for a relaxing stay and long mountain hikes. ▮ ▮	11	●	■	●	■
ILLETAS: *Europe Playa Marina* €€ Paseo Illetas 68, 07015. ☎ 971 402 611. FAX 971 402 800. W www.europehotels.org @ ipm@europehotels.com Next to the sea on the outskirts of Illetas, this large hotel is surrounded by woodland. All the rooms have views of the sea. ▮ ▮ ▮ ▮	159	●		●	■
MANACOR: *La Reserva Rotana* €€€€€ Camí de S'Avall, 07500, 3 km (2 miles). ☎ 971 845 685. FAX 971 555 258. W www.reservarotana.com @ info@reservarotana.com This 17th-century mansion house hotel has its own golf course and can even organize balloon flights. The upmarket cuisine and fine local wines are something to write home about. ▮ ▮ ▮ ▮ ▮	21	●	■	●	■
MANACOR: *Son Aimoxa Vell* €€€ Ctra. Cales de Mallorca–Manacor, 07500, 5 km (3 miles). ☎ 971 846 242. This large, 16th-century country residence has been converted into a luxury hotel. There is a broad expanse of garden and the stylish rooms have all been decorated with modern furnishings. ▮ ▮ ▮ ▮ ▮ ▮	15	●	■		■
MONTUÏRI: *Sa Rota d'en Palerm* €€ Crta. Lloret de Vistalegra-Montuïri, 07518, 1 km (half a mile). ☎ 971 726 934. FAX 971 185 034. W www.sa-rota.com This small country resort has a uniquely inviting feel. The original home is Italian in feel and the grounds and bungalows have been beautifully landscaped. A large pine forest dominates the hilltop behind. ▮ ▮	8	●	■	●	■
PALMA: *Hostal Brondo* € C/ Ca'n Brondo 1, 07001. ☎ 971 719 041. FAX 971 721 579. This colourful, British-run place has undergone a complete refurbishment, affectionately preserving the original rococo architectural elements. It is ideally located for taking in all the historic sights in central Palma.	12	●	■	●	
PALMA: *Hotel Born* € C/ Sant Jaume 3, 07012. ☎ 971 712 942. FAX 971 718 618. @ hotel_born@hotmail.com This 16th-century palace of the Marquis of Ferrandell (Ca'n Maroto) was restored in the 18th century and has a classic Mallorcan courtyard entrance with palm trees, marble floors, and Ionic columns in the lobby. Many fine antique touches include carved stone fire surrounds, frescoed ceilings and oriental carpets, and chandeliers. Patio seating for breakfast. ▮	29	●	■	●	
PALMA: *Dalt Murada* €€ C/ Almudaina 6A, 07001. ☎ 971 425 300. FAX 971 719 708. W www.daltmurada.com A wonderful converted mansion that feels just like staying in the home of an aristocratic friend. Works of art that have been in the family for centuries adorn every wall. There are spectacular views of the cathedral and the historic centre. ▮ ▮	10	●		●	
PALMA: *Palau Sa Font* €€ C/ Apuntadores 38, 07012. ☎ 971 712 277. FAX 971 712 618. W www.palausafont.com "Art and design in the heart of the historic centre" is the phrase that captures the essence of this beautiful hotel. Subtly graced with warm Italianate colours and accented with remarkable pieces of sculpture. The atmosphere here is peaceful but always welcoming. ▮ ▮ ▮	19	●		●	■

PALMA: *Portixol* €€€ 23
C/ Sirena 27, 07006. 971 271 800. FAX 971 275 025. W www.portixol.com
This wonderful, bright and airy design hotel is situated on its own little
port. Service is cheerful and efficient and rooms are exceedingly well
equipped. TV 📋 Y ⛽ 🍴

PALMA: *Palacio Ca Sa Galesa* €€€€ 12
Carrer de Miramar 8. 971 715 400. FAX 971 721 579.
W www.palaciocasagalesa.com @ reservas@palaciocasagalesa.com
Set in a wonderfully restored 17th-century merchant's house close to the
cathedral and Arab baths, the Palacio Ca Sa Galesa hotel is luxurious and
tastefully decorated. The fine city views only add to the sense of grandeur.
TV 📋 Y ⛽ 🍴 P

PALMA: *Arabella Sheraton Golf Hotel Son Vida* €€€€€ 93
Carrer de la Vinagrella s/n, 07013. 971 787 100. FAX 971 787 200.
W www.arabellasheraton.com @ golfhotel.sonvida@arabellasheraton.com
Considered to be one of Palma's best hotels, its rooms all have balconies
and luxurious furnishings, and are divided into seven price categories. The
restaurant's Spanish and Mallorcan cuisine is excellent. Y ⛽ 🏊 🍴 🎾 ♿ 🛗

PALMA NOVA: *Delfin Playa* €€ 144
Hermanos Moncada 17, 07181 Calvià. 971 680 100. FAX 971 680 112.
This medium-standard hotel situated near the beach is surrounded by
gardens and offers a good place to relax. TV Y ⛽ 🏊 🍴

PEGUERA: *Cala Fornells* €€ 94
971 686 950/954. FAX 971 68 75 25.
W www.calafornells.com @ hotel@calafornells.com
This hotel is situated on an attractive coastline notable for its coves.
Its comfortable rooms and private beach make it worth recommending.
TV 📋 🏖 🏊 🍴 🎾 🛗

PEGUERA: *Palmira Cormoran* €€ 129
C/ José Maria Pemán 15–17, Urbanización La Romana, 07160.
971 686 650. FAX 971 687 261.
W www.palmirahotels.com/cormoran.html @ reservas@palmirahotels.com
A modern hotel with a pleasant atmosphere. TV 📋 Y ⛽ 🍴 🛗

PLATJES DE PEGUERA: *Petit Cala Fornells Hotel* €€ 24
971 685 405. FAX 971 685 443. @ petitcf@baleares.com
Standing on a high escarpment above a small bay, this is a quiet hotel.
All the rooms have terraces with views out to sea.

PLATJES DE MURO: *Grupotel Parc Natural* €€€ 146
Ctra. Alcúdia–Artà s/n, 07458. 971 892 017. FAX 971 890 345.
W www.grupotel.com @ parcnatural@grupotel.com
This is an excellent place for families with children and for anyone who
looks forward to a holiday in peaceful surroundings. The restaurant serves
local specialities. TV 📋 Y ⛽ 🏊 🍴 🎾 🛗

POLLENÇA: *Son Brull* €€€ 25
Crta Palma-Pollença PM 220, 07460, 50 km (31 miles).
971 535 353. FAX 971 531 068. W www.sonbrull.com
This brand-new, self-proclaimed "avant-garde" design hotel lives up to its
every aspiration and then some. From the beautiful restoration of the
historic manor house to the infinity pool and the really exciting aesthetic
details, this is spectacular option. TV 📋 Y ⛽ 🎾 ♿

POLLENÇA: *Son Sant Jordi* €€ 8
C/ Sant Jordi 29, 07460. 971 530 389. FAX 971 535 109.
@ s.santjordi@hspollensa.com
This tiny hotel is big on style and has thought of every comfort, including a
garden and pool in the back. Loads of refined antiques combined with
rustic features give it a unique look. TV 📋 Y ⛽

PORT D'ANDRATX: *Hotel Villa Italia* €€€ 17
Camino de San Carlos 13.
971 674 011. FAX 971 673 350. W www.hotelvillaitalia.com
@ hotelvillaitalia@hotelvillaitalia.com
This large 1920s villa stands on a slope of a hill with an extensive view
over the bay and Port d'Andratx harbour. The rooms are decorated with
antique furniture; those in the Castillo section are furnished in a rustic style.
Y ⛽ TV 🍴

For key to symbols see back flap

<table>
<tr><td colspan="2">

Price categories for a standard double room per night including breakfast, service and tax.

€ below 75 euros
€€ 75–150 euros
€€€ 150–225 euros
€€€€ 225–300 euros
€€€€€ over 300 euros.

</td><td colspan="5">

CREDIT CARDS
Accepted credit cards usually include American Express, MasterCard, Visa, Diners Club.

OPEN ALL YEAR
The hotel is open throughout the year.

ROOM WITH A VIEW
Hotel rooms have good views, including country vistas or sea views.

SWIMMING POOL
Hotel has a pool for the exclusive use of its guests.

</td></tr>
<tr><td colspan="2"></td><td>NUMBER OF ROOMS</td><td>CREDIT CARDS</td><td>OPEN ALL YEAR</td><td>ROOM WITH A VIEW</td><td>SWIMMING POOL</td></tr>
</table>

	NUMBER OF ROOMS	CREDIT CARDS	OPEN ALL YEAR	ROOM WITH A VIEW	SWIMMING POOL
PORT DE POLLENÇA: *Mirimar* €€ Passeig Anglada Camarassa 39. ☎ 971 866 400. FAX 971 864 075. W pollensanet.com/mirimar Stylish hotel with wood-beam ceilings, a sea-view terrace and lush gardens. The patios are graced with antiques and Mallorcan ceramics, and rooms are traditionally furnished, quiet, comfortable. Private beach access. TV ▤ Ⅰ Ⅱ	84	●			
PORT DE SÓLLER: *Es Port* € C/ Antonio Montis s/n, 07108. ☎ 971 631 650. FAX 971 631 662. W www.hotelesport.com The hotel occupies a 17th-century manor house surrounded by a garden just 100 metres from the beach. The gardens and reception area are charming and the rooms, in a modern extension, clean and comfortable. Ⅰ ◆ P ◊	14	●	■		■
PUIGPUNYENT: *Gran Hotel Son Net* €€€€ Puigpunyent, 07194. ☎ 971 147 000. FAX 971 147 001. W www.sonnet.es @ recepcion@sonnet.es In a building dating back to 1672, the hotel's celebrity guests include King Juan Carlos and Claudia Schiffer. The facilities range from golf and Spanish lessons to health and beauty treatments. TV ▤ Ⅰ Ⅱ ◊ 24 ⚲	25	●	■		■
SANTA MARÍA DEL CAMÍ: *Read's* €€€€ Ca'n Morgues. ☎ 971 140 261. FAX 971 140 762. W www.readshotel.com Where else does a *trompe-l'oeil* lion gaze on you affectionately as you enjoy your Jacuzzi, or does your bathroom come equipped with a silver Moroccan rosewater sprinkler. Elegant yet unostentatious, this is Mallorcan resort living at its very finest. Excellent dining, too. TV ▤ Ⅰ Ⅱ ◊ ⚲	23	●	■	●	■
SES SALINES: *Es Turó* €€ Ctra. Palma–Santanyí, 07640. ☎ 971 649 531. W www.esturo.com The first-floor rooms of this typical *finca* provide a lovely view of the sea. The traditional Mallorcan cuisine is particularly good. TV ▤	10	●			■
SÓLLER: *Ca's Puers* €€€ Carrer Isabel II 39, 07100. ☎ 971 638 004. FAX 971 630 429. W www.caspuers.com This elegant patrician town mansion has been impeccably refurbished. Located right off the central town square and behind the main church, it features a well-known restaurant. Each spacious room – all located on many different levels – is decorated in uniquely elegant style. TV ▤ Ⅰ Ⅱ	6	●		●	
SÓLLER: *Ca's Xorc* €€€ Ctra. Sóller–Deiá, 07100, 56 km (35 miles). ☎ 971 638 280. FAX 971 632 949. W www.casxorc.com Located above Sóller Valley, eye-to-eye with the Serra de Tramuntana, this elegant country house offers breathtaking views. A real rustic retreat with all the amenities, including garden niches, an ancient, a wonderful wine cellar, and one of the area's best restaurants. TV ▤ Ⅰ Ⅱ	13	●		●	■
VALLDEMOSSA: *Vistamar de Valldemossa* €€€€€ Ctra. Valldemossa–Andratx, 07170, 3 km (2 miles). ☎ 971 612 300. FAX 971 612 583. W www.vistamarhotel.es @ info@vistamarhotel.es This 18th-century *finca* has maintained its old world atmosphere, with locally produced furniture and art. The gardens and swimming pool perch over a green gully looking towards the sea. TV ▤ Ⅰ Ⅱ P	16	●			■
MENORCA					
BINIANCOLLA: *Sur Menorca* €€ Sant Lluís, 07710. ☎ 971 159 111. FAX 971 159 121. @ hsm@infotelecom.es All rooms have balconies and sea views at this pleasant hotel. Apartments and bungalows are in the gardens. The hotel offers free bus transport to the beach. Ⅰ Ⅱ ◆ Ⅳ ▦ 24	244			●	■

CALA ALCAUFAR: *Alcaufar Vell*   €€   6
Ctra. Cala Alcaufar, 7 km (4 miles), 07710 Sant Lluís. 【 *971 151 874.*
Situated 2 km (1 mile) from Punta Prima beach, this is an elegant *finca*
with a family atmosphere and stylish interiors. ▮ ▮

CALA EN PORTER: *Sa Païssa*   €   27
【 *971 377 389.* ⓦ www.sapaissa.com ⓐ sapaissa@sapaissa.com
This family-friendly hostel has a warm welcome and good food. ▮ ▮ ▮

CALA GALDANA: *Audax*   €€€   244
【 *971 154 646.* ⒻⒶⓍ *971 154 647.* ⓦ www.rtmhotels.com ⓐ rtm@rtmhotels.com
This modern hotel is set back a little from the beach. The rooms are
spotlessly clean and tastefully furnished. There is an attractive split-level
pool with good views of the bay. ▮ ▮ ▮ ▮ ▮ ▮

CALA GALDANA: *Cala Galdana & Villas d'Aljandar*   €€€   202
07750 Ferreries. 【 *971 154 500.* ⒻⒶⓍ *971 154 526.*
ⓦ www.galdana.com ⓐ galdana@infotelecom.es
A large hotel complex with excellent service. The beautiful Cala Galdana
Bay beach is nearby. ▮ ▮ ▮ ▮ ▮ ▮ ▮

CALA EN BOSCH: *Lago Garden*   €€   320
C/ Alisios s/n, 07760. 【 *971 387 013.* ⒻⒶⓍ *971 387 241.* ⓦ www.gardenhotels.com
Recently renovated, this hotel has comfortable rooms and apartments,
many of which have views of the port. ▮ ▮ ▮ ▮

CALA EN BOSCH: *Princesa Playa Apartment Hotel*   €€€   225
Gran Vía Son Xoriguer 17, 07760. 【 *971 387 271.* ⒻⒶⓍ *971 387 270.*
ⓦ www.infotelecom.es/princesa_playa/hotel.html ⓐ princesaplaya@princesaplaya.net
The Princesa Playa is a large apartment complex, scenically set amid lush
greenery, a short walk from the beach. An ideal place for families to
holiday. ▮ ▮ ▮ ▮ ▮ ▮

CALA MORELL: *Sant Ignasi*   €€€   20
Ctra. Cala Morell, 07760 Ciutadella, 3 km (2 miles). 【 *971 385 575.* ⒻⒶⓍ *971 480 537.*
ⓦ www.santignasi.com ⓐ santignasi@santignasi.com
This elegant hotel occupies a late 18th-century house and is surrounded by
a fine garden where meals are served during the summer. ▮ ▮ ▮

CIUTADELLA: *Alfonso III*   €   46
Camí de Maó 53, 07760. 【 *971 380 150.* ⒻⒶⓍ *971 481 529.*
ⓦ www.supersonik.com/hotel/alfonso ⓐ halfonso@supersonik.com
This modern hotel is moderately priced and is situated in the town centre. It
offers all the basic facilities and is clean and comfortable. ▮

CIUTADELLA: *Hesperia Patricia*   €€   44
Paseo San Nicolas 90-92, 07760. 【 *971 385 511.* ⒻⒶⓍ *971 481 120.*
ⓦ www.hesperia-patricia.com ⓐ hotel@hesperia-patricia.com
Part of the "Hesperia" chain of hotels, this is near the harbour and is
particularly convenient for business travellers. ▮ ▮ ▮ ▮ ▮

CIUTADELLA: *Rural Morvedra Nou*   €€€   18
Camí Sant Joan de Misa, 07760. 【 *971 359 521.* ⒻⒶⓍ *971 359 174.*
ⓦ www.infotelecom.es/morvedra
Situated 8 km (5 miles) south of Ciutadella, this hotel is located in a late 17th-
century house. The restaurant serves good regional cuisine. ▮ ▮ ▮ ▮

FERRERIES: *Aparthotel Loar*   €   30
Av. Verge de Toro 2, 07750. 【 *971 374 181.* ⓦ www.hotel-loar.com
This apartment-hotel is located in the centre of Ferreries. It provides
comfortable accommodation and has its own swimming pool.

FERRERIES: *Son Triay Nou*   €€   4
Ctra. Cala Galdana, 3 km (2 miles), 07750. 【 *971 155 078.* ⓦ www.sontriay.com
Situated in a rather remote spot, the pretty colonial-style *finca* provides an
ideal base for hikers. The rooms are simply furnished but comfortable, and
there is a good tennis court and swimming pool. ▮ ▮

FORNELLS: *Hostal Fornells*   €€   17
C/ Mayor 17, 07748 【 *6408 965 877.* ⒻⒶⓍ *6408 965 878.*
ⓦ www.windsurf-fornells.com ⓐ hostalfornells@windsurf-fornells.com
The Hostal Fornells is an ideal place for anyone who enjoys windsurfing,
and many of the guests are sports enthusiasts. Most rooms have balconies
with views of the sea. ▮ ▮ ▮

		Number of Rooms	Credit Cards	Open All Year	Room With a View	Swimming Pool
Price categories for a standard double room per night including breakfast, service and tax. € below 75 euros €€ 75–150 euros €€€ 150–225 euros €€€€ 225–300 euros €€€€€ over 300 euros.	**CREDIT CARDS** Accepted credit cards usually include American Express, MasterCard, Visa, Diners Club. **OPEN ALL YEAR** The hotel is open throughout the year. **ROOM WITH A VIEW** Hotel rooms have good views, including country vistas or sea views. **SWIMMING POOL** Hotel has a pool for the exclusive use of its guests.					
MAÓ: *Miramar* €€ Carrer Moll del Fonduco 44, 07720. ☎ 971 362 900. ☎FAX 971 351 240. W www.hotel-miramar.com @ reception@hotel-miramar.com All the rooms and terraces have sea views at this hostel situated near Maó's harbour. There is a casino nearby. 🛏 📺 🍴		36	●		●	▨
MAÓ: *Port Mahón* €€ C/ Fort de L'Eau 13, 07702. ☎ 971 362 600. ☎FAX 971 351 050. W www.sethotels.com @ portmahon@sethotels.com Situated in a stylish building, this quiet hotel is on the outskirts of town, close to the harbour with views over the port. The gardens are wonderful and the Port Mahón is one of the best hotels in the capital of Menorca. 📺 ▤ 🛏 🍴		82	●			▨
SANT LLUÍS: *Biniarroca Hotel* €€€ Camí Vell 57, 07710 San Luís. ☎ 971 150 059. ☎FAX 971 151 250. W www.biniarroca.com @ hotel@biniarroca.com This 15th-century farmhouse is surrounded by a beautiful garden. The interior of the Biniarroca Hotel is decorated with works of art. 📺 ▤ 🍴 🛏		12	●			▨
SON XORIGUER: *Hotel Pueblo Menorquín* €€€ ☎ 971 387 080. ☎FAX 971 387 079. W www.pueblomenorquin.com The Hotel Pueblo Menorquín has comfortable, well-equipped bungalows set in a lovely garden, just a short distance from the beach. It also offers guests a wide range of health and relaxation therapies. 📺 ▤ 🍴 🛏 🍴 ⬤		53	●	▨		▨
SON XORIGUER: *La Quinta Menorca* €€€€ Avda. Son Xoriguer s/n, 07769 Ciutadella. ☎ 971 055 000. ☎FAX 971 055 001. W www.laquintamenorca.com @ recepcion@laquintamenorca.com In addition to the usual amenities, this luxurious hotel is particularly well known for its excellent restaurant. A good place to unwind, La Quinta Menorca also offers guests a variety of relaxation therapies. 📺 ▤ 🛏 🍴 🍴 ⬤		82	●			▨
URBANIZACIÓN SA CALETA: *Apartamentos Blanc Palace* €€ C/ Aries 2. ☎ 971 482 511 ☎FAX 971 480 412. W www.blancpalace.com This modern apartment complex makes a good base for family holidays. 📺 🍴 🛏 🍴		125	●			▨
IBIZA						
BAHÍA DE SANT ANTONI: *Osiris Ibiza* € Playa Es Puet s/n, 07820 Sant Antoni de Portmany. ☎ 971 340 916. ☎FAX 971 341 685. W www.hotelosiris.com @ hosiris@teleline.es This inexpensive hotel is next to Es Puert beach. Its balconies provide beautiful views over the bay. 📺 🍴 🛏 🍴 24 ♫		97	●		●	▨
BAHÍA DE SANT ANTONI: *Hotel Nautilius* €€ Cala de Bou, 46/48,07830. ☎ 971 340 400. @ hotelnautilius@clubgreenoasis.com The Hotel Nautilius is a modern hotel belonging to the Green Oasis chain, situated near the beach, a mere 3 km (1.8 miles) from Sant Antoni. 🍴 🛏 24 ♿ ♫		168	●		●	▨
BAHÍA DE SANT ANTONI: *Stella Maris Paraiso* €€€ Cala Gració, Apartado 149, 07820. ☎ 971 340 600. ☎FAX 971 342 731. W stmaris@ctv.es The Stella Maris Paraiso is a large complex consisting of bungalows and apartments hidden amid the greenery of a tropical park, near the beach. With its comfortable rooms, you are bound to enjoy a good night's rest. ▤ 🍴 🛏 🍴 ♫		130	●		●	▨

CALA MOLÍ: *Hostal Cala Molí* €€ 8
San José, 07830. ☎ 971 806 002. FAX 971 806 150. @ reservas@calamoli.com
The hostel combines a magnificent setting on the high shore above the sea, with a family atmosphere provided by the owners and regular guests. Nearby are several attractive bays and beaches, including Cala Tarida, Cala Vedella and Cala Moli. TV 🍸 🍽 P 🛏

CALA PORTINATX: *Apartaments del Rey* €€ 130
Cala Portinatx s/n, 07810. ☎ 971 320 561. FAX 971320 684.
@ delrey@ibiza-hotel-guide.com
This four-storey hotel complex is situated near the beach and close to the town centre. The accommodations have kitchens and bathrooms.
TV 🍽 🍸 🍴 📶 24

CALA PORTINATX: *Presidente* €€ 270
Sant Joan de Labritja, 07810. ☎ 971 320 575. FAX 971 320 577.
W www.ecohoteles.com @ hotelpresidente@ecohoteles.com
This hotel is just a short way from the beach. TV 🍽 🍸 🍴 🍷 📶

CALA TARIDA: *Green Oasis Cala Tarida* €€ 192
Plaza del Mar s/n, 07829. ☎ 971 806 268. FAX 971 806 135.
W www.greenoasis.com
A large hotel consisting of low buildings set in a garden that disguises the size of the entire complex. All of its simple rooms have recently been fully refurbished. TV 🍸 🍴 🍷 📶 24

CALA VEDELLA: *Club Aquarium* € 125
San José, 07830. ☎ 971 808 100. FAX 971 808 094. @ clubaquarium@inicia.es
Club Aquarium offers a number of apartments, which are found in the quiet garden. It is near Cala Vedella and is an ideal place for family holidays with plenty of facilities for all age groups. 🍸 🍴 🍷 📶 24

CALÓ D'EN REAL: *Village* €€€ 20
San Josép de sa Talaia, 07830. ☎ 971 808 001. FAX 971 808 027.
W www.hotelvillage.net @ village@ctv.es
This "village" is located a short way from some natural rock pools. The rooms are in various price ranges, and all are tastefully decorated and furnished with antiques. The restaurant is good. TV 🍽 🍸 🍴 🍷 🍷

ES CALÓ D'ES MORO: *Blau Parc* € 96
C/ Velázquez 9, Sant Antoni de Portmany, 07820. ☎ 971 348 131.
FAX 971 348 134. W www.grupolasirena.com
This small hotel, situated near Es Caló d'es Moro beach, opened in 2000. The rooms are simple but comfortable. TV 🍽 🍸 🍴 P

EIVISSA: *El Corsario* €€ 15
Poniente 5, 07800. ☎ 971 301 248. FAX 971 391 953. @ elcorsario@ctv.es
The hotel occupies a former pirate's den in the heart of Dalt Vila. Its rooms have a simple but tasteful decor. Beautiful view of Ibiza Bay and the town.

EIVISSA: *Royal Plaza* €€ 117
C/ Pedro Frances 27–29, 07800. ☎ 971 310 000. FAX 971 314 095.
W www.ibiza-spotlight.com/royalplaza
This modern hotel situated at the centre of Eivissa offers comfortable rooms with modern furnishings. All the rooms have modern sockets for hooking up to the Internet. 🍽 🍸 🍴 🍷 🍷 P 🛁

EIVISSA: *El Palacio* €€€€ 7
Calle del la Conquista 2, 07800. ☎ 971 301 478. FAX 971 391 581.
W www.elpalacio.com @ bielbienne@bluewin.ch
A hotel with stylish decor, situated at the centre of historic Dalt Vila. The apartments have been arranged to suit the supposed tastes of former movie stars, including Greta Garbo, Marilyn Monroe and James Dean.

FIGUERETES: *Figueretes Hotel* €€ 76
Paseo ses Pitiusas s/n, 07800. ☎ 971 301 243. FAX 971 300 558.
@ hotelfigueretes@telefonica.net
A modest hotel close to the beach, the rooms offer a good rest after a day spent on the beach or a night in nearby Eivissa. TV 🍸 🍴 🍷 🍷 24 P

PLATJA D'EN BOSSA: *Apartamentos Dausol 1 & 2* €€ 50
C/ de la Murtra 6, 07800. ☎ 971 301 831. @ hotelreservations@hotmail.com
A basic, no-frills complex of two buildings with swimming pools near the beach. Close to the clubs Space and Bora-Bora (*see p121*). 🍸 🍴 24

For key to symbols see back flap

Price categories for a standard double room per night including breakfast, service and tax.

€ below 75 euros
€€ 75–150 euros
€€€ 150–225 euros
€€€€ 225–300 euros
€€€€€ over 300 euros.

CREDIT CARDS
Accepted credit cards usually include American Express, MasterCard, Visa, Diners Club.

OPEN ALL YEAR
The hotel is open throughout the year.

ROOM WITH A VIEW
Hotel rooms have good views, including country vistas or sea views.

SWIMMING POOL
Hotel has a pool for the exclusive use of its guests.

	NUMBER OF ROOMS	CREDIT CARDS	OPEN ALL YEAR	ROOM WITH A VIEW	SWIMMING POOL
PLATJA D'ES FIGUERAL: *Invisa Hotel Club Cala Blanca* €€ San Carlos, 07850. ☎ 971 335 100. FAX 971 335 040. W www.invisa-hoteles.com @ cblanca@invisa-hoteles.com Thoroughly renovated in 1991, this large hotel complex has comfortable rooms and many facilities including several pools, a children's play area and nightly entertainment. TV ▤ ▮ ▮ ▮	320	●			▪
PLATJA TALAMANCA: *Victoria Hotel* €€ Apartado De Correos 256, 07800. ☎ 971 311 912/962. FAX 971 311 901. @ victoria@hotelvictoria-ibiza.com This hotel is very close to the beach and offers a friendly family atmosphere. The simply furnished rooms all have sea views. TV ▮ ▮ ▮	140	●			▪
PLATJA TALAMANCA: *Argos* €€ C / La Mola s/n, Eivissa, 07800. ☎ 971 312 162. FAX 971 316 201. @ argoshotel@sord.ibiza.com The hotel has a reasonable restaurant and is close to the historic centre of Eivissa, on the other side of the bay. All of the rooms are newly redecorated and refurbished. TV ▤ ▮ ▮ ▮	106	●	▪	●	▪
PORT DES TORRENT: *Aparthotel Nereida* €€ San José. ☎ 971 343 362. FAX 971 344 161. @ nereida@ibiza-hotels.com The large, comfortable apartments, mostly with sea views, make this an ideal place for family holidays. TV ▮ ▮ ▮ ▮ ▮	136	●		▪	▪
PORT DE SANT MIQUEL: *Galeón* €€ Sant Joan de Labritja, 07815. ☎ 971 334 534. FAX 971 334 535. @ sanmiguelresort@etn.es The hotel, perched on a high shore, was awarded a prize for its architecture in 1970 and was recently refurbished. The garden terraces command views of Sant Miquel's beautiful bay. TV ▤ ▮ ▮ ▮	189	●			▪
PORT DE SANT MIQUEL: *Hacienda Na Xamena* €€€€€ ☎ 971 334 500. FAX 971 334 514. W www.hotelhacienda-ibiza.com @ hotelhacienda@retemail.es This luxury hotel, opened in 1981, enjoys a magnificent cliff setting. Most of the rooms have terraces, some have their own jacuzzis (which have been positioned to make the most of the sunsets). There are two restaurants, three swimming pools and a sauna/spa. ▤ ▮ ▮ ▮ ▮ P ▮	62	●			▪
SANT ANTONI DE PORTMANY: *Hotel Arenal* € Avda. Dr. Fleming 16, 07820. ☎ 971 340 112. FAX 971 345 734. W www.savinesarenal.com @ arenal@infonegocio.com The simply furnished hotel is near the town beach and the promenade with its numerous bars. It is close to the Es Paradis club. ▮ ▮ ▮ ▮ P ▮	155	●	▪		▪
SANT ANTONI DE PORTMANY: *Hotel-Club Els Pins* € Carrer des Caló, s/n, 07820. ☎ 971 340 301. FAX 971 340 550. W www.ibiza-hotels.com/elspins This hotel is situated on the coast in its own large garden. Many of the rooms have stunning views across the bay. TV ▮ ▮	170	●			▪
SANT ANTONI DE PORTMANY: *Vistabella* €€€ Camí de Benarnussi s/n, 07820. ☎ 971 342 324/976. FAX 971 346 609. W www.vistabella.net @ vistabella@ctv.es This complex of luxury bungalows is set in a quiet spot, about a mile from the town centre. It is an excellent place to relax. ▤ TV P	11		▪		▪
SANTA EULÀRIA DES RIU: *Riomar* €€ Platja del Pinos, 07840. ☎ 971 330 327. FAX 971 332 826. W www.hotelriomar.com @ info@hotelriomar.com The hotel stands on the outskirts of Santa Eulària des Riu, near the river that flows through the town. All the rooms are simply furnished and have terraces with sea or mountain views. ▮ ▮ ▮ ▮	120	●		●	▪

SANTA EULÀRIA DES RIU: *Duquea Playa* €€ | 32
C/ Sant Llorenc, 07840. 917 319 337. FAX 917 319232.
W www.duquesaplaya.com
Recently built near the town centre, this hotel is situated midway between the harbour and the beach. All the rooms have balconies providing views of the sea or the mountains. TV ▤ ▯▯ ▮

SANTA EULÀRIA DES RIU: *S'Argamassa Palace* €€ | 25
Urbanización S'Argamassa s/n, 07840. 971 330 271. FAX 971 332 794.
W www.sargamassa-palace.com @ sapalace@retemail.es
This modern hotel has well-appointed apartments. TV ▤ ▯▯ ▮

SANTA EULÀRIA DES RIU: *Tres Torres* €€€ | 118
Bahía Ses Estaques, 07840. 971 330 326/454. FAX 971 332 085.
W www.ecohoteles.com @ hoteltrestorres@ecohoteles.com
Tres Torres is a modern hotel close to Santa Eulària des Riu's harbour and also to the beach. TV ▮ ▯▯ ▮

SANTA EULÀRIA DES RIU: *Palladium* €€€ | 48
C/ Los Lirios 1, Siesta–Santa Eulària des Riu, 07840. 971 338 260.
A luxurious hotel occupying an historic building, the Palladium offers a range of health and relaxation treatments and excellent service. TV ▯▯ ◐

FORMENTERA

CALA SAONA: *Cala Saona* €€ | 116
971 322 030. FAX 971 322 509. @ hotelcalasaona@teleline.es
The hotel stands on the shores of one of Formentera's most beautiful bays, just a short way from the beach and surrounded by a pine forest. It provides a friendly, family atmosphere. TV ▤ ▮ ▯▯ ◐

ES PUJOLS: *Hostal Roca Plana* €€ | 47
C/ Espalmador 41–55, 07871.
971 328 335. FAX 971 328 401. @ rocaplana-hs@formentera.net
This quiet hostel is for less demanding visitors and overlooks the beach. ▮

ES PUJOLS: *Sa Volta* €€ | 25
Miramar 94, 07871. 971 328 125/143. FAX 971 328 228. @ savolta@interbook.net
Renovated in 1999, the hotel has well-equipped and comfortable rooms.
TV ▤ ▮ ▯▯

LA SAVINA: *Hostal La Savina* €€ | 39
Avda. Mediterrania 22–40, 07871. 971 322 279. FAX 971 322 279.
This family hostel, which has been operating for 50 years, is close to the Llevant and Illetes beaches. Its pretty terrace overlooks the port.

PLATJA MIGJORN: *Cases Turístiques Castelló* € | 10
971 187 614. @ saplatgeta@yahoo.es
Situated in a quiet corner near Torre d'es Pi d'es Catala, the hotel is a complex of apartments and studios and is close to the beach. TV

PLATJA MIGJORN: *Hostal Costa Azul* € | 27
971 328 024. FAX 971 328 994.
This modest hotel has a good restaurant. The beach is close by. TV

PLATJA MIGJORN: *Insotel Club Formentera Playa* €€€€ | 333
971 328 000. FAX 971 328 035. W www.insotel.com @ formenteraplaya@insotel.com
This hotel complex, built in 1996 near the Migjorn beach, consists of the main building and a number of studios. The standard of the rooms and apartments varies with the price. TV ▤ ▮ ▯▯ ▯▯ ◐ ▤ P ♿

PLATJA DE SA ROQUETA: *Lago Playa* €€ | 60
971 328 507. FAX 971 328 842. @ lagoplaya@interbook.net
A good value hotel, Lago Playa stands north of Es Pujols, close to the beaches of Sa Roqueta, Llevant and Illetes. ▮ ▯▯ P

SANT FERRAN: *Apartamentos Mayans* € | 23
Ctra. Cala En Baster, 07871. 971 328 439. FAX 971 328 719.
This pleasant hostel is just a short walk from the centre of Sant Ferran. TV

SANT FERRAN: *Illes Pitiuses* €€ | 25
Avda. Joan Castelló Guasch 48, 07871. 971 328 189/740. FAX 971 328 017.
This German-run hotel has a family atmosphere and well-equipped rooms, all with their own private bathroom. TV ▤ ▮ P

WHERE TO EAT

Restaurant
sign in Alcúdia

THE RESORTS AND large town centres found in the Balearic Islands offer a good selection of restaurants, able to satisfy even the most demanding of palates. While the resorts do, of course, cater for visitors who have come for the beaches rather than the food, good quality local cuisine is in plentiful supply. Restaurants serving local specialities can be easily spotted thanks to their signs: *Cuina Mallorquína*, or *Cuina Menorquína*. Those restaurants that are open all year are likely to be more authentic than seasonal establishments, though they can also be pricier. On Ibiza or Formentera, gourmets have fewer opportunities to sample traditional local cuisine, but even here there are restaurants that are well worth recommending.

A simple *finca* restaurant in Mallorca

LOCAL CUISINE

THE DELICIOUS cuisine of the Balearic Islands can be quite time-consuming to prepare but is well worth the wait. Many of the dishes are Catalan in origin. *Ensaimadas*, delicious spiral pastries that are dusted with icing sugar, are commonplace. So, too, are the spicy pork sausages *(sobrasadas)*. Hearty soups, another essential part of any menu, are prepared in a different way on every island. Rustic 'one-pot' dishes are also popular. The best known of these is *caldereta de llagosta (see p101)*.

Although the number of restaurants offering lobster and other seafood is so great that one would expect these dishes to be inexpensive, in fact this is far from the truth. The price paid for lobster here is similar to that charged by restaurants in Paris or London. It is also worth remembering that dinner in a restaurant that specializes in local cuisine will cost more than a meal eaten in a small restaurant by the beach.

WHEN TO EAT

AS WITH THE REST OF Spain, lunchtime in the Balearic Islands is usually between 1:30pm and 3pm. Some restaurants may be closed after 3pm. Many others will be full and you may have to wait a long time to be served. Outside traditional mealtimes, the menu selection can be limited. As an alternative, bars can provide a good variety of food and snacks while beachside restaurants are good for snacks at any time of the day.

Dinner on the islands usually starts after 9pm, when the temperature drops. This is when the restaurants, cafés, gardens and bars fill up. For Spaniards this is a time to meet with friends. Restaurants tend to fill up for Sunday lunch and booking is essential at this time.

PLACES TO EAT

THERE IS A BOUNDLESS choice of places to eat in the Balearic Islands. This is especially true during the high season, when many restaurants are open that are closed during the other months of the year. In the cheaper bars it is worth trying *tapas* or *raciones* (snacks) as these are most likely to be freshly prepared (a *racion* is often enough for two). When venturing into a bar that is popular with the locals, you should try the set price *menú del día* (menu of the day). This is a full three-course meal, accompanied by a drink. Often these menus are very good value and may cost as little as seven euros.

Many of the best restaurants are far from the resorts and do little to advertise themselves to visitors. Though the menus may look the same as beachside restaurants, the prices and quality can vary enormously. Most of these can be found

A modest restaurant in Estellencs

Restaurant garden in Eivissa, Ibiza

away from the beaches, hidden in alleys or down narrow streets near the harbours. Some are located in small villages outside the big towns or on main roads. Lunch or dinner in one of these restaurants can turn into an expedition but it is often well worth the trip. Apart from your favourite dishes, you may also like to try the *especialidad del día* (daily special) or order a dish recommended by the chef.

Many visitors prefer to use their hotel's restaurant for breakfast and dinner, and take their lunch in bars and restaurants close to the beach. Some hotels have wonderful restaurants, others are just adequate. One point in hotel restaurants' favour is that they can offer a wide selection of food, low prices, fast service and a friendly atmosphere. Most of them serve a safe, international cuisine and you are likely to see *paella*, pizza, fish and chips, roast chicken and curry all on the same menu. These restaurants successfully compete with the popular fast-food chains. Restaurants that are near or on less crowded beaches tend to offer much better food, but the choice may be limited.

VEGETARIANS

THE FOOD OF THESE islands tends to be on the heavy side and is based mainly on pork and fish, but it also has a lot to offer vegetarians. It is easy to make a meal of *tapas* consisting of vegetables such as artichokes, broad beans, aubergines, peppers, tomatoes or *tortilla española* (Spanish omelette). One of the simplest vegetarian dishes is *tumbet* (a tomato-rich vegetable stew). Local vegetarian cuisine worth recommending includes Eggs a la Sóller, Sant Juan noodles, and Mahón-style beans *(see pp156–7)*. Most restaurants, even those next to beaches, offer some vegetarian dishes. If there are none on the menu you can always ask for a vegetable or fruit salad.

Paella served in a huge dish at a beachside restaurant, in Ibiza

PRICES AND TIPPING

IN BEACHSIDE restaurants, prices are reasonable. A lunch will cost around 15 euros. The *menú del día* may be even cheaper. The sky is the limit on prices charged by some of the top restaurants; it all depends on your choice of menu. Some regional dishes and seafood may be expensive. The price of the latter will depend on the weight of the ordered lobster or fish.

Mallorca tends to have the highest prices, but even here you should remember that in a provincial restaurant the same meal may cost much less than in a popular resort. The final price includes service charges and tax and is therefore higher than the sum of the menu items. Normally, the tip does not exceed 10 per cent; it is usual to round up the bill.

Most restaurants welcome credit cards. Even some bars will accept this form of payment, but small sums are normally paid in cash. Some small restaurants, especially those not geared up for tourists, may not accept credit cards, however, so it is best to check in advance.

BOOKING

THERE ARE A large number of restaurants on the Balearic Islands and there should not be any problem in finding a table. Nevertheless, it is worthwhile booking a table in advance to avoid disappointment, particularly when you want to dine in a specific restaurant or one that is especially popular or some distance away.

DISABLED PERSONS

THE ISLANDS' RESTAURANTS are not adapted for the needs of disabled people. They do not have wheelchair ramps and the tables inside tend to be placed close together. The most accessible are the bars and small restaurants situated along seaside promenades, with outside tables.

Bahía Mediterráneo restaurant in Palma, Mallorca

What to Eat in the Balearic Islands

Sugar-dusted ensaimada

THE FOOD OF THESE islands is Mediterranean in origin, but differs quite markedly from Italian, Canary Island or even Spanish regional food. Much of it is Catalan and many dishes are pork based. Understandably, given the island culture, fish and seafood are also popular.

Vegetarians will also be able to find much to their taste. Snacks are plentiful and freshly-baked pastries are well worth trying, as are the many kinds of *tapas* available from bars. The simplest snack is *pa amb oli* – a slice of bread spread with olive oil.

Cebolla rellena a la ibicenca *are white onions stuffed with cooked meat and slowly roasted; they should be served piping hot.*

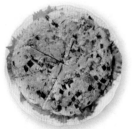

Tortilla de sardinas *is a hearty type of omelette made with sardines, olives, capers, onion and garlic.*

Tarta con verduras *is a dish consisting of fresh vegetables on a pastry base. It can be eaten either hot or cold.*

Habas al estilo de Mahón *is made with beans and may have potatoes, onion, artichokes and sometimes sobrasada (sausage).*

Arroz brut *is made with partridge and rabbit with additional* sobrasada *and* butifarra *(sausage), which are stewed in a clay pot, together with a selection of vegetables, wild mushrooms and rice.*

Artichoke

Slices of **sobrasada** (pork sausage)

Saffron rice

Large helping of quartered partridge

Wild mushrooms

Tumbet *is similar to ratatouille and is made with peppers, aubergines (egg plant), tomatoes and potatoes.*

Huevos fritos al modo de Sóller *are fried eggs with* sobrasada *(pork sausage), served with pea sauce.*

Berenjenas rellenas *consists of aubergines stuffed with onion, bread and herbs, often also with pork, served with tomato sauce.*

Empanada mallorquína *is a delicious pie filled with a stuffing made of lamb, bacon and* sobrasada *(pork sausage).*

Serviola a la mallorquína *is a baked fish served with tomato sauce garnished with raisins and pine nuts.*

Sopa mallorquína *is served as a soup with vegetables. Sometimes it is also made with meat or chickpeas* (garbanzos).

Fideua *is a tasty paella made with noodles and various types of fish and crab, and served with shrimps.*

Sola a la mallorquína *is a stewed fish served with fried potatoes and vegetables and garnished with garlic and raisins.*

Saffron and almond sauce

Pieces of *sobrasada*

Fried chicken leg

Fried piece of leg of lamb

Roasted new potatoes

Sofrito ibicenco *is a dish originating from Ibiza, made with lamb and chicken. The meat is fried along with chopped* sobrasada *and* butifarra *(sausages), potatoes and liver. It is later stewed in a sauce made with almonds, caraway seeds, saffron and garlic.*

Calamares a la balear *consists of squid packed with a stuffing made with raisins and stewed in white wine. It is often served with roast potatoes.*

Codorniles emborrachados *are succulent partridges roasted in a clay pot with wine and brandy, and served with an aromatic sauce.*

WHAT TO DRINK

Although the Balearic Islands are famous for their gin *(see p106)*, they also offer a choice of other interesting alcoholic beverages. Their wines are good value and are particularly worth trying. Wines from Mallorca, especially the Binissalem region, are considered the best. It is also worth trying the herb liqueurs, *hierbas*. Each island produces its own type and there is a really large selection. Some are extremely potent! In many shops you can taste the liqueurs before deciding to buy. A chilled glass of dry sherry is a pleasant aperitif and goes well with *tapas*.

Red wine from Binissalem

Hierbas, a herb liqueur

Choosing a Restaurant

T HE FOLLOWING RESTAURANTS have been chosen for their fine food, with particular emphasis on regional cuisine, as well as for the quality of their location and decor. Establishments are listed in the order in which the islands appear in the guide, and then in alphabetical order according to location and price. For more details on food and restaurants, see pages 154–7.

	OPEN ALL YEAR	CREDIT CARDS	REGIONAL CUISINE	GARDEN OR TERRACE	PARKING

MALLORCA

ALCÚDIA: *Sa Pedrera* €€€
Ctra. Sta. Margalida–Alcúdia, 6 km (4 miles). 971 185 159.
The restaurant at the Casal de Santa Eulàlia hotel serves lunch in the cool cellars of the old house or on a beautiful terrace, beneath sun umbrellas. Mallorcan and international dishes are on the menu. 1:30pm–4pm daily.

| | ● | ■ | ● | ■ |

ALCÚDIA: *Es Convent* €€€€
Carrer del Progrés 6. 971 548 716. W www.esconvent.com
A hotel restaurant serving good Mediterranean cuisine, including typical Balearic dishes. 1pm–3pm & 8pm–10:30pm daily.

| | ● | ■ | ● | ■ |

BUNYOLA: *L'Hermitage* €€€€€
Hotel l'Hermitage, Crta. Alaró–Bunyola, Orient. 971 180 303.
Off the beaten track, but with soaring views and some of the island's best cuisine. Cozy medieval rooms and luxuriant terraces. Dec & Jan.

| | ● | ■ | ● | ■ |

CALA GAMBA: *Club Nautico Cala Gamba* €€€€€
Paseo Cala Gamba, Coll d'en Rabassa. 971 261 045.
This restaurant is very popular with gourmets visiting Mallorca. Its large windows provide a view of the entire town and the harbour.

| | ● | | | ■ |

CALA SANT VICENÇ: *Cavall Bernat* €€€€
Hotel Cala Sant Vicenç, Maressers 2. 971 530 250. W www.terreno-lounge.com
The brilliant French chef here does the Suau family proud with his original interpretations of age-old Mediterranean dishes. Jan & Feb.

| | ● | ■ | ● | |

CALVIÀ: *Sant Joan* €€€€€
Plaça de la Iglesia 5. 971 670 927.
Mainly French and Galician dishes, prepared by chefs Patrik Tisseraud and Eric Lymberis. Tue–Sat evening, Sun midday (winter); Tue–Sun evening (summer).

| | ● | | | ■ |

CIUDAD JARDIN: *Marisqueria Ca'n Jordi* €€€€
C/ Isla de Cipre 37. 971 491 909.
An excellent fish restaurant, popular with politicians and businessmen. Its guests include King Juan Carlos. from 1pm daily.

| | ■ | | | ■ |

DEIÀ: *El Olivo* €€€€
Hotel La Residencia, Finca Son Canals. 971 639 392.
Dine in the romantic garden or in the converted olive mill. The cuisine is first-rate, featuring imaginative takes on Mallorcan and Mediterranean tradition.

| | ■ | ● | ■ | ● | ■ |

FELANITX: *Son Colom* €€
Ctra. Felanitx–Campos, 1 km (half a mile). 971 58 00 47. W www.soncolom.com
This pleasant restaurant has a friendly atmosphere and serves Mediterranean dishes prepared with local produce. Sat evenings.

| | | | | ■ |

FELANITX: *Vista Hermosa* €€€€
Ctra. PM 401, 6 km (4 miles). 971 639 392.
With its mountaintop gardens and huge terrace, this international restaurant is one of the island's most beautiful. Nov & Dec.

| | ● | ■ | ● | ■ |

FORNALUTX: *Per Amunt* €€
Carrer Bellavista 1. 971 631 952.
A split-level restaurant with a terrace that provides a magnificent view of the Serra de Tramuntana. Pizza, pasta, Greek salad and even Mexican specialities. noon–3pm, 7pm–11pm Fri–Wed; 7pm–11pm Thu.

| | | | ● | |

GÉNOVA: *Ses Albergínies* €€€€
C/ Rector Vives 2. 971 404 779.
This restaurant in an appealing little village is worth a trip, especially if combined with a visit to the Fundació Pilar i Joan Miró (see p58). Reserve ahead.

| | ■ | ● | ■ | |

Price per person for a three-course meal, including wine and tax (without tip). € up to 15 euros €€ 15–20 euros €€€ 20–25 euros €€€€ 25–30 euros €€€€€ over 30 euros.	**OPEN ALL YEAR** Restaurant is open throughout the year. **CREDIT CARDS** Eurocard, MasterCard, Visa, Diners Club all accepted. **REGIONAL CUISINE** Menu includes choice of Balearic Islands cuisine. **GARDEN OR TERRACE** Meal can be served on a terrace, in a garden or courtyard. **PARKING** Restaurant has its own parking.				

		OPEN ALL YEAR	CREDIT CARDS	REGIONAL CUISINE	GARDEN OR TERRACE	PARKING
ILLETAS: *Illetas Playa* Avda. Illetas 75. 971 709 896. Situated by the beach, the restaurant serves mainly Spanish cuisine, but also offers delicious pizzas.	€		●		●	
JARDINES DE ALFÀBIA: *Ses Porxeres* Ctra. De Sóller, 17 km (11 miles). 971 613 762. W www.sesporxeres.com Occupying an old Mallorcan building, Ses Porxeres is one of the best restaurants on the island. It enjoys a fine view over the nearby valley and produces some excellent Catalan dishes. Aug and Mon, also Sun evening.	€€€€		●	■	●	■
LA BONANOVA: *Samantha's* C/ Francisco Vidal Sureda 115. 971 700 000. @ samanthas@telefonica.net Located in an old villa, the restaurant prides itself on its tasty Spanish and Mediterranean cuisine. 1pm–3:30pm & 8pm–11pm daily.	€€€€€	■	●	■		
MANACOR: *La Reserva Rotana* Camí de S'Avall, 3 km (2 miles). 971 845 685. Go for the *menú del día* for a sample of what this wonderful kitchen can turn out. The menu changes every day. Dec & Jan.	€€€€		●	■	●	■
MANACOR: *C'an Mateu* Ctra. Vieja de Manacor, 21 km (13 miles). 971 665 036. The restaurant is surrounded by a tropical garden, which includes a playground and swimming pool. Serving typical Mallorcan cuisine, it has frequently been awarded the *Cuina mallorquina* award.	€€€€€	■	●	■	●	■
MONTUÏRI: *Puig de Sant Miquel* Ctra. Palma–Manacor, 31 km (19 miles) . 971 646 314. This quiet restaurant, standing on a hill, specializes in Mallorcan cuisine. Its *cabrito* (roast goat) is certainly worth trying.	€€€	■		■	●	■
PALMA: *Ca'n Joan de S'Aigo* C/ Can Sanç 10. 971 710 759. This antique coffee house hails from the 1700s and serves delicious traditional pastries (especially the lighter-than-air *ensaimadas*). Tue.	€	■		■		
PALMA: *Diner* C/ Sant Magi 23. 971 736 222. Two creative young American women have brought the American Dream of the 1950s to the island – a bright and shiny new diner, with milkshakes, burgers, hash browns, even peanut butter and jelly sandwiches. 24/7.	€		●			
PALMA: *La Bóveda* C/ Boteria 3 or Passeig Sagrera 3, off Plaça Llotja. 971 720 026. Popular *tapas* bar, one of several on this short backstreet, with long, wide windows and wine stacked high along the back wall.	€	■	●	■	●	
PALMA: *Celler Pagés* Off c/ Apuntadors at c/ Felip Bauza 2. 971 726 036. Traditional Mallorcan food with a semi-*nouvelle* delicacy that surprises with its deft lightness. The fish, game and vegetable dishes are all worthy. Sun.	€€		●	■		
PALMA: *Celler Sa Premsa* Plaza Obispo Berenguer de Palou 8. 971 723 529. Situated in a converted garage, this rustic-looking restaurant offers an extensive Mallorcan menu.	€€	■		■		
PALMA: *Casa Gallega* C/ Pueyo 6. 971 714 377. Excellent *tapas*, as well as a great number of lunch dishes, it is difficult to decide whether to choose the fish or meat dishes. Not that it matters as they are all excellent and the helpings are really huge.	€€€		●			

For key to symbols see back flap

<table>
<tr><td colspan="2">

Price per person for a three-course meal, including wine and tax (without tip).

€ up to 15 euros
€€ 15–20 euros
€€€ 20–25 euros
€€€€ 25–30 euros
€€€€€ over 30 euros.

</td><td colspan="5">

OPEN ALL YEAR
Restaurant is open throughout the year.

CREDIT CARDS
Eurocard, MasterCard, Visa, Diners Club all accepted.

REGIONAL CUISINE
Menu includes choice of Balearic Islands cuisine.

GARDEN OR TERRACE
Meal can be served on a terrace, in a garden or courtyard.

PARKING
Restaurant has its own parking.

</td></tr>
</table>

	OPEN ALL YEAR	CREDIT CARDS	REGIONAL CUISINE	GARDEN OR TERRACE	PARKING
PALMA: *Forn de Sant Joan* €€€ C/ Sant Joan 4. 971 728 422. A family-run restaurant serving *tapas* or fulls meal in an attractive choice of rooms. Wonderful bar spills onto the street. ☐ *Mar–Oct daily; Nov–Feb Thu–Sun.*		●	■		
PALMA: *Aramís* €€€€ C/ Montenegro 1. 971 725 232. One of the finest of the new breed of Spanish restaurants. Imaginative, international menu. Reservations recommended. ● *Sun & Mon and 1st week of Aug.*		●	■		
PALMA: *Caballito del Mar* €€€€ Paseo Sagrera 5. 971 721 074. Situated in the old part of Palma, the restaurant serves grilled or baked fish and seafood. The desserts, including cheesecake, are excellent. ▯▤		●		●	
PALMA: *La Cuchara* €€€€ Paseo Mallorca 18. 971 710 000. W www.lacuchara.com One of two restaurants of the same name, serving international cuisine. ▯ ☐ *1pm–4pm & 8pm–midnight daily.*		●		●	
PALMA: *La Lubina* €€€€ Muelle Viejo s/n. 971 723 350. Situated on the quay, this restaurant's guests include the rich and famous who moor their yachts in the local marina. A frequent winner in various gastronomic competitions, it specializes in seafood and fish. ▯		●		●	■
PALMA: *Mangiafuoco* €€€€ Plaza Vapor 4. 971 451 072. Truffles are flown in weekly to create the culinary magic this place can offer. It is set on a square with its own windmill overlooking the bay. There is also an excellent wine cellar full of remarkable vintages. ● *Jan.*		●			■
PALMA: *Chopin* €€€€€ Carrer Ca'n Puigdorfila 2. 971 723 556. @ chopinrte@hotmail.com Situated in the town centre, this elegant restaurant combines Swiss and Mediterranean cuisine. The fish and pasta dishes are particularly good. ▯ ▯		●		●	
PALMA: *Koldo Royo* €€€€€ Paseo Marítimo 3. 971 732 435. @ Koldo.royo@atlas-iap.es Specializing in Mallorcan and Spanish dishes with a modern twist, this restaurant is worth visiting not only for the food but for the fine bay views. ▤ ▯ V ☐ *lunch and dinner Mon–Fri, dinner Sat.*	■	●		●	
PALMA: *Portixol* €€€€€ C/ Sirena, 27. 971 271 800. W www.portixol.com Memorable *nouvelle* Mediterranean food in a seaside setting. Fish is a speciality. Excellent service and carefully chosen wines.	■	●	■	●	■
PALMA: *Terreno Lounge* €€€€€ C/ Bellver 8. 971 454 787. W www.terreno-lounge.com A luxurious setting with patio, pool, linens and tropical plants. Mediterranean fare is beautifully prepared. ● *1 month in winter – Jan or Feb.*		●	■	●	
PETRA: *Hotel & Restaurant Sa Plaça* €€€ Plaça Ramon Llull 4. 971 561 646. Overlooking the main square, this hotel restaurant offers top-notch international cuisine. Its specialities include shrimp in chocolate. ● *Aug.*				●	
POLLENÇA: *La Fonda* €€€ C/ Antoni Maura 31. 971 534 751. Mallorcan food is the specialty here, with a different menu every week. The wood-beamed medieval interior features a mix of contemporary expressionistic art and rustic antiques. ● *Dec & Jan.*		●	■	●	

POLLENÇA: *Son Brull*   €€€€
Crta. Palma-Pollença PM 220, 50 km (31 miles). 971 535 353.
The newest gourmet establishment to join the Suau family line-up. The themes
are still Mediterranean, and the ingredients are homegrown. ● *Dec & Jan.*

POLLENÇA: *Bens d'Avall*   €€€€€
Ctra. Sóller–Deià. 971 632 381.
The spectacular terrace, with its Classical balustrade, affords one of the
island's greatest views. Here, fresh fish is cooked in a wood-burning oven.

PORT D'ALCÚDIA: *Jardín*   €€€€
Tritones s/n. 971 892 391.
Attractively presented Spanish and international cuisine such as duck in
orange sauce, partridge with vegetables or cod in garlic sauce with asparagus.

PORT D'ANDRATX: *Villa Italia*   €€€€
Camino de San Carlos 13. 971 674 011.
Unforgettable views combined with a superb cuisine make this a standout
choice. Delicious Italian creations, such as ravioli with *porcini* mushrooms,
mozzarella, *panna cotta*, or chicken *scallopini*.

PORTITXOL: *Dos Mares*   €€€
Passeig Barceló i Mir 19.
You can enjoy tasty fish and Mallorcan cuisine in a friendly family
atmosphere at this restaurant. ▼

PORTOCOLOM: *Sa Cuina*   €€€€
Ctra. s'Horta–Portocolom, C/ Vapor de Santueri s/n. 971 824 080.
The food served here is a combination of traditional Mallorcan dishes and
modern international cuisine. The decor is a nice mix of traditional and
contemporary design. ○ *12:30pm–3:30pm & 7–11:30pm daily.* ● *Oct–May: Thu.*

PUERTO PORTALS: *Tristán*   €€€€
971 675 547.
The island's only restaurant to have been awarded two Michelin stars is a
favourite with the king and various glittering sets. The views of the yacht-
filled harbour are appropriately dazzling, too. ● *Nov–Feb.*

PUIGPUNYENT: *L'Orangerie*   €€€€
Gran Hotel Son Net. 971 147 000.
Expertly and creatively prepared taste treats await you in this mountain
retreat, only minutes from the centre of Palma. Spectacular views.

SANTA MARÍA: *Read's Hotel & Restaurant*   €€€€€
Ca'n Moragues. 971 140 261. W www.readshotel.com
International cuisine complemented by wonderful service, for a memorable
dining experience. The restaurant has recently earned a Michelin star. ▼ ▼

SENCELLES: *Sa Cuina de n'Aina*   €€€€
Carrer Rafal 31. 971 872 992. W www.sacuinadenaina.com
This cozy restaurant, with several rooms and a fireplace, specializes in meat
dishes. ▤ ♿ ▼ ○ *1pm–4pm & 7pm–11pm Tue–Sun.*

SINEU: *Molí de'n Pau*   €€€
Ctra. Santa Margarita 25. 971 855 116.
This restaurant, occupying an old windmill, offers Spanish cuisine and
typical Mallorcan dishes. ▼ ○ *Tue–Sun.*

SÓLLER: *Ca's Puers*   €€€€€
Carrer Isabel II, 39. 971 638 004. W www.caspuers.com
The beautiful garden is a knockout, and the service impeccable. The menu
includes such delicacies as saffron jelly, braised artichokes and vegetable
tagliarini. The restaurant has a well-deserved Michelin star. ● *Dec–Feb.*

SÓLLER: *Ca's Xorc*   €€€€€
Ctra. de Deià, 56 km (35 miles). 971 638 280. W www.casxorc.com
Some of the island's finest dining, high in the Tramuntana mountains.
During lunch the views are breathtaking. At dinnertime there is a romantic
ambience. ▼ ○ *for lunch & dinner time daily.* ● *15 Nov–15 Dec.*

VALLDEMOSSA: *C'an Costa*   €€€€
Ctra. Valldemossa–Deià, 3 km (2 miles). 971 612 263.
This restaurant occupies an old oil factory and serves Mallorcan cuisine at
its very best. ○ *noon–4pm & 7:30–11pm.*

For key to symbols see back flap

<table>
<tr><td colspan="2">

Price per person for a three-course meal, including wine and tax (without tip).

€ up to 15 euros
€€ 15–20 euros
€€€ 20–25 euros
€€€€ 25–30 euros
€€€€€ over 30 euros.

</td></tr>
</table>

OPEN ALL YEAR
Restaurant is open throughout the year.

CREDIT CARDS
Eurocard, MasterCard, Visa, Diners Club all accepted

REGIONAL CUISINE
Menu includes choice of Balearic Islands cuisine.

GARDEN OR TERRACE
Meal can be served on a terrace, in a garden or courtyard.

PARKING
Restaurant has its own parking.

	OPEN ALL YEAR	CREDIT CARDS	REGIONAL CUISINE	GARDEN OR TERRACE	PARKING
MENORCA					
CALA BINIANCOLLA: *Adrián* €€ Cala Biniancolla 31. 971 159 053. info@restaurante-adrian.com Standing on the shore of the bay, the restaurant serves tasty home cooking. ▤ ▼ ◯ *Apr–Oct: 6pm–midnight Mon–Sat; noon–midnight Sun & public holidays.*		●	■	●	■
CALA EN BOSCH: *Ca n'Anglada* €€€€ 971 381 402. The new Mediterranean cuisine offered by this restaurant concentrates mainly on fish dishes. It should prove popular with those who enjoy culinary experiments and dishes served in an extravagant but fun way.	■			●	■
CALA EN PORTER: *Sa Païssa* €€ Avda. Central. 971 377 389. A large hotel restaurant with fast, efficient service; the cuisine is international in flavour. ◯ *May–Oct: from 9am daily.*		●		●	
CALA GALDANA: *Es Barranc* €€€ 971 154 643. esbarranc@teleline.es. This restaurant serves very good Menorcan food, beautifully presented. The lobster is particularly recommended. ▼ ▼ ♿		●	■	●	
CALES COVES: *Opera Dua* €€€ Passaig del Rio, s/n. 971 377 375. opera@infotelecom.es A smart, warm interior maintained in a rustic style. The menu includes a full array of Italian dishes, as well as a good selection of Italian wines. ▼	■	●		●	■
CIUTADELLA: *El Camilón* €€ Plaça Colom 47. 971 380 922. This well-known and popular restaurant offers international cuisine with a French influence.				●	
CIUTADELLA: *La Guitarra* €€ C/ Dolors 1. 971 381 355. Diners in this atmospheric cellar restaurant can enjoy typical Balearic dishes (duck, lamb, snails). The most famous Menorcan dish – *caldereta de llagosta* (lobster stew) – is particularly delicious. It also serves international cuisine. ◯ *Mon–Sat.*	■	●	■		
CIUTADELLA: *Grill las Brasas* €€€ Avda. Los Delfines. 971 388 01 This rustic–style restaurant specializes in hearty grilled meats and Castilian cuisine. ▼ ◯ *May–Sep: 1pm–4pm & 6:30pm–midnight.*		●	■	●	
ES CASTELL: *Sa Foganya* €€€ C/ Ruiz y Pablo 97. 971 354 950. The grilled food, both meat and fish, is definitely worth trying here at Sa Foganya. ▼ ▼	■	●	■	●	
FERRERIES: *Mesón El Gallo* €€€ Ctra. Cala Galdana, 1.5 km (1 mile). 971 373 039. This restaurant opened more than 25 years ago in a 200-year-old farmhouse and specializes in meat dishes, prepared in the traditional style. The steak with Mahón cheese is very popular.			■		■
FERRERIES: *Liorna* €€€€ Carrer de Dalt 9. 971 373 912, 971 155 222. A restaurant-cum-art gallery, the interior here is smart and up-to-date with a subtle, romantic atmosphere. The food is mainly Italian with a hint of Modern European.	■	●		●	

FORNELLS: *Ca'n Miquel* €€€
Paseo Marítimo s/n. **(** *971 376 623.*
A good restaurant, specializing in fish and rice dishes. Its *caldereta de llagosta* (lobster stew) is particularly good.

FORNELLS: *Sa Llagosta* €€€€
Carrer Gabriel Gelabert 12. **(** *971 376 566.*
One of the many restaurants in Fornells serving meat and seafood, including the famous *caldereta de llagosta* (lobster stew).

FORNELLS: *Es Pla* €€€€
Passeig des Pla. **(** *971 376 655.*
Situated on the bay, the restaurant serves mainly Menorcan food. It is occasionally visited by King Juan Carlos.

MAÓ: *La Bombilla* €€
Plaça Bastio y Sant Roc 31. **(** *971 364 576.*
This modest restaurant, situated in the old part of Maó, offers quite a good selection of *tapas* and *platos combinados*. **◻** *10am–4pm & 5pm–midnight.*

MAÓ: *Taj* €€
Sinia des Muret 23. **(** *971 354 070.*
An Indian restaurant with a waterfall in its child-friendly back garden. Takeaway food is available. **◻** *from 7pm daily.*

MAÓ: *Asador* €€€
Ctra. de Aeropuerto. **(** *971 367 903.*
This smart restaurant combines Castilian cuisine and grilled meats.

MAÓ: *La Minerva* €€€€
Moll de Llevant 87. **(** *971 351 995.*
Housed in a former flour mill, this restaurant is spacious and upmarket. It offers typical Mediterranean cuisine as well as Modern European dishes.

SANT CLIMENT: *Es Moli de Foc* €€€€€
C/ Sant Llorenç 65. **(** *971 153 222.*
Occupying a modest house with a lovely patio, this sophisticated restaurant offers most of the traditional Balearic dishes as well as some French cuisine.

SANT LLUÍS: *La Rueda* €€
C/ Sant Lluís 30. **(** *971 150 349.*
An elegant restaurant, La Rueda offers a large selection of *tapas*. Also recommended are its typical Menorcan dishes, served in the upstairs restaurant. **●** *Tue.*

IBIZA

BAHÍA DE SAN ANTONIO: *Venice* €€
(*971 348 578*
The service here is fast but it is also a good place to linger. Particularly recommended are its delicious lasagne and many types of pizza. **◻** *from 6pm.*

CALA BENIRRÀS: *Benirràs Restaurante* €€
Situated by the beach, Benirràs Restaurante has a lovely view over the surrounding area. Recommended dishes include squid with garlic and herbs, and the local cheesecake - a real treat! **◻** *May–Oct: 11:30am–11:30pm.*

CALA JONDAL: *Tropicana* €€€
(*971 187 520.*
Another restaurant close to the beach, this one has good fish dishes, in particular its *parilla de pescado*. On Sundays it resounds with a Brazilian beat. **◻** *Mar–Sep: from 11am.*

CALA LLONGA: *La Casita* €€€€
Urbanización Valverde 60. **(** *971 330 293.* **@** *la-casita@ctv.es*
The restaurant La Casita occupies an old farmhouse and is an ideal place for a romantic evening. Though the chef is Austrian, the menu is based on the regional cuisine of Ibiza and changes every Friday throughout summer and autumn, with a grill on Thursdays. **◻** *4pm–midnight Mon, Wed–Fri, noon–midnight Sat–Sun.*

For key to symbols see back flap

						OPEN ALL YEAR	CREDIT CARDS	REGIONAL CUISINE	GARDEN OR TERRACE	PARKING

Price per person for a three-course meal, including wine and tax (without tip).

€ up to 15 euros
€€ 15–20 euros
€€€ 20–25 euros
€€€€ 25–30 euros
€€€€€ over 30 euros.

OPEN ALL YEAR
Restaurant is open throughout the year.

CREDIT CARDS
Eurocard, MasterCard, Visa, Diners Club all accepted.

REGIONAL CUISINE
Menu includes choice of Balearic Islands cuisine.

GARDEN OR TERRACE
Meal can be served on a terrace, in a garden or courtyard.

PARKING
Restaurant has its own parking.

CALA DE SANT VICENT: *Can Gat*   €€
971 320 123.
Next to the beach and furnished in a traditional style, this restaurant is typically Ibizan. The seafood and fish dishes are its strongest points.
Apr–Nov: 1pm–5pm & 8pm–11.30pm daily.

CALA TARIDA: *Ca's Mila*   €€€
971 806 193.
A large, popular restaurant situated by the beach with a rustic-style interior. Its terrace overlooks the entire bay. *1pm–4pm & 7pm–midnight daily (summer); Sat–Sun (winter).*

CALA VEDELLA: *Maria Luisa*   €€€
971 808 012.
This family-run restaurant at the end of the beach has particularly good fish, crab and lobster dishes. Booking is recommended at the weekend.
noon–5pm & 6pm–midnight daily.

EIVISSA: *Es Caliu*   €€
Ctra. Eivissa–Sant Joan. 971 325 075.
A typical Ibizan restaurant serving tasty grilled food and good daily specials. *Jul–Aug: evenings daily.*

EIVISSA: *Formentera*   €€
Avda. De Andenes 5. 971 311 024.
This family-run restaurant near the harbour specializes in regional cuisine. Recommended dishes include the ray with vegetables, and you certainly can't go wrong with any of the desserts. *1pm–4pm & 7pm–midnight daily.*

EIVISSA: *Hong Kong*   €€
C/ Vincente Cuervo 13. 971 311 756.
Should you wish to depart from the traditional Ibizan fare, the Shanghai and Cantonese food served here is of a good quality. The *menú del día* (menu of the day) is especially good. Takeaway food is also available.

EIVISSA: *Can den Parra*   €€€
C/ San Rafael 3. 971 391 114.
A romantic restaurant at the heart of Dalt Vila. The grilled rabbit and steak with goat's cheese are particularly good. Booking is advisable during August. *May–Oct 8pm–1am daily.*

EIVISSA: *La Brasa*   €€€
C/ Pere Sala 3. 971 301 202.
Situated near Passeig de Vara de Rey, this restaurant has an elegant interior and a charming garden. The meat- and fish-based menu varies with the season. Booking is recommended. *1pm–1am Mon–Sat; 7pm–1am Sun.*

EIVISSA: *Living Life*   €€€
Avda. Vuit d'Agost. 971 316 289.
The Art Deco style interior and international cuisine lends this restaurant a contemporary feel, which is only added to by the presence of sushi on the menu. *Mar–Sep: 9pm–3am.*

EIVISSA: *Studio*   €€€
C/ de la Virgen 4. 971 315 368. reststudio@teleline.es
The Studio's colourful interior is modelled on an Arabic style. Meals are served either inside, on the terrace or on the balcony. All the food is beautifully presented. Reservations are recommended. *from 8pm. Last orders at 1:30am.*

Restaurant	Price	OPEN ALL YEAR	CREDIT CARDS	REGIONAL CUISINE	GARDEN OR TERRACE	PARKING
Can Gat	€€		●		●	
Ca's Mila	€€€		●		●	
Maria Luisa	€€€	■	●		●	
Es Caliu	€€	■		■	●	■
Formentera	€€	■	●	■	●	
Hong Kong	€€	■				
Can den Parra	€€€		●		●	
La Brasa	€€€	■	●		●	
Living Life	€€€		●			
Studio	€€€	■	●		●	

EIVISSA: *El Cigarral* €€€€
Fray Vincente Nicolas 9. (971 311 246.
This restaurant is renowned for its excellent cuisine and elegant decor.
El Cigarral specializes in Mediterranean-style food. 📋 ● *Sun afternoon.*

EIVISSA: *La Oliva* €€€€
Calle Santa Cruz 2. (971 305 752. @ ursurene@teleline.es
This popular restaurant stands at the very heart of the Old Town and
enjoys a good reputation thanks to chef René Salle who skilfully combines
traditional Ibizan recipes with Provençal cuisine. Booking is recommended.
○ *7:30pm–1am daily.*

ES CANA: *Mandarin* €€€
The exquisite Chinese cuisine served here at the Mandarin can be
enjoyed while sitting in comfortable armchairs and listening to
traditional Chinese music.

FIGUERETES: *De Gouwe Haan* €€
C/ Galicias.
Catering especially for the European market, you can pick from Dutch
cuisine with Indonesian specialities; also steak, *schnitzel*, fish and
vegetarian food. With such a wide selection, it seems there is no dish you
cannot order here. **V**.

FIGUERETES: *Soleado* €€€
Paseo Ses Pitiusas s/n. (971 394 811. @ soleado.ibz@teleline.es
This restaurant by the beach enjoys wonderful views of Formentera. The
Provençal-based cuisine is light and tasty, and beautifully presented.
○ *Apr–Oct.*

MARINA BOTAFOCHA: *Café Sidney* €€€
(971 192 243. @ cafe.sidney@ctv
A modern restaurant serving international cuisine. The three-course
fixed menu is changed every week. Recommended dishes include salads,
particularly the turkey breast or marinated salmon with avocado.
Booking is recommended for the Italian evenings and on Sundays.
Ⓨ ○ *9am–3am (summer); 10am–2am (winter).*

PLATJA DES NIU BLAU: *Bora-Bora* €€
(971 339 772. @ restborabora@terra.es
This restaurant and club, situated by the beach, is a good place to relax
after the stresses of a night out. It serves mainly simple fish dishes and
paella, and there is a large selection of cocktails and other drinks.
○ *10am–midnight.*

SANT ANTONI DE PORTMANY: *S'Embarcador* €€€
Paseo Maritimo, s/n. (971 803 260.
S'Embarcador, a modern restaurant situated by the beach near the Bahia
Hotel, specializes in good quality Mediterranean cuisine with a decent
range of dishes.

SANT ANTONI DE PORTMANY: *Rias Baixes* €€€€€
Cervantes 12. (971 340 480. @ riasbaixas@eresmas.com
The restaurant's interior is a skilful blend of homely atmosphere and
elegance. Most Spanish and Balearic dishes are made according to
traditional recipes. ● *Mon during lunchtime.*

SANT ANTONI DE PORTMANY: *Rincon de Pepe* €€
(971 314 665.
One of many "West End" restaurants. The international cuisine is
dominated by Spanish dishes. The traditional local desserts are excellent.
○ *Easter–early Nov: daily.*

SANT ANTONI DE PORTMANY: *Tijuana* €€
C/ Ramon y Cajal 28. (971 342 473.
Two restaurants serving spicy Tex-Mex food including chilli con carne,
tortillas and salsa.

SANT ANTONI DE PORTMANY: *Deva's Indian Restaurant* €€€
C/ Burgos 14. (971 343 747.
This is a classic, old-style Indian restaurant and bar with dishes from
various regions throughout India. Deva's provides a welcome alternative
for those seeking a change from the Mediterranean food available
elsewhere. ○ *7pm–midnight Tue–Sun.*

For key to symbols see back flap

<table>
<tr><td>

Price per person for a three-course meal, including wine and tax (without tip).

€ up to 15 euros
€€ 15–20 euros
€€€ 20–25 euros
€€€€ 25–30 euros
€€€€€ over 30 euros.

</td><td>

OPEN ALL YEAR
Restaurant is open throughout the year.

CREDIT CARDS
Eurocard, MasterCard, Visa, Diners Club all accepted.

REGIONAL CUISINE
Menu includes choice of Balearic Islands cuisine.

GARDEN OR TERRACE
Meal can be served on a terrace, in a garden or courtyard.

PARKING
Restaurant has its own parking.

</td></tr>
</table>

	OPEN ALL YEAR	CREDIT CARDS	REGIONAL CUISINE	GARDEN OR TERRACE	PARKING
SANT ANTONI DE PORTMANY: *Grill Sant Antoni* €€€ C/ Bisba Torres 5. ☎ 971 340 451. This rustic restaurant offers a homely atmosphere. Its rich and varied menu includes flame-grilled local specialities; also steak, shrimp and *paella*.		●	■	●	
SANT AUGUSTIN: *Club Victoria* €€€€ Ctra. Sant Augustí–Cala Tarida, 3 km (2 miles) ☎ 971 340 900. Enjoying a magnificent bird's-eye view over the entire area, this restaurant's menu includes a number of Scandinavian dishes. ○ May–Oct: 7:30pm–11pm.		●		●	
SANT RAFAEL: *L'Elephant* €€€€ Plaça de l'Església. ☎ 971 198 056. A smart restaurant whose terrace provides views over Dalt Vila from its roof-bar. Its French cuisine is especially good. ☷ ○ Apr–Nov: 8pm–1am daily.		●		●	■
SANTA EULÀRIA DES RIU: *Mirage* €€ Paseo del Puerto. ☎ 971 332 922. @ amanda_a_hayes@yahoo.com Close to the harbour, this restaurant is a good place to have breakfast as well as dinner. There is music and dancing in the evenings. ○ until 4am.				●	■
SANTA EULÀRIA DES RIU: *Mariner's Beach Bar* €€€ Mariner's Beach. ☎ 971 331 984. The restaurant, situated by the beach, offers Mediterranean cuisine. In the evenings it livens up considerably and puts on displays of flamenco dancing.	■			●	
SANTA EULÀRIA DES RIU: *Ca Na Ribes* €€€€ Sant Vincent 44. ☎ 971 330 006. A smart restaurant with a lovely patio full of greenery, this restaurant has been in operation since 1926. It features a separate tea room and bar. The sole fillet with shrimp in champagne sauce is highly recommended. ○ Apr–Oct: 1pm–3:30pm & 7pm–11pm. ● Wed.		●		●	
SANTA EULÀRIA DES RIU: *The Royalty* €€€€ Sant Jaume 51. ☎ 971 331 819. This smart, pleasant restaurant has good international cuisine and friendly service. ○ 8am–1am daily.	■	●		●	
SANTA EULÀRIA DES RIU: *Celler C'an Pere* €€€€€ Sant Jaume 63. This is an authentic, family-owned cellar restaurant that offers a good selection of classic dishes. ☷	■	●		●	
SANTA EULÀRIA DES RIU: *S'Argamassa Palace* €€€€€ Urbanización S'Argamassa. ☎ 971 330 271. @ sapalace@retemail.es An elegant hotel restaurant specializing in Mediterranean cuisine, which offers a wide selection of dishes. ▤	■	●		●	
SANTA INES: *Sa Capella* €€€€ Ctra. Sant Antoni de Portmany–Santa Ines ☎ 971 340 057. Sa Capella occupies a 16th-century stone church. Meals are also served on the terrace. The delicious fish and meat dishes are exquisitely presented. ○ Apr–May & Sep–Oct: 8pm–midnight; Jun–Aug: 8:30pm–12:30am.		●		●	■
FORMENTERA					
CALA SAONA: *Es Pla* €€€€ Ctra. Cala Saona. ☎ 971 322 903. The pizzas and pastas are particularly good here and the garden terrace is great in the summer. ○ May–Oct: noon–3:30pm & 7pm–midnight daily.				●	

ES CALÓ: *Pascual* €€
971 327 014.
This restaurant is worth visiting in order to sample its lobster stew *(caldereta de llagosta)* and seafood cooked in a clay pot. Served in the open air on the pine-fringed terrace, they taste delicious! *1pm–4pm & 7pm–11pm daily.*

ES PUJOLS: *La Barca* €
Paseo Marítimo Es Pujols 24/30. *971 328 502.*
This small restaurant, located close to the beach, specializes in good quality Mediterranean cuisine.

ES PUJOLS: *Sa Barraca* €€
971 328 027.
A good bet for some *tapas*, this restaurant also offers a wide selection of Spanish wines. *8pm–3am.*

ES PUJOLS: *Caminito* €€€
Ctra. Es Pujols–La Savina. *971 328 106.* www.rte-caminito.com
caminito@rte-caminito.com
With a courtyard and an indoor barbecue, this restaurant's menu is based on meaty Argentinian food. Particularly recommended are the beef dishes, including *Asado de tira Bife* and *Parrillada de carne.*
Apr–Nov: 8pm–12:30am

ES PUJOLS: *Ma Vie* €€€
Calle Punta Primas. *971 328 529.*
A romantic interior and friendly service, plus an extensive menu with an impressive selection of fish dishes, makes Ma Vie a perfect choice for a special meal.

ES PUJOLS: *Restaurant & Grill Timón* €€€
Avda. Miramar. *971 328 982.*
This very popular restaurant specializes in delicious grilled beef dishes. Booking is recommended to avoid disappointment. *12:30pm–3pm & 7pm–11pm.*

LA MOLA: *El Mirador* €€€€
Ctra. La Mola, 14 km (9 miles). *971 327 037.*
The restaurant, situated on the side of a hill, enjoys staggering views over the entire island. Its star dish is grilled fish served with green sauce.
May–Oct: 1pm–4pm & 8pm–11:30pm.

LA SAVINA: *Bellavista* €€€
Paseo Maritimo 8. *971 322 236.*
Bellavista serves tasty food, and the menu includes favourite local dishes including as *arros a banda* (rice with seafood). *noon–5pm & 6:30pm–1am daily.*

PLATJA MIGJORN: *Blue Bar* €€
Ctra. Sant Ferran, 8 km (5 miles). *971 187 011.*
This bar, situated by the beach and boasting a large terrace, is famous for its good music. Dishes worth recommending include the pasta served with various choices of sauce. *noon–midnight daily.*

PLATJA MIGJORN: *Sa Platgeta* €€
C/ Camari. *971 187 614.* saplatgeta@yahoo.es
A modest bar on a quiet part of the beach, Sa Platgeta is surrounded by pine trees. It serves tasty hors d'oeuvres.

SANT FERRAN: *Sa Finca* €€€€
Cala Embaster. *971 329 028.*
The menu at Sa Finca features mainly fish and beef dishes, typical of Formentera. *7pm–midnight Mon–Sat (summer); 1pm–3pm & 6pm–11pm (winter).*

SES ILLETAS: *Es Moli de Sal* €€€
971 187 491.
Situated on top of a hill, this upmarket restaurant is housed in an old windmill. You get a splendid view of the sea from the terrace. The menu of Es Moli de Sal is dominated by fish and seafood. The owners ferry their guests to and from their yachts and boats to the restaurant, free of charge.
May–Oct: 1pm–5pm & 8pm–11:30pm daily.

Es Caló: Pascual		●	■	●	
Es Pujols: La Barca		●		●	
Es Pujols: Sa Barraca	■	●	■	●	
Es Pujols: Caminito		●		●	■
Es Pujols: Ma Vie		●		●	
Es Pujols: Restaurant & Grill Timón	■	●	■	●	■
La Mola: El Mirador		●		●	■
La Savina: Bellavista	■	●		●	■
Platja Migjorn: Blue Bar				●	
Platja Migjorn: Sa Platgeta		●		●	
Sant Ferran: Sa Finca	■	●		●	
Ses Illetas: Es Moli de Sal		●			■

SHOPPING IN THE
BALEARIC ISLANDS

As elsewhere in Spain, the islands produce a wide variety of good leatherware, with Inca, in Mallorca, having a worldwide reputation for footwear. Items of clothing including hippy jewellery found on market stalls are most in evidence on Ibiza, which is also known for its fashion label, Ad Lib. Locally produced ceramics

Ceramic lantern

also make good souvenirs and are available on all of the islands, as are other island crafts including embroidery and basketwork. Local produce should also not be ignored, and bringing home a string of garlic, some spicy sausages or a good bottle of Mallorcan wine is as good a way to remember the holiday as anything.

Ceramics shop in Maó, Menorca

WHERE TO BUY

Souvenirs of the Balearic Islands can be bought almost anywhere and the number of small shops offering all sorts of knick-knacks and mementos is truly amazing. They can be found in the historic parts of towns, in tourist centres and near harbours and beaches. Almost every hotel has its own boutique. There are also numerous shops selling clothes and anything that may be useful on the beach, including mattresses, mats, hats, beach balls and sun-block creams.

The items offered by boutiques can also be found in larger shopping centres, where you can buy food and various factory products. Palma has the largest choice of shops while Maó, in Menorca, has quite a few

outlets and can cater for most holidaymakers' tastes.

Factory shops are good places to buy souvenirs. They offer slightly lower prices and a much larger selection of goods. The specialist centres are also great places to hunt for souvenirs including pottery or synthetic pearls.

Boutiques and restaurants along a seaside promenade

OPENING HOURS

The large shops in tourist centres are usually open from 9am until 9pm. Some close for a siesta between 2pm and 5pm. Boutiques have similar opening hours. Shops along the beaches open virtually non-stop. These are the most reliable places to buy food and other basic articles. During high season most shops remain open seven days a week.

Provincial towns and villages do not have such regular opening hours and are more attuned to the pace of life of the local people than to holidaymakers. Shops in small villages may also close at weekends.

HOW TO PAY

When shopping in boutiques, small shops, food stores and markets it is customary to pay in cash. Only some larger stores, such as hypermarkets or factory shops, or those selling jewellery, cosmetics and books accept credit cards.

MARKETS

Markets are an integral feature of the Mallorcan scenery. They are held at weekly intervals, mostly in the provincial towns and villages of the island. They mainly serve the local population, although during high season they also offer many goods aimed at tourists. Besides everyday domestic items, most of them sell fruit, vegetables and sometimes locally produced sauces and preserves. Markets tend to start in the mornings and end early in the afternoon.

Hippy markets are held mainly on Formentera and Ibiza. Aimed squarely at visitors, they offer colourful clothes reminiscent of the fashions popular in the 1960s, as well as every type of ornament, including brooches, earrings, necklaces, belts and bracelets made of shells. These bustling markets are organized during the high season only and, unlike traditional Mallorcan markets, they are held every day.

Hippy bazaar in San Francesc on Formentera

FOOD

THE BALEARIC ISLANDS offer a number of unique food products that are specific to the region. The delicious *ensaimada* pastry, popular with tourists, is packed in distinctive octagonal boxes, making it easy to transport. Gourmets may be tempted by *sobrasada* – a spicy pork sausage produced in several varieties and used in many Balearic dishes. Strings of dried peppers, or olives prepared in a variety of ways, attract those who wish to bring back culinary souvenirs. All these products can be bought in markets and food

Shop selling local delicacies in Palma

stores. Shops that sell exclusively Balearic food are very attractive. The sheer number and variety of colourful products on display will tempt anyone to step inside.

The most popular alcohols produced on the islands include gin from Maó and herb liqueurs. You can taste the local gin in the Maó distillery *(see p96)*. Liqueurs are produced in a great number of varieties on all the islands and can be sampled in the shops that sell them. Balearic wines are also well worth trying. The best wines come from the Binissalem region on Mallorca, where a grand wine festival is held every year in September. There are only two wine producing regions in the Balearic Islands – Binissalem and Pla i Llevant, both on Mallorca. Wines that are especially worth sampling include those from the cellars of Jaume de Punitró, Marcià Batle, Vins Nadal, Herederos de Ribas, Pere Seda and Miguel Gelabert.

Dried peppers

SOUVENIRS

THESE DAYS IT is difficult to buy genuine local handicrafts on the Balearic Islands.

Sometimes you can find them in markets, but they have been largely replaced by factory-made articles that imitate handicrafts. These include ceramics decorated with traditional patterns, typical of the islands. The most characteristic pottery items – the *siurells* produced mainly on Mallorca – are colourful whistles in the shape of people or animals, painted in white, red and green. They can be bought in many places at the markets, in small shops and in large stores that sell Balearic pottery. Popular, but expensive, is the glassware produced by the three glassworks on Mallorca. At the Gordiola glassworks near Algaida you can witness the production process *(see p87)*. Equally popular are articles made of olive wood, such as bowls and mortars produced by the Olive-Art factory near Manacor.

Also close to Manacor is a factory producing high-quality simulated pearls that can be bought in many souvenir shops, as well as in smart boutiques all over Europe *(see p81)*.

Among the most popular souvenirs are espadrilles (traditional footwear) from Ibiza. Souvenirs from Menorca include leather goods such as wallets, handbags, jackets and sandals. T-shirts and baseball caps with humorous slogans and pictures are also popular.

What to Buy
in the Balearic Islands

T HE CHOICE OF SOUVENIRS in the Balearic Islands is vast, but it can be difficult to find genuine local handicrafts among them. However, it is still possible to buy items from each of the islands that is characteristic of the place. In Mallorca, these include simulated pearls, glassware, dolls and wines from the Binissalem region; in Menorca – leather goods, textiles and local gin; in Ibiza – hippy souvenirs or club clothes.

Doll in regional costume

Ceramics

Ceramic items are among the most popular souvenirs. The variety of forms and designs is staggering. Many of those on offer have not actually been produced on the islands and it is best to buy from one of the local manufacturers.

Plate decorated with cobalt

Colourful plate

Condiment container

Glass

The high quality glassware produced on the Balearic Islands was once as popular as that made in Venice. To this day, the most popular articles of glassware are modelled on traditional designs.

"Gordioli" goblet

Leaf-shaped bowl

Pestle and mortar

Wooden Articles

Articles made of olive wood are very popular with visitors to the islands. They have a distinctive colour and are very durable. The choice is, however, limited to a few designs.

"Lafiore" pots

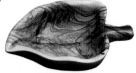

Sandals

Leather wallet

Leather Goods

Menorca is famous for its leather goods. The factory shops sell virtually everything that can be made of leather including wallets, coats and jackets. Many articles are made to order for large international companies.

Warm leather gloves

Woman's handbag

Hippy Jewellery

A large number of hippy products sold in Ibiza and Formentera have been produced by a flourishing cottage industry, though less authentic products are beginning to dominate. Even so, it is still worth visiting these markets, if only for their atmosphere.

Earrings

Box from India

Black pearl necklace

Belt with shells

Ring

Simulated Pearls

Simulated pearls are Mallorca's signature item. Though expensive, every item comes with a certificate of authenticity. You can buy ready-made jewellery as well as single pearls that you can use to make your own necklace or bracelet.

Necklace of simulated pearls

Wickerwork

Wickerwork is very popular with visitors to the Balearics and wickerwork items are among the most genuine Balearic products. The baskets of various shapes and sizes are particularly attractive.

Beach basket

Straw hat

Clothes

Clothes, including T-shirts with a variety of slogans and original designs, such as the ones sold on Menorca with the "Ecológica de Menorca" sign, are also popular. Club clothes likewise make interesting souvenirs.

Cap with "Mallorca" inscription

Printed T-shirts

Alcohol

A large selection of alcoholic drinks is on offer. Each island produces its own herb liqueur (hierbas). All adult visitors to Menorca might try the local gin. Connoisseurs will not miss the chance to try Mallorcan wines, particularly the best of them – the red wine from Binissalem, but also white and rosé varieties from the same vineyards.

Herb liqueur

Almond liqueur

Local red wine

ENTERTAINMENT IN THE BALEARIC ISLANDS

I BIZA IS LISTED IN the *Guinness Book of Records* as the world's most entertaining place. This is no doubt due to the number of nightclubs, bars and pubs packed into this small island. The other islands of the archipelago have plenty of entertainment on offer, however, and there are many clubs, concerts and shows to choose from.

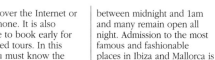

Horsedrawn cab in Palma

The range of entertainment available to visitors is much wider than this, however. At the height of the holiday season, the larger resorts open up casinos, concert halls, cinemas and theatres and also organize folklore, theatre and cinema festivals. On top of this, and perfect for the kids, are the many aquaparks and other amusement parks to enjoy.

Shelves of the many liqueurs on offer in a shop

INFORMATION

I T IS A GOOD IDEA to find out what is on offer before you leave as local tourist information offices may not always have details of forthcoming cultural events, particularly if they are held in another town. The Internet has a wealth of information on concerts, amusement parks and festivals and may sometimes include first-hand accounts of particular attractions.

Current details may often be found in the local press. Keep your eyes peeled, too, as many events are advertised on posters. Other valuable sources on what is happening are hotel reception areas.

BOOKING TICKETS

T ICKETS TO SOME of the major clubs in Ibiza, such as Amnesia and Privilege, can be booked before you go on

holiday, over the Internet or by telephone. It is also advisable to book early for any guided tours. In this case, you must know the organizer's telephone number or go to the local office. The same applies to concerts and music festivals. Hotel receptions will often be happy to do the booking for you. The earlier you book, the better your chances of getting a ticket. In many cases, tickets are only sold a short time in advance. Admission to many open-air events is often free.

Entry ticket to Jardines d'Alfàbia

NIGHTLIFE

N IGHTLIFE flourishes on the islands. Ibiza is particularly famous for it, but Mallorca also has many nightclubs (*discotecas*). The clubs usually open their doors

between midnight and 1am and many remain open all night. Admission to the most famous and fashionable places in Ibiza and Mallorca is relatively expensive. Lesser known venues tempt guests in with various gimmicks or free drinks. Earlier in the evening you can visit bars and pubs.

For those who do not fancy the clubs, there are also casinos and many venues that put on artistic programmes.

MUSIC AND THEATRE

D ESPITE APPEARANCES, the cultural life on the Balearic Islands is not limited to pubs, clubs and religious festivals. Classical music, opera and theatre are all very popular with the locals, particularly on Mallorca and Menorca. Theatres and opera

Tourist information office in Sant Antoni de Portmany, Ibiza

Partygoers enjoying themselves at Amnesia, Ibiza

houses can be found in many places. Their repertoire includes mainly modern Spanish drama and there are frequent performances by visiting theatre and opera companies from mainland Spain, as well as from other European countries including Germany, Italy and the UK.

The leading theatres are the **Teatre Principal** in Palma and **Teatre Principal de Maó** in Menorca. During the summer season, when the theatres close, theatre festivals come to take their place. These are mostly international events. Many of these include theatre workshops, which offer plenty of opportunities for audience participation.

Lovers of classical music will also find something on the islands. World-class musicians and orchestras frequently appear in the concert halls, such as the Auditórium de Palma de Mallorca. In addition, many music festivals and concerts are organized during the holiday season. In Menorca, there are three major festivals during the summer season – in Maó, Ciutadella and Fornells. Festivals taking place between June and September are held in concert halls, theatres and churches. Among the important musical events in Mallorca are the classical music festivals in Palma (Feb–Mar) and the Chopin Festival in Valldemossa (Aug). Other events include international festivals of music in Deià and Pollença during the summer.

POPULAR MUSIC

LOVERS OF JAZZ and rock have no cause to complain in the Balearic Islands, particularly during the summer season. Occasionally, top rock groups or pop stars make an appearance. You should enquire about dates and venues in the local tourist information office or look up events in the local press. There are also numerous local regular events, such as a Rock 'n' Roll Festival in Maria de la Salut, in Mallorca, while cities such as Palma have many live music venues.

Some events have become a permanent fixture in the islands' cultural calendar. Anyone who loves jazz may know about Sant Climent in Menorca. Twice a week during the summer months and less frequently during the winter, "jam sessions" are held here. Another very popular event in Mallorca is the International Jazz Festival held every year during May and June, in Cala d'Or.

FIESTAS

WHEN VISITING the islands, it is worth including one of the fiestas in your itinerary. These are held not only as celebrations of patron saints, but may also commemorate historic events or celebrate important harvests (such as the grape harvest festival in Binissalem and the melon festival in Vilafranca de Bonany). These colourful, bustling celebrations, accompanied by music, dancing and feasting, can go on for several days during which time the town's business life grinds to a halt as the local population joins in the fun.

Street processions with people dressed in regional costumes or their Sunday best are often spiced up by the *dimonis* – devils that personify evil, which are defeated in the end. This happens during the fiestas in Montuïri and Santa Margalida. An important element of many fiestas are the horse races and shows. The most interesting of these are held during the Sant Joan fiesta in Ciutadella (Jun). The majority of fiestas, as well as other cultural and entertainment events, are held during the summer months, at the peak of the holiday season. Important events taking place outside the tourist season include the Procession of the Three Magi (Jan), the carnival (Feb) and the celebrations associated with Holy Week.

Sign for a horse show

Participants in a colourful fiesta

AMUSEMENT PARKS

No VISIT TO THE islands would be complete without a trip to a water-park or theme park, especially if you have children. Marineland in Mallorca provides the opportunity to see the performing dolphins and sea lions and look at the colourful fish in the aquarium, while the thrills and spills of the water-parks can be great fun, especially when it is hot.

During the high season there are also many funfairs with carousels and circus troupes with acrobats and magicians. Magnificent horse shows are staged in Menorca.

Another form of entertainment in the islands is afforded by a visit to one of the numerous caves, especially in Mallorca. Some of these have their own light and music shows.

MUSEUMS

THE ISLANDS' MUSEUMS are sometimes overlooked since they are not set up as tourist attractions. Some of the collections are quite modest, presenting the history of the town or region and its associated folklore. However, there are museums on the islands that are definitely worth visiting. These include the private art collection in Casa March, in Mallorca.

This has a collection of some of the greatest 20th-century artists. Equally interesting is the Museu de Mallorca in Palma *(see pp52-3)*, which displays works of art from prehistoric times up to the present day, illustrating the cultural development of the island. The Museu de Menorca in Maó is of a similar character, but its collection is more limited in its scope *(see p96)*.

Another worthwhile museum is the Museu de la Natura de Menorca, in Ferreries *(see p106)*. It has a modern display showing all that is typical of the island's natural environment, culture and traditions. It is a nice idea

Logo of Menorca's natural history museum

Glass-bottomed boat ride

to pop in here before you start exploring the island.

Children will probably be more interested in visiting the Waxwork Museum in Binissalem, in Mallorca. Here, they can see wax likenesses of a number of famous people who are in one way or another associated with the island.

EXCURSIONS

THOSE LOOKING FOR an active holiday will have no trouble finding plenty of outlets able to provide details of walking or cycling trails, and even organize excursions. For anyone looking for a less strenuous excursion, there are plenty of coach tours. It is, of course, possible to hire a car and drive to some of the most interesting places around the islands. You can also ask at tourist offices about guided tours. You might, however, bear in mind that some groups may contain a number of nationalities and you should be prepared to listen to a commentary in a variety of languages. Of all the tours and excursions on offer, possibly the most pleasant are boat cruises. These include glass-bottomed boat rides, and even submarine trips. The most pleasurable of

these are sailing trips to remote little bays. This way you can circumnavigate the whole of Ibiza or Menorca.

CHILDREN

THE SPANISH ARE famously fond of children and kids are welcomed in restaurants, especially at lunchtimes. In terms of attractions, Mallorca has the lion's share with water-parks, dolphin shows, caves and long promenades for cycling. Fun shows, including mock pirate battles and jousting tournaments, are organized for the enjoyment of younger visitors. Out of season, there are visits by circuses and fairs to the islands and some of the larger clubs runs special youth afternoons at the weekends.

The other islands have fewer attractions but there is still plenty for the kids. Menorca has pony rides and riding shows, while Ibiza's beaches and all the associated seaside attractions, such as snorkelling, beach games and banana rides, will keep most children happily occupied for the duration.

Slides in a water-park in Ibiza

DIRECTORY

NIGHTCLUBS IN MALLORCA

BCM
Avda. S'Olivera, Magaluf.
[971 711 856.
British-run entertainment complex – the biggest club on the island.

Menta
Avda. Tucan, Alcúdia.
Two dance floors, seven bars and an indoor pool.

Palladium Palace
C/ Gaviotas 1, Peguera.
[971 686 557.
A smaller club that gets packed at the weekends.

Titós
Paseo Marítímo, Palma.
[971 730 017.
Upmarket club with a cocktail bar and a great view of the bay from the club's glass elevator.

See pp120-21 for details of clubs on Ibiza.

THEATRES

Café Teatre Sans
C/ Can Sanç 5, Palma, Mallorca.
[971 727 166.

Centro Dramático di Marco
Patronato de asistencia Palmesana. C/ Ramon Llull 11, Palma, Mallorca.
[971 726 008.

Fundació Teatre Principal de Maó
C/ Costa d'en Deià 40, Maó, Menorca.
[971 355 603.
See p94 for further details.

Orfeó Maonès
C/ de Gràcia 155, Maó, Menorca.
[971 363 942.

Teatre De Vilafranca
Sant Martí 25, Vilafranca de Bonany, Mallorca.
[971 832 072.

Teatre del Mar
Capitàn Ramonell Boix 90, "Es Molinar", Palma, Mallorca. [971 248 400.

Teatre Municipal de Manacor
Avda. del Parc s/n, Manacor, Mallorca.
[971 554 549.

Teatre Principal
Plaza Hospital 4, Palma, Mallorca.
[971 713 346.
See p49 for further details.

MAJOR CONCERT HALLS

Auditori d'Alcúdia
Plaça de la Porta de Mallorca 3, Alcúdia, Mallorca. [971 897 185.

Auditórium de Palma de Mallorca
Paseo Marítimo 18, Palma, Mallorca.
[971 734 735.

Auditórium Sa Màniga
C/ Son Galta 4, Cala Millor, Mallorca.
[971 587 373.

Centro Cultural Andratx
C/ Estanyera, Andratx, Mallorca. [971 137 770.

SHOWS

Casino Mallorca
Urb. Sol de Mallorca s/n, Magaluf, Mallorca.
[971 130 000/012.

Castillo Comte Mal
Crta. De S'Esglaieta, 3 km (2 miles), Palmañola, Mallorca. [971 617 766.

Club Escola Menorquína
Ctra. Ferreries–Cala Galdana, Menorca.
[971 155 059/497.

Pirates Adventure Show
Magaluf, Mallorca.
[971 130 411.

Son Amar
Ctra. de Sóller, 10 km (6 miles), Palmañola, Mallorca.
[971 617 533.

Son Martorellet
Ctra. Ferreries–Cala Galdana, 1.5 km (1 mile), Menorca.
[609 049 493.

AMUSEMENT PARKS

Acuario de Mallorca
C/ Gambí 7, Porto Cristo, Mallorca.
[971 820 971.

Aguamar
Platja d'en Bossa, Ibiza.
[971 300 671.

Aquacity
Autostrada Palma–S'Arenal, exit 13, Mallorca.
[971 440 000.
One of the world's largest water-parks, which includes a mini-zoo.

Aqualandia
Cap Martinet –Talamanca, Eivissa, Ibiza.
[971 192 411.

Aquapark
Ctra. de Cala Figuera, Magaluf, Menorca.
[971 131 371.
Long-established water-park on the edge of town.

Aquapark Menorca
Urb. Los Delfines, Ciutadella, Menorca. [971 388 705.

Aquarium Cap Blanc
Ctra. De Cala Gració, Sant Antoni de Portmany, Ibiza.
[608 434 466.

Club Hipico Songual
Ctra. Establiments–Puigpunyent, 2 km (1 mile), Mallorca. [971 798 578.

Exotic Parque – Los Pajaros
Hospitalet Vell, Calas De Mallorca.
[971 183 492.

Golf Fantasía
C/ Tenis 3, Palma Nova–Calvià, Mallorca.
[971 135 040.
Crazy golf with a choice of three circuits.

Jumaica Tropical Park
Ctra. Portocolom–Porto Cristo, Mallorca.
[971 833 355.

Marineland
C/ Gracillaso de la Vega 9, Costa d'en Blanes, Calvià, Mallorca. [971 675 125.
See p59 for further details.

Natura Park
Santa Eugènia, Mallorca.
[971 144 532.

Safari-Zoo Reserva Africana
Sa Coma, Mallorca.
[971 810 909.
See p80 for further details.

Son Gual Parc Prehistoric
Ctra. Palma–Manacor, Mallorca.
[971 663 171.

Western Water Park
Ctra. Cala Figuera–Sa Porrassa, 12–22, Mallorca. [971 131 203.

Xiqui Park
Joan Miro 3, Palma, Mallorca. [971 283 888.

CRUISES

Barcos Azules
Passeig Es Través 3, Port de Sóller, Mallorca.
[971 630 170.
Island boat trips.

Excursions a Cabrera
Colònia de Sant Jordi, Mallorca. [971 649 034
See p83 for further details.

Nemo Submarines
C/ Galeón 2, Magaluf, Mallorca. [971 130 244.
Two-hour exploration by submarine. Expensive.

OUTDOOR ACTIVITIES

THE WARM climate and diversity of the landscape on the Balearics make them an excellent place for all types of sport. The most popular of these are, of course, water sports and you will find windsurfing, sailing and diving are all well catered for. Those looking for an activity holiday of this kind will have

Tourist trail signpost

the chance to practise their favourite sports under professional supervision. Cycling, horseriding and golf are also popular in the islands and many travel bureaux and agents offer equipment hire, from yacht charter to bicycle rental. Some hotels also have their own facilities and can often hire out equipment.

Surfer in Cala Major, in Mallorca

WINDSURFING

THE CONDITIONS for windsurfing are not as good here as they are in the Canary Islands because the local winds are not strong enough for advanced surfers. As a consequence, the Balearic Islands are not popular with professionals, but this makes them a very good place for beginners to pick up some of the basic techniques.

Though the number of schools is rather limited, all of the islands have at least one school that teaches windsurfing and offers equipment hire. Surfing enthusiasts will also find suitable spots in the Balearic Islands, but don't expect the "ultimate wave".

SAILING

SAILING IS THE MOST popular water sport in the Balearic Islands. Major international regattas include the King's Cup and the Princesa Sofia

Trophy held in Mallorca. These are high-profile events and attract many of the world's leading sailors; King Juan Carlos is a frequent competitor. The Trofeo Conde Barcelona, held in August, features regattas with classic sailing boats. Almost every coastal town has its own marina and these are visited by yachts from all over Europe. Many vessels remain here for the winter.

Of course you do not have to own a yacht in order to cruise the Balearic Islands. Many firms offer sea-going vessels for charter. Smaller inshore catamarans can be rented by the hour on local beaches. You can also find many clubs or schools that are able to teach you the rudiments of sailing.

The popularity of sailing is so great that during the high season the marinas tend to be very busy, even though the mooring charges are extremely high. Some boats moor in sheltered bays, accessible only by sea.

FISHING

DESPITE THE FACT that the local waters teem with fish, fishing is not a popular sport here. A few agents organize trips, however. Further information is available from the Asociación Balear de Chárters, e Pesca y de Recreo *(see p179)*.

BEACH ACTIVITIES

DURING THE HIGH season, beaches employ lifeguards so it is safer to bathe and swim. Most beaches are sandy and situated in small bays. Sailing yachts and fishing boats sometimes anchor at the mouth of the bay and these are only a hazard if you swim out too close to them. The beaches can be busy and are sometimes short of space for beach sports. Nevertheless, a few of them have areas designated for volleyball, and even on busy beaches you can still find space to kick a ball around or play frisbee.

Catamarans on Es Pujols beach in Formentera

Beach volleyball, popular throughout the islands

DIVING AND SNORKELLING

THE CLEAR, CLEAN coastal seawaters combined with the diversity of underwater flora and fauna create ideal conditions for diving and the sport is as popular as sailing throughout the islands. Every seaside resort has at least one diving centre *(centro de buceo)* where you can hire equipment, go for a test dive with an instructor or enrol on a course. A one-week stay would be sufficient to complete the beginners' course in scuba diving. The organizers ensure proper supervision by a qualified instructor and provide all the necessary equipment.

People hoping to dive in deeper waters must hold a proper diving certificate, such as PADI, CUC, CMAS/FEDAS or SSI. Holders of these certificates can join expeditions, some of which explore underwater caves. One of the best places to dive is the water around Cabrera, about 18 km (11 miles) off the coast of Mallorca. In 1991, Cabrera and its surrounding waters were awarded the status of a national park – the first park of its kind in Spain. Diving here requires the permission of the park ranger.

A much cheaper but equally exciting way of getting a glimpse of underwater life is to go snorkelling. A snorkeller can observe the wonders of the deep while floating on the surface of the water almost anywhere. Perhaps the most interesting places are the small

bays rarely visited by tourists, where nature has hardly been touched by the hand of humans. A word of warning: snorkelling can be dangerous if you are distracted and collide with nearby rocks.

Motorboat with parachute waiting for the adventurous to paraglide

OTHER WATER SPORTS

OTHER WATER SPORTS that are popular with visitors include taking out a high-speed water-bike or paragliding. Paragliding behind motorboats (similar to hang-gliding) offers a wonderful way to see the islands. You can also take water-skiing lessons or (an easier option) bump along on a rubber raft, towed by a speeding boat.

Alternatively, visitors might like to join a sea trip by kayak. The most interesting routes go to the islands such as Conillera, near Ibiza, or Dragonera, off Mallorca. Equally exciting are trips to the waters of Formentor (Mallorca) and Cavalleria (Menorca).

HIKING

HIKING AROUND THE islands is becoming popular. The best area for hiking is probably the mountainous regions of Mallorca. The trails leading through the Serra de Tramuntana are difficult, but they offer a wonderful experience and breathtaking scenery. Trekking across the mountains along rough paths requires suitable footwear and clothing and should not be undertaken alone as there are potential hazards such as sudden changes in the weather and unexpected ravines.

Menorca also offers many hiking trails. Most of these lead through the local nature reserves, of which the island has 18. The regions of S'Albufera, Cap de Favaritx and Cap de Cavalleria are truly magnificent areas for hiking. Many agents organize themed excursions, such as bird-watching trips. If setting off without a guide, you should make sure you have a good map, as many tourist trails are not signposted.

Snorkelling in shallow waters in Menorca

Two-wheeled Sport

Cycling is very popular hereabouts and renting a bicycle from one of the numerous hire firms is inexpensive. Cycling is an excellent way to explore the towns or get to a nearby beach. On Formentera it is the most popular form of transport, along with the scooter.

More ambitious cyclists may want to undertake longer trips and all types of terrain can be encountered on the islands, from long, flat stretches of coast through to steep mountain roads. The islands also offer many interesting trails for mountain bikes, although the routes leading through the wild mountain terrains on Mallorca, or the coastal crags of Menorca are best undertaken with a guide. Agents who organize these tours generally offer guides and equipment.

Cyclists in a boulevard in Playa de Palma, Mallorca

Climber on a rock face near Valldemossa, Mallorca

Horse Riding

Horse riding is another popular island sport and there are several riding centres on the islands that provide facilities for beginners as well as for advanced riders. The riding areas and trails are deliberately set amid beautiful scenery but you should not expect romantic gallops along the beach. All horse riding is done under the supervision of an instructor. There are many riding centres in Menorca and this is where they breed the famous Menorcan black horses that play such a prominent part in many fiestas. As well as riding lessons and outings, many centres also stage displays of horse breaking. For those who fancy a flutter, regular horse-races are held on Mallorca and Ibiza.

Golf

There are many golf courses in Mallorca, Menorca and Ibiza and their beautiful setting and excellent facilities attract great numbers of players. Mallorca's golf courses are particularly popular. Out of a total number of 21 courses on the Balearic Islands, 18 are on Mallorca. Here, you might see royalty, famous actors, prominent politicians and sports personalities at play.

Every golf course has an equipment hire facility and school. However, if you want to take lessons during the high season, or play one of the more interesting courses, you should book in advance.

Other Sports

The warm climate and varied terrain mean that most sports can be enjoyed somewhere in the islands. The steep rocks along the coast of Mallorca and the inland regions are good places for rock climbing, providing various degrees of difficulty. Surprisingly, for such a dry region, there are even places that are good for canoeing, a very popular sport in Spain but one which requires a high level of fitness. When planning these expeditions you should seek advice from the organizers, who will not only inform you about the best routes but will also ensure suitable supervision.

The good aerodynamic conditions on Mallorca make the island suitable for hang-gliding and paragliding (see p177). These sports are not popular in the other islands of the archipelago. The best lifting currents are encountered in the inland regions. This is where beginners' courses are held and where you can also meet experienced hang-gliders. The islands' weather conditions are also favourable for ballooning. A number of companies and some of the more exclusive hotels on the island can organize hot-air balloon flights.

Mallorca's caves are a paradise for pot-holers but only a handful of caves are open to the general public since most are reserved for specialist adventurers. Cave exploration can be dangerous and is only recommended for trained people with the proper equipment.

Enjoying a golf lesson

DIRECTORY

BALLOONING

**Mallorca
Ballons**
971 818 182.

DIVING

Big Blue
C/ Marti Ros García 6,
Palma Nova, Mallorca.
971 681 686.
www.bigbluediving.net

**Crystal Seas
Scuba**
Cala en Bosch,
Menorca.
971 387 038.
www.crystalseas-
scuba.com

**Diving Center
San Miquel**
Port de Sant Miquel, Ibiza.
971 334 539.
www.divingcenter-san-
miguel.com

**Formentera
Diving**
c/Almabraba 71, Puerto
de la Savina, Formentera.
971 323 232.
www.formenteradiving.
com

**Menorca
Diving Club**
Maritimo 98, Fornells.
971 376 412.
www.menorcadiving-
club.com

Octopus
Canonge Oliver 13,
Port de Sóller,
Mallorca.
971 633 133.
info@octopus-
mallorca.com

Skualo
Paseo Cap d'Es Toll 11,
Porto Cristo, Mallorca.
971 815 094.
FAX 971 822 739.

Sub Menorca
Club Elité Falcó, Son
Xoriguer.
609 656 916.
FAX 971 387 809.
submenorca@aol.com

FISHING

**Asociación
Balear de
Chárters, e Pesca
y de Recreo**
C/ Antoni Riera Xamena 6,
1st floor, Palma, Mallorca.
670 356 530.
www.mfont atlas-iap.es

**Federación
Española de
Pesca y Casting**
Navas de Tolosa 3,
Madrid.
915 328 352.
www.fepyc.es

Mestral
Muelle comercial 46–48,
Ciutadella, Menorca.
971 381 485.

GOLF

**Asociación de
Campos de Golf
de Baleares**
Ctra. Cala Figuera s/n,
Magaluf, Mallorca.
971 130 148.
FAX 971 130 176.

Canyamel Golf Club
Avda. D'Es Cap Vermell,
Urbanización Canyamel,
Mallorca.
971 841 313.
FAX 971 841 314.

**Club de Golf Son
Termens**
Ctra. de S'Esglaieta,
10 km (6 miles), Bunyola,
Mallorca.
971 617 862.

**Federación Balear
de Golf**
Avda. Jaume III, 17–10
Despacho 16, Palma,
Mallorca.
971 722 753.
FAX 971 711 731.
www.fbgolf.com

Golf de Ibiza
Ctra. Jesus–Cala Llonga,
8 km (5 miles), Ibiza.
971 196 118.

Golf Santa Ponsa I
Urbanización Golf
Santa Ponsa, Mallorca.
971 690 211.

**Real Golf
de Bendinat**
C/ Campoamor s/n,
Urbanización Bendinat,
Mallorca. 971 405 200.
bendinat@bitel.es

HIKING

Dia Complert
c/San Luis Gonzaga 5,
Maó, Menorca.
609 670 996.
diacomplert@infotele-
-com.es
www.diacomplert.net

Ecoibiza
C/ Abad y Lasierra 35,
Eivissa, Ibiza.
971 302 347.

Mallorca Activa
Son Pereto 9, Palma,
Mallorca.
971 783 160.
FAX 971 783 159.
info@
mallorcaactiva.com

**Mallorca
Aventura**
929 731 313.

HORSE RIDING

Ca'n Paulino
Ctra. Vieja de Algaida s/n,
Mallorca.
971 121 002.

**Equus Balearic
Mallorca**
C/ General Riera 3,
Palma, Mallorca.
971 751 909.
FAX 971 756 195.

Picadero Sant Tomàs
Camino Viejo, 3 km (2
miles), Ciutadella,
Menorca.
971 188 051.

**Pony Club
Calvià**
Finca Sa Punta, Calvià,
Mallorca.
609 646 248.
FAX 971 670 401.
Children's lessons only

Rancho Ca'n Dog
Ctra. Sant Joan, 14 km (9
miles), Ibiza.
639 574 046.

SAILING

Centro Wet Four Fun
Platja d'Es Pujols,
Formentera.
971 321 809.
www.wet4fun. com

**Club Náutico
el Arenal**
C/ Roses s/n, S'Arenal,
Mallorca.
971 440 142.

**Club Náutico
Ciutadella**
Cami de Baix s/n,
Ciutadella, Menorca.
971 383 918.
cncciutadella
@wanadoo.es

**Club Náutico
Porto Cristo**
C/ Vela 29, Porto Cristo,
Mallorca. 971 821 253.

**Club Náutico Sant
Antoni**
Paseo Marítimo s/n, Sant
Antoni de Portmany, Ibiza.
971 340 645.

**Escuela Balear
de Náutica**
C/ Aragó 28 bajos, Palma,
Mallorca.
971 909 060.
www.escuelabalear-
nautica.com

**Real Club Náutico
de Palma**
Muelle de Sant Pere s/n,
Palma, Mallorca.
971 726 848.

WINDSURFING

**Centro de vela
Anfibios**
Platja d'en Bossa, Ibiza.
971 303 915.
www.anfibios.com

**Club Náutico Sa
Ràpita**
Explanada del puerto s/n,
Sa Ràpita, Mallorca.
971 640 001.
FAX 971 640 821.

Windsurf Fornells
Bahia Fornells, Menorca.
971 188 150.
FAX 971 375 581.

SURVIVAL
GUIDE

PRACTICAL INFORMATION

THE BALEARIC ISLANDS are one of Europe's most popular holiday destinations. The islands have invested heavily in tourism and are geared up to receive multitudes of visitors. Hotel and catering facilities are extensive and there are plenty of attractions for the whole family to enjoy. In general, the islands are safe for visitors, although as with any other busy resort destination, holidaymakers are vulnerable to

Informació Turística →

Tourist information sign

crimes such as bag-snatching. Such crimes can be avoided if you take sensible precautions. A well-developed information service, especially on the Internet, makes researching and planning a trip here a relatively straightforward business. During the peak period tour operators tend to snap up the available accommodation, but outside the summer season it is fairly easy to book a room in advance.

WHEN TO VISIT

EACH SEASON OF THE year has something to offer. Nevertheless, the tourist season is at its busiest from July until September. It peaks in August, which coincides with the hottest weather on the islands. The hotels, bars and restaurants fill up, beaches are full of sun-lovers and the clubs are crowded. At the height of the season you are more likely to hear German or English being spoken than Spanish or Catalan.

Anyone who dislikes crowds should plan their visit for the period before the high season or when things begin to quieten down. In May, June, late September and early October, the weather is still warm enough for sunbathing. Springtime is between January and April. This is the best time

West End in Sant Antoni de Portmany, Ibiza

for hiking as the flowers are in bloom although there can be heavy rain and storms at this time of year. The islands are quietest during the autumn months and December.

VISAS

REGULATIONS covering admission to the Balearic Islands are the same as for the rest of Spain. Nationals of all the European Union member states do not require a visa to enter the Balearic Islands for tourist visits of up to 90 days. People from other non-EU countries including Australia, Canada, Ireland, Israel, Japan, New Zealand and the USA are likewise not required to obtain a visa before entry. If in doubt, you should contact the Spanish Embassy or seek advice from a travel agent. Anyone who does require a visa must apply in person at the consulate in their own country.

CUSTOMS REGULATIONS

CUSTOMS REGULATIONS state in detail the limits on goods imported to and exported from the Balearic Islands. Such information may be obtained from Spanish Embassies and travel agents. Specific customs queries may be referred to the *Departamento de Aduanas e Impuestos Especiales* (Customs and Excise Department) in Madrid. Remember that only adults are entitled to export alcohol and cigarettes in the quantities allowed by the regulations.

Nationals of non-EU countries may apply for VAT refunds on goods purchased in any of the islands' shops bearing the sign "Duty Free for Tourists". The refund is worked out on the basis of the *formulari*, stamped by the Customs Officer at the point of departure. The refund can be claimed at the airport, at any branch of Banco Exterior, or on returning home, by post or via bank transfer.

Strolling through Ciutadella, Menorca

◁ The marina in Cala d'en Bosch harbour, Menorca

LANGUAGE

THE OFFICIAL JOINT language of the Balearic Islands is Spanish (Castilian). For many locals, however, the everyday language is Catalan. This bilingual culture can be felt when using local maps, where the names of places may be given in one or the other language. Catalan, in its turn, is divided into variants specific to each of the islands. In Mallorca it is known as *Mallorquín*, in Menorca as *Menorquín* and in Ibiza as *Eivissenc*.

During Franco's regime Catalan was banned and you risked a prison sentence if you were caught speaking it. Nevertheless, the local population has never abandoned its use and learning a few courtesy phrases in Catalan is a good way to win over the locals.

In tourist areas English and German are readily understood. Information signs and restaurant menus are generally multilingual. Greater problems with communication may be experienced away from the busiest areas. But even in the provinces, increasing numbers of people can speak at least one major European language as well as Spanish.

TOURIST INFORMATION

YOU WILL FIND Tourist Information offices *(Informació turisticats)* in all of the larger towns and resorts. These offer free maps and information packs; they also have details of current cultural events, entertainment and available accommodation. However, the information they provide may be somewhat general in nature and usually limited to the town where the tourist office is or its immediate vicinity. If you want to go on an organised hike or cruise it is best to enquire with the agent who organizes them *(see p175)*.

Horse-cab ride in Palma, Mallorca

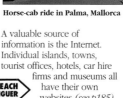

Signposts on Menorca

A valuable source of information is the Internet. Individual islands, towns, tourist offices, hotels, car hire firms and museums all have their own websites *(see p185)*. They usually include photographs with text written in several languages. It is therefore much simpler to do your research before leaving home, than once you are already there. While using websites you should check when they were last updated because some may quote last year's prices. The best websites are those run by the provincial government of the Balearic Islands and the Tourism Promotion Department "Ibatur" *(Institut Balear de Promoció del Tourisme)*.

YOUTHS/STUDENTS

THE BALEARICS are an ideal destination for young holidaymakers. The fine weather, great beaches and clubs attract thousands of young people from all over Europe. Some also come in search of seasonal employment, combining work with pleasure. Holders of the International Student Identity Card (ISIC) and the Euro under-26 card are entitled to many benefits when visiting the Balearic Islands.

They can get discounts on ferry travel, entrance charges to museums and galleries and tickets to some of the other tourist attractions. Some travel agents offer cheap flights to cardholders.

CHILDREN

AS WITH MUCH OF Europe, children are welcome in most places except the big clubs, which of course, have age restrictions for obvious reasons. Most hotels can provide cots, some have all-day care, babysitting and special entertainment for youngsters. It is nevertheless worth checking in advance what facilities are available at any given hotel.

Restaurants in hotels and in towns are also good at providing for the needs of children. They have highchairs and have special menus for children. When hiring a car, you should have no problem getting a child seat.

Children visiting one of Menorca's historic sights

Market in Inca, Mallorca, with local produce

FACILITIES FOR THE DISABLED

T HE BALEARIC ISLANDS are not particularly hospitable to disabled people. Most hotels and restaurants are not adapted to serve guests who use wheelchairs. Many public places such as museums, galleries and shops are also inaccessible. When planning a visit, it is useful to use the services of an organization that deals with the problems of disabled people. **RADAR** (Royal Association for Disability and Rehabilitation) is a good first stop for advice. Or you can approach **COCEMFE** (The Spanish Association for the Disabled). Another helpful agency is **Viajes 2000**.

Public transport also presents problems for people in wheelchairs and moving from town to town can be difficult. Disabled visitors to Mallorca can use the services of a specialized company, such as EMT Special Bus Service.

EXCURSIONS

T RAVEL AGENTS WHO sell holidays to the Balearic Islands usually also offer a choice of excursions for an additional fee. These are mostly day-long sightseeing trips, cruises, safaris, or visits to casinos, theatres or clubs. However, the prices you pay for these may be higher than those quoted by local tourist agents, and it is worth browsing through leaflets displayed at the hotel reception desk, or calling in at one or two local tourist offices to check what is on offer.

ISLAND TIME

A LL THE ISLANDS are one hour ahead of Greenwich Mean Time (GMT), six hours ahead of Eastern Standard Time and nine hours ahead of Pacific Standard Time. The changeover to summer time, as with mainland Spain, takes place on the last Sunday in March. The clocks are put back on the last Sunday in September.

RESERVADO

Parking sign for the disabled

In terms of vocabulary, the word used to describe the early hours after midnight is *la matinada*. *El mati* means morning (up to 1pm); late afternoon and evening are *la tarda*, while night is referred to as *la nit*.

OPENING HOURS

M USEUMS and historic monuments are generally open from Tuesday to Sunday, from 10am to 2pm and again from 4pm to 6pm. As with most offices, they close for public holidays and fiestas. Tourist information offices have similar opening hours.

Some sectors of business are reassessing their traditional opening hours. Big department stores, for example, and hypermarkets tend to forgo the siesta and are generally open until 8 or 9pm, though most still close on Sundays.

Theme parks and gardens are open seven days a week and they do not close for siesta. Most clubs open their doors late at night and stay open until morning. Many offices associated with tourism work shorter hours during the winter; some close altogether.

ELECTRICAL SUPPLY

T HE MAINS VOLTAGE on the islands is generally 220V AC. A three-tier standard travel convertor will enable you to use foreign equipment. Mains sockets require the European-style two-pin, round-pronged plugs.

RELIGION

L IKE THE REST of Spain the Balearic Islands are Roman Catholic and religion plays an important part in community life. All religious festivals are lavishly celebrated and at these times the offices in town remain closed. Church opening hours vary. Some, like the cathedral church in

Tourists resting in Dalt Vila, in Eivissa

Eivissa, have set sightseeing hours. Others, including Palma cathedral, expect a donation or charge an admission fee. Many churches are open only for services, i.e. early mornings or evenings (6pm–9pm).

When planning to visit a particular religious building you should check its opening hours in advance. Hotel reception desks and tourist information centres can sometimes provide details.

Church statue

will usually allow non-guests to use their toilet facilities, but it is polite to ask permission first. When looking for a toilet you should ask for *servicios* or *aseos*. Doors leading to the men's toilets are marked *señores* or *caballeros*; to the ladies', *señoras* or *damas*. If there are no written signs, the doors will be marked with a picture of a male or female silhouette. (Sometimes you might see an amusing cartoon of a pipe-smoking man or a long-haired women with a fan.)

Special toilets designed for the disabled are a rarity on the islands, even in hotels, to say nothing of restaurants. In

the future things should improve, however, as all newly-built hotels must by law be fully accessible to travellers with disabilities.

Customers relaxing at a café in Plaza Mercal, Palma

TOILETS

PUBLIC TOILETS ARE few and far between, even in large towns. Bars and restaurants

---

DIRECTORY

EMBASSIES IN MAINLAND SPAIN

Australia
Santa Engracia 120, Madrid.
℡ 914 416 025.
FAX 914 425 362.

United Kingdom
Calle de Fernando El Santo 16, 28010 Madrid.
℡ 917 008 200.
FAX 917 008 272.

CONSULATES

France
Mallorca: Avda. Argentina 45, 1st floor, 07013 Palma.
℡ 971 730 301/302.
FAX 971 780 099.

Menorca: C/ Deià 30, 07702 Maó.
℡ 971 354 387.
FAX 971 366 262.

Ibiza: C/ Abad i Lasierra 35, 1st floor, 07800 Eivissa.
℡ 971 301 216.
FAX 971 301 216.

The Netherlands
Mallorca: C/ San Miquel 36, 6th floor, 07002 Palma.
℡ 971 716 493, 971 728 364.
FAX 971 726 642.

Menorca: C/ Angel 12, 1st floor, 07703 Maó.
℡ 971 354 363.
FAX 971 362 408.

Ibiza: Via Púnica 2 pral B, 07800 Eivissa.
℡ 971 300 434.
FAX 971 391 322.

Germany
c/Porto de Pi 8, 3rd floor, 07012 Palma, Mallorca
℡ 971 707 737.
FAX 971 707 740.

Menorca: C/ Des Negres 32, 07703 Maó.
℡ 971 361 668, 971 365 812.
FAX 971 369 012.

Ibiza: C/ D'Antoni Jaume 2, 2–9th floor, 07800 Eivissa. ℡ 971 315 763.
FAX 971 315 763.

United Kingdom
Mallorca: Plaça Mayor, 3-D, 07002 Palma.
℡ 971 712 085/445.
FAX 971 717 520.

Menorca: Sa Casa Nova, Cami Biniatap, 30, 07720 Es Castell.
℡ 971 363 373.
FAX 971 354 690.

Ibiza: Avda/ Isidoro Macabich 45, 1st floor, 07800 Eivissa.
℡ 971 301 818.
FAX 971 301 972.

ORGANIZATIONS FOR THE DISABLED

COCEMFE
C/ Luis Cabrera 63, Madrid.
℡ 917 443 600.
FAX 914 131 996.

RADAR
12 City Forum, 250 City Road, London, EC1V 8AF.
℡ 020 7250 3222.

Viajes 2000
Paseo de la Castellana 228–230, Madrid.
℡ 913 231 029

TOURIST INFORMATION

Mallorca
C/ Santo Domingo 11, Palma.
℡ 971 724 090.
FAX 971 226 963.

Caseta Pl.Espanya, Palma.
℡ 971 754 329.

Menorca
Roullada D'Alt 24, Maó.
℡ 971 363 790.
FAX 971 367 415.

Plaça Catedral, Ciutadella.
℡ 971 382 693.
FAX 971 382 667.

Ibiza
Passeig de Vara de Rey 13, Eivissa.

℡ 971 301 900.
FAX 971 301 562.

Passeig de ses Fonts. Sant Antoni de Portmany.
℡ 971 343 363.

Formentera
Ajuntament. Sant Francesc.
℡ 971 322 027.

TOURIST INFORMATION WEBSITES

W www.balearics.com
W www.balearicsinfo.com
W www.balearweb.com
W www.caib.es
W www.visitbalears.com

Mallorca
W www.mallorcanow.com
W www.mallorca2000.com
W www.a2zmallorca.com

Menorca
W www.menorca.net
W www.menorca.org
W www.idomenorca.com

Ibiza
W www.eivissa.de
W www.ibizaes.com
W www.ibiza-online.com
W www.ibiza-spotlight.com
W www.ibizaholidays.com

Formentera
W www.guiaformentera.com

Personal Security and Health

THE CRIME LEVEL ON the Balearic Islands is lower than in other regions of Europe. Thefts do occur in the most crowded places and even in hotels, but they can be minimized by taking sensible precautions. Credit cards and money are best hidden away. Never leave anything visible in your car when you park it. It is also advisable to avoid carrying excessive amounts of cash. When in need, you can always ask a policeman for help. Basic medical help and advice is usually provided by a pharmacist. Holders of valid medical insurance can receive treatment in public hospitals and clinics.

PERSONAL PROPERTY

BEFORE TRAVELLING abroad it is wise to make sure you have adequate holiday insurance in order to protect yourself financially from the loss or theft of your property. Even so, it is also advisable to take common-sense precautions against loss or theft in the first place. Traveller's cheques are a far safer option than cash. If you have two credit cards, do not carry them together and make sure you keep a separate note of credit card cancellation numbers. Particular care should be exercised in crowded places such as airports and bus stations. Patrolling policemen often remind visitors about the need to be careful. There are also cases of tourists falling victim to theft when drunk. Never leave a bag or handbag unattended and do not put a purse or wallet on a tabletop in a café. The moment you discover a loss or theft, report it to the local police. The police will give you a *denuncia* (written statement), which you will need to make an insurance claim. If you have your passport lost or stolen, report it to your consulate.

Beach notice board in Cala Millor

SPANISH POLICE

THE ISLAND POLICE are friendly towards tourists. They are always ready to give advice and help. However, in case of any infringement of the law they can be very firm and it is best not to try to argue with them.

As in the rest of Spain there are three types of police on the islands. The *Policía Nacional* (state police), the *Policía Municipal*, also known as the *Policía Local* (local police), and the *Guardia Civil* (National Guard). The force encountered most frequently by tourists is the *Policía Municipal*. Their officers are mostly encountered in small towns, and patrol the streets of crowded tourist resorts; they have a separate branch for traffic. The *Policía Nacional* wear brown uniforms. They deal with more serious incidents and matters concerning foreign visitors; they also guard various important buildings in large cities. The *Guardia Civil*, dressed in green uniforms, patrol rural areas. You can see them while travelling the roads and wild areas of the Balearic Islands.

State police car or *Policía Nacional*, frequently seen around the islands

Lifeguard on duty at Sant Elm beach, Mallorca

BEACHES

DURING THE HIGH season most beaches have lifeguards. Many beaches have swimming areas marked by buoys, although this does not mean that swimming outside these areas is prohibited. Many beaches have Red Cross stations. Notice boards at the entrance to the beach give information on facilities such as showers or wheelchair access *(see left)*. Many smaller beaches do not have lifeguards. Nevertheless, swimming is usually safe, as beaches are generally situated in small coves with calm waters.

The majority of the Balearic Islands' beaches are sandy. However, those along the northern shores of the islands are often rocky. You should exercise special care when swimming off rocky beaches. It is also recommended that you use footwear when entering the water and that you watch out for underwater rocks when snorkelling.

The sun should be taken seriously while on the beach. Between 12noon and 6pm it is best not to stay exposed for too long. It can take only minutes to get sunburnt and children are especially vulnerable. Be sure to apply a high-factor sunblock cream and also make use of an umbrella. Deckchairs and umbrellas can often be hired for a fee. Drink plenty of water to avoid dehydration.

MEDICAL CARE

BOTH NATIONAL AND private healthcare are available in Spain. Visitors from EU countries are entitled to free national health treatment. They must, however, remember to travel with a certified copy of an E111 or E112 form (the latter applies to chronic conditions). These can be obtained in the UK from the Department of Health or from a post office before you travel. Please note that Spanish healthcare does not cover all expenses such as the cost of dental treatment. Having private health insurance can also avoid time-wasting bureaucracy. Visitors from outside the EU should always carry valid medical insurance.

In case of illness, you should report to a hospital or clinic. At night, patients are seen by the *Urgencias* (Emergency). You can also telephone the Cruz Roja (Red Cross) for help.

Red and white ambulance on Formentera

Decorative pharmacy sign

PHARMACIES

PHARMACIES HAVE THE SAME opening hours as other shops. They carry a green or red cross with the word *farmàcia*, or sometimes *apotecaria*. Details about those open at night and on public holidays can be found in the windows of all pharmacies. Most pharmacists in large towns speak at least one foreign language. This is important, since when dealing with minor medical problems, pharmacists are entitled to give advice and even dispense necessary medicines. In this instance, consulting a pharmacist may be enough. Balearic pharmacies sell several medicines over the counter that in other countries are available only on prescription. Away from the big towns, a *farmàcia* may be found in any small town or village. Here, opening hours may be shorter and they are not often open at weekends. In smaller towns and villages the pharmacist may be less used to dealing with tourists and communication may be a problem as a result.

FIRE HAZARDS

THE BALEARIC ISLANDS have a dry Mediterranean climate, with mild winters and hot summers. The summer heat often causes droughts since rain falls sporadically between October and February. This creates conditions where fire can spread extremely quickly. Parched woodlands, combined with the general layout of the land, makes firefighting very difficult. Often fire fighting necessitates airplanes and helicopters dropping vast amounts of water. It is vital, therefore,

Firefighting airplane on Ibiza

when travelling on the islands or using picnic facilities, to remember to take great care to prevent a fire from starting. Before leaving, carefully check the remains of any bonfire and be sure to pick up glass, particularly bottles, that may also cause fire. It goes without saying that you should be especially careful when extinguishing cigarettes in country areas.

The island Fire Brigade is called *Bomberos*, and as elsewhere in the world, it has an easy-to-remember emergency telephone number *(see below)*.

DIRECTORY

EMERGENCY NUMBERS

Police, Guardia Civil, Red Cross, Ambulance & Fire Brigade

📞 *112*

PHARMACIES

Mallorca
Farmacia La Rambla C.B.
Rambla Ducs de Palma,
Palma de Mallorca.
📞 *971 729 126.*

Menorca
Farmacia Sequi Puntas
Avda. Vives Llull 16 RDSI, Maó.
📞 *971 360 993.*

Ibiza
J.A. Marítur
C/ Anibal 11, Eivissa.
📞 *971 310 371*

Formentera
Climent Gonzalez A.M.
Avda. Constitucion 26.
📞 *966 792 311.*

Communication and Banks

Logo of a local bank

THE QUALITY OF TELEPHONE services in the Balearic Islands is high. Thanks to the transfer to digital technology in 1998 the line quality is generally good. The banking services on the islands are equally efficient and many foreign banks, mainly German, have branches here. The Spanish postal system does not function quite so well and it may take a week or more for a letter posted in the Balearic Islands to reach its destination. When communicating with Spanish companies it is best to use fax or e-mail.

Bright and easy-to-spot post box belonging to the Spanish *correos*

TELEPHONES

MOST OF THE TELEPHONES in the Balearic Islands are owned and maintained by the Spanish company Telefónica, although in some of the busier resorts you may see phones belonging to other companies. This competition means that even in a small place you should have no problem finding a public telephone – if not in a street kiosk, then in a bar or restaurant.

The most common telephones are coin- or card-operated types. Since 2001, telephones that once accepted Spanish pesetas have been adapted to take euros. The card-operated telephones are of various types, as there are two types of phonecards. One has a black magnetic strip with an encoded value. The other has a PIN number that must be entered before the connection can be made.

When dialling a number you should remember that in Spain you must always dial the full nine-digit number, even if you are in the same area. The code for the Balearic Islands is 971. A call from Mallorca to Menorca will cost the same as one from Palma to Andratx. When telephoning the Balearic Islands from the UK, Ireland and New Zealand you must first dial 0034 (the country code for Spain) and then the

Telephone kiosk

subscriber's number starting with the area code (i.e. 971). When calling a mobile phone number you should dial the country code, followed by the subscriber's number. To phone the UK from the Balearic Islands dial 0044, then area code (minus the 0) then number; to phone Ireland dial 00353, then area code (minus the 0) then number; to phone the US or Canada dial 001, then area code then number.

There are four tariffs for international calls. These apply respectively to EU countries, other European countries and northwest Africa, North and South America, and the rest of the world. International calls are cheapest at night, between 10pm and 8am, on Saturdays after 2pm and on Sundays. A call from a public telephone costs 35 per cent more than one made from a private phone, but is still cheaper than from a hotel.

Colourful logo of Telefonica

POSTAL SERVICE

THE SPANISH postal system is one of the worst in Europe and you should not be surprised if postcards and letters sent from the islands take a week to reach the addressee. Sometimes they can take even longer. If a message is

urgent, it is much better to send it by fax or e-mail. You can also send express (*urgente*) or a registered (*certificado*) mail.

Post offices are open Mondays to Saturdays, between 9am and 7pm, with a break for the siesta. If you only want to buy a stamp, you would be better off looking for a kiosk that bears the sign *timbre*, or asking at a hotel reception desk. Postal charges depend on where the item is being sent to and fall into bands that include the EU, the rest of Europe, the USA and the rest of the world. Post offices also accept telegrams, registered mail and parcels. Letters and cards can be mailed in a yellow post box.

Many hotels, as well as some shops, offer services of companies other than the Spanish post. They are, however, no more efficient. If you use one of these and buy an appropriate stamp, remember to post your letter in the correct box. Otherwise it will not be delivered.

CURRENCY

IN MARCH 2002, the Spanish peseta was replaced by the common EU currency, the euro. Notes have several denominations, ranging from 5 to 500 euros. Euro banknotes look the same in all European countries, but the coins have a different reverse. The Spanish ones are inscribed *España*.

BANKS AND CASH DISPENSERS

MOST BANKS ARE OPEN from 9am until 2pm. Some have longer opening hours or work in the afternoons on a rota system. After the switch to the euro, most bureaux de change closed. Now the easiest way to change currency is in a bank, at the counter marked *cambio*.

To do this you will need to show your passport or other ID. Most banks charge a small commission for this.

Alternatively, you can withdraw money from one of the many cash dispensers that work 24 hours. They all dispense money and accept all major credit cards. Some charge a commission on withdrawals with cards issued by rival banks. If you want to avoid this, you should find out if any Spanish bank has an agreement with your own bank before travelling.

One of the many cash dispensers available on the islands

CREDIT CARDS AND TRAVELLER'S CHEQUES

THE MOST POPULAR credit cards are Visa and MasterCard. However, most cash dispensers, as well as shops, hotels and restaurants, will also accept American

Express or Diners. When you pay with a card, cashiers will usually pass your card through a reading machine. Sometimes you may be asked to punch in your PIN number. Some smaller places, such as market stalls and independent shops may not accept credit cards.

Traveller's cheques are by far the safest way of carrying money. When you lose a cheque you don't automatically lose the money and it can be quickly replaced. These may be cashed in banks and bureaux de change. The most popular cheques traveller's cheques are American Express, Visa and Thomas Cook. Banks charge a commission for cashing a cheque.

RADIO AND TELEVISION

NUMEROUS PUBS AND cafés have a television and it is easy to watch major sporting events live, including many English and German league soccer matches. Hotels have a larger selection of TV channels. Besides Spanish national TV, such as TVE1, TVE2, there are a number of local channels including Catalan TV3 and Canal 33. These broadcast mainly Spanish news and light entertainment.

You can tune into the BBC's World Service 24 hours a day on 648kHz medium wave and also on 98.5FM.

NEWSPAPERS

SEVERAL LOCAL NEWSPAPERS are published on each of the islands. These cover mainly local issues and can be valuable sources of information for visitors who

Popular dailies published in the Balearic Islands

want to find out about forthcoming cultural and sporting events. They also publish useful addresses and telephone numbers. Some of the local newspapers have foreign language supplements.

In many towns, kiosks and hotels sell Spanish national papers as well as British and German newspapers, which are available all of the time. Most of the popular EU publications arrive on the Balearic Islands with a minimum delay.

Kiosks selling papers in Passeig d'es Born in Palma, Mallorca

TRAVEL INFORMATION

MOST VISITORS arrive on the Balearic Islands by air. This is not only the fastest but often also the cheapest way of getting here. The airports are on Mallorca, Menorca and Ibiza. Served by international airlines, these are mostly charter flights, though there are also regular scheduled flights from the UK. Alternatively, you can fly

Spanair's logo

to mainland Spain and change planes. During peak season, Palma's airport is one of the busiest in Europe. Sea links are equally convenient, but you must first get to the Spanish coast. The routes from Barcelona, Dénia and Valencia to the Balearic Islands are served by large ferries that may carry cars, and also by fast catamarans.

Palma Airport's departure hall, Mallorca

AIR TRAVEL

REGULAR LINKS between large Spanish cities and the Balearic Islands are provided by the Spanish carrier **Iberia**. There are also regular flights between the Balearic Islands (mainly Mallorca) and countries that provide the greatest numbers of visitors such as Germany and Britain, as well as Austria, Switzerland, France and the Netherlands.

The Balearic Islands are featured by a wide range of European tour operators – ask your travel agent for advice. Package holidays operate year-round and feature both scheduled and charter flights. Palma is also served by low-cost airlines **easyJet** and **bmibaby** with flights from London Gatwick, Stansted, Luton, Bristol, East Midlands, Manchester and Liverpool.

Flights from the UK take under three hours. These relatively short flight times mean that the islands are not only popular for annual holidays, but also for "mini-breaks". Flights from the US require changing planes in London or Madrid.

FLIGHTS BETWEEN THE ISLANDS

ONE OF THE carriers providing flights between the islands is **Spanair**. The flight from Mallorca to Menorca takes only 30 minutes. For that reason this is a convenient way of travelling. Before island hopping, it is a good idea to find out what type of aircraft you are going to fly in. Some are quite small and you may not be able to take large hand luggage. Travelling in a small, packed and stuffy light aircraft can be a little unpleasant for anybody who suffers from claustrophobia or other health problems. Even in the best of weather, the flight may be bumpy and a small aircraft makes this more noticeable.

However, flying between the islands will not only save you time but will also give you the chance to see magnificent views of the archipelago.

Multi-lingual information sign at Palma's airport

AIRPORTS

SON SANT JOAN AIRPORT on Mallorca is situated on the outskirts of Palma, around 11 km (7 miles) from the centre of the island's capital. The nearby motorway provides a fast road link to Palma. Terminal A is used for scheduled flights; Terminal B is for charter flights. The airport has many shops, car hire agents and tourist information centres.

Over the last few years the airport has been constantly extended for the needs of tourists. Despite its size, it is difficult to get lost here. Individual zones are well sign-posted, but be prepared for long walks when making your way from one sector of the airport to another. Menorca's airport is near the island's capital – Maó. This is

Colourful aircraft at Ibiza's airport

Ferries in Maó's harbour, Menorca

DIRECTORY

AIRPORTS

[W] www.aena.es

Mallorca – Son Sant Joan
[C] 971 789 099/000.

Menorca
[C] 971 157 000.

Ibiza
[C] 971 809 000.

AIRLINES

bmibaby
[W] www.bmibaby.com

easyJet
[W] www.easyjet.com

Iberia
[C] 902 400 500.
[W] www.iberia.com

Spanair
[C] 902 131 415.
[W] www.spanair.es

FERRY LINES

Balearia
[W] www.balearia.net

Iscomar
[W] www.iscomar.com

Trasmediterranea
[W] www.trasmediterranea.es

Umafisa Lines
[W] www.umafisa.com

the smallest of the Balearic airports. Ibiza's airport is a dozen or so kilometres from Eivissa and is far busier. The traffic increases particularly during weekends, when club-goers from all over Europe arrive for the Saturday-Sunday revel. The aircraft touching down here are often painted in the most fantastic designs. When taking off or landing in Eivissa you get a bird's-eye view of the town and of Dalt Vila. Frequent bus services operate from all the main airports and can take you straight to the city centres.

FERRIES

ANYONE WHO plans to take their own car or motorcycle to the islands must use a ferry. These run frequent and regular services between large towns on the Spanish mainland and the harbours of Mallorca, Menorca and Ibiza. Journey times are quite reasonable; it takes seven hours by ferry from Barcelona to Palma for example.

The large ferries operated by **Trasmediterranea** sail from Barcelona and Valencia to Palma and Maó. They also provide transport to Ibiza. The latter may be reached from Barcelona (11 hours) or Valencia (about four hours). **Balearia** and **Umafisa**, two smaller ferry companies, also have services to the islands. If you're in a hurry, you can also use Trasmediterranea's new high-speed ferry service, which carries up to 900 passengers and 265 cars and can take you from Valencia to Ibiza in three hours.

BALEARIA

Logo of Balearia
ferry lines

Inter-island services are equally diverse. You can choose a fast Trasmediterranea catamaran or a slower ferry run by a company like **Iscomar**. Both of them have bars for passengers.

Using ferries to hop from island to island will always be cheaper than flying and it can be a very pleasant option. Arriving by sea and catching your first glimpse of Maó's ancient harbour is an experience that is hard to forget. Some islands can only be reached by sea. These include Cabrera, Formentera and Dragonera. A journey by ferry from Ibiza to Formentera takes about an hour; by catamaran it takes about 30 minutes. Ticket prices for ferries providing links between the islands are reasonable, but going by a catamaran will cost you more. Price differences between competing companies are greater for longer routes, but prices depend mostly on the time of year. The lowest prices can be obtained after high season, from October until

December, and again from the end of January until the end of March. In the period from Easter until the beginning of July – known as the "half-season" – the ferry prices tend to go up again. Children up to the age of 12 are entitled to a 50 per cent reduction, and infants travel free.

Pleasure boat - an enjoyable way to travel to smaller ports

Getting Round the Islands

THE BALEARIC ISLANDS have only two railway lines, both of which are in Mallorca. The first is an historic line from Palma to Sóller; the other links Palma with Inca. In order to explore the more remote parts of the island, as well as the remaining islands of the archipelago, you will need a car, a scooter or a bicycle. On Formentera, a scooter and bicycle are the best means of transport. When travelling round the islands, you should pay particular attention to the numerous motorbike riders. Weekend motorbike rallies and races are held in Mallorca, although they are strongly opposed by the *Guardia Civil*.

Scenic, winding road leading to Sa Calobra, Mallorca

ROADS

ROADS AND SIGNAGE on the Balearic Islands are generally good, although there is a shortage of hard shoulders. As a consequence, stopping along the road in order to admire the scenery can be difficult and dangerous and is not recommended. The only free motorway runs along the coast of Badia de Palma, encircling Mallorca's capital. Its second segment links Palma with Inca. To use the segment between Alfàbia and Sóller that passes through the tunnel under Serra de Tramuntana, you have to pay a toll. During the morning and afternoon rush hour in the areas around Palma and other industrial towns like Inca or Manacor, you may experience traffic jams.

Take great care when you are trying to reach some beaches or sights off the beaten track. The roads leading to them can be narrow, steep and winding. Problems can arise when two cars try to pass each other. Some beaches and sights inland can only be reached along unmade, bumpy roads and to travel to these requires a four-wheel drive vehicle.

MAPS

WHEN HIRING A CAR you will normally be given an outline road map of the island. It will show the main roads on which it is safe to drive. Unfortunately the maps are not always up to date and it is advisable to buy one of the maps sold in bookshops, souvenir shops or petrol stations. The folding B&B

Maps are particularly good. Please note that town and street signs now appear in Catalan rather than Spanish (Castilian), so make sure you get a map marked in Catalan.

CAR AND SCOOTER HIRE

COMPANIES WILL BE falling over themselves to rent you a car almost as soon as you have landed, as all major car hire companies, **Avis**, **Hertz** and **Europcar** have their desks at the airports. It is, however, worth taking your time to search for a small local firm that may offer you a better price.

The price of car hire depends on the time of year, the size of the car and the length of hire. Advance booking can also affect the price. It is worth not only comparing the prices quoted by the various companies but checking exactly what the quote includes.

When hiring a car, you will have to show your passport and valid driver's licence. You should also carefully check the conditions regarding insurance and any restrictions about driving on rough tracks or taking the car from one island to another. Be sure to inspect the condition of the car, as you will have to return it in the same condition or pay a fine. The terms and conditions of hire can vary greatly from company to company. Check carefully before signing any contract.

Scooters are a very popular form of transport, particularly on Formentera and Ibiza. Hire

Scooters on the streets of Eivissa, Ibiza

Petrol station run by the Cepsa chain

rates for these are much lower and they can transport you to places that cars cannot reach. Many people learn to ride a scooter during their holidays.

RULES OF THE ROAD

DRIVING ON THE Balearic Islands is no different to driving in any other European country. You should remember the speed limits, which are 120 km/h (74 mph) on motorways, 90 km/h (55 mph) on major roads and 50 km/h (30 mph) in towns. The fines for breaking the speed limits are high, just as they are for drunken driving. The highest permitted blood alcohol level is 0.05 per cent.

Sign for a parking meter

BUYING PETROL

PETROL STATION PUMPS are generally operated by the staff. Only a few are automatic and open 24 hours. Menorca, Ibiza and Formentera have very few petrol stations. The same applies to the Serra de Tramuntana region of Mallorca. When touring these areas you should remember that a car uses more fuel on mountainous terrain than on a flat road. It is therefore worth filling the tank before setting off.

TOWN DRIVING

IF AT ALL POSSIBLE, you should avoid driving in large town centres and popular resorts. Many streets in historic towns are narrow, with one-way traffic. Cars parked alongside pavements make driving conditions even more difficult. Popular

resorts are always crowded and it can be very difficult to find a parking space.

Most car parks charge fees, and there are fines for non-payment. Paid car parking spaces along pavements are marked with a blue line. Generally, the parking fees apply from 9am to 1pm and from 5pm to 8pm on weekdays, and from 9am to 1pm on Saturdays. In many towns, such as Eivissa, parking in these spaces is limited to a set time. A yellow line painted along the pavement means that parking is prohibited. In Palma and Maó use one of the underground car parks. Here, there is no time limit on parking, but you may have to wait in a long queue.

BUSES

BUS LINKS BETWEEN major towns as well as between large and small towns are very good. Buses between small towns and villages, where there are not many direct connections, are less efficient. Of the large towns, only Palma has its own municipal bus network. Travelling by bus is not expensive. You should bear in mind that during weekends

Bicycle and "quadcycle" on a promenade

DIRECTORY

HIRING A CAR

Avis
W www.avisworld.com
Betacar
W www.betacar.es
Hertz
W www.hertz.com
Spain Car Rental
W www.spaincarrental.com

BUS STATIONS

Empresa Municipal de Transportes Urbanos de Palma
Plaça Espanya. Palma, Mallorca.
C 971 177 777.
Transportes Menorca
Vassallo s/n. Maó, Menorca.
C 971 380 393.
Autobuses
Sant Antoni de Portmany, Ibiza.
C 971 380 393.

TRAIN STATIONS

Palma-Inca
C 971 752 245.
Tren de Sóller
C 971 752 028.

the services are much less frequent. When planning a further journey, particularly on Mallorca, check your options for the return journey.

Ibiza has a special night bus service during high season, taking guests to the most popular clubs and ferrying them between Sant Antoni de Portmany and Eivissa.

TAXIS

FOR TRAVELLING AROUND town or visiting nearby sights, it is best to hire a taxi. Most taxis in Palma have a black and cream colour scheme. The driver is obliged to turn on the meter at the start of the journey and the sum displayed is the one you pay. For disabled people, taxi transport is by far the most convenient, as you can order a specially adapted vehicle. Taxis to the airport may charge an additional airport and luggage fee.

Acknowledgments

DORLING KINDERSLEY would like to thank the following people whose contributions and assistance have made the preparation of this book possible.

CONSULTANT Chris Rice

FACTCHECKER John Gill

PROOFREADER Stewart Wild

INDEXER Helen Peters

ADDITIONAL CONTRIBUTORS Tony Kelly, Andrew Valente, Jeffrey Kennedy

ADDITIONAL PHOTOGRAPHY Joe Cornish, Neil Lucas

ADDITIONAL DESIGN & EDITORIAL ASSISTANCE Jo Cowen, Anna Freiberger, Conrad van Dyk

SENIOR EDITOR Jacky Jackson

MANAGING EDITOR Helen Townsend

PUBLISHING MANAGER Kate Poole

SPECIAL ASSISTANCE
WIEDZA I ŻYCIE would like to thank the following people for their help in creating this guide.

Martin & Toni Cornell, Zbigniew Dybowski, Joanna Egert-Romanowska, Christiane Hagen, Martin Hagmüller, Javier Lopez Silvosa, Barbara Sudnik

The publisher would also like to thank the people and institutions who allowed photographs of their property to be reproduced, as well as granting permission to use photographs from their archives:

AENA, Gabinete de Comunicación-Aeropuertos de Baleares; Aeropuerto de Palma de Mallorca (Elisabet Royo Romero); AFP in Warszawie (Piotr Ufnal); Aguamar in Platja d'en Bossa; Amic Hotels in Palma (Andreu Llabrés); Amnesia in Sant Rafael (Stéphane Schweitzer, Aymeric Huot-Marchand); Banys Àrabs in Palmie (Doña Pilar); National Library in Warsaw (Iwona Grzybowska); Centre Perles in Palma (Lluc Antonio Bibiloni, Carolina Gato); Corbis – Agencja Free in Warsaw (Gabriela Ściborska); Coves de Campanet (Maria Antònia Siquier); Eden in Sant Antoni de Portmany (Gemma); El Divino in Eivissa; Els Calders (Javier Marqués); Es Paradis in Sant Antoni de Portmany; Fundació Pilar i Joan Miró in Cala Major (Núria Sureda, Joan Insa); Grupo Aspro-Ocio (Omar García Melcon); Ibatur (Esteve Rigo Ribas); La Granja (Manuel Moragues Marqués); La Residencia in Deià (Arantza Zamora); La Reserva Puig de Galatzó (Heike Killisch); Modas Leather in Ferreries (Suzanne Sparkes-Keeble); Museu d'Art Espanyol Contemporani in Palma (Antonio Barcelo); Museu de Lluc in Monasteri de Luc (Elvira González); Museu de Mallorca in Palma (Guillem Rosselló Bordoy); Museu de Menorca in Maó (Anna Fernandez); Naviera Universal Española, S.L. in Barcelona (Núria

Alvarez); paulunderhill.com (Paul Underhill); Safari-zoo Mallorca (Miquel Brunet Alós)

PICTURE CREDITS
t=top; tl=top left; tc=top centre; tr=top right; c=centre; cl=centre left; cr=centre right; cb=centre below; ca=centre above; clb=centre left below; crb=centre right below; cla=centre left above; cra=centre right above; b=bottom; bl=bottom left; bc=bottom centre, br=bottom right, ba=bottom above, la=left above

AENA 190cl; AFP 187b; Amic Hotels 142t, 143t Amnesia 120t, 173t

Biblioteka Naradowa in Warsaw Krzysztof Konopka 67clb

Carlos Minguel 24ca, 24cb, 25c, 25cb, 25bl, 25br Corbis 34c, 35c, 35bl, 120ca, 121b; Franz-Marc Frei 29t; Roger Halls 111t; Bob Krist 17b; Kelly-Mooney 37ca; Vittoriano Rastelli 133b; Hans Georg Roth 31c, 91b; James A. Sugar 21b, 29c, 37cb; Cueva des Hams 79 tl

El Divino 120b

Fundació Pilar i Joan Miró 58b

Grupo Aspro-Ocio 41bl, 59tl, 59bl, 59br, 87t, 88cb, 89b

Ibatur 26b, 27c, 28t, 173b

Piotr Kiedrowski 157bc, 171cb
Juliusz and Hanna Komarniccy 12, 20c, 26c, 171la
Wesley Kutner 15b, 16c, 17t, 154c, 155b

La Reserva Puig de Galatzó 61t, 61c
Andrzej Lisowski 14c, 15t, 17c, 19br, 23br, 28b, 96ca, 120cb, 121c, 129b, 143c, 155t, 155c, 177t, 182b, 183b, 184b, 190b, 192b

Paweł Murzyn 10c, 10b, 13b, 18bl, 18br, 20b, 23ba, 25tl, 29b, 40ca, 89tl, 119b, 128c, 172cl, 176c, 182c

Robert Pasieczny 22 cb, 34b, 37bl, 41t, 45, 64t, 64ca, 66t, 68b, 70cp, 172t, 174t; Paulunderhill.com 120t

Biel Salas Servera 22t, 23c, 23ca, 23cb, 24t, 24b, 25tr, 84 tl, 84b, 85t

Andrzej Zygmuntowicz and Ireneusz Winnicki 5c, 101b, 156tr, 156cla, 156ca, 156cra, 156crb, 156br, 157bl, 157tc, 157tr, 157ca, 157cb, 157cr, 157bl

JACKET: Front: CORBIS: Nik Wheeler cl; DK PICTURE LIBRARY: bc; Joe Cornish cr; B. Zaranek main image. Back: DK PICTURE LIBRARY: Colin Sinclair t/b. Spine: DK PICTURE LIBRARY: B. Zaranek

All other images © Dorling Kindersley
For further information see:
www.dkimages.com

Phrasebook

IN AN EMERGENCY

Where is the telephone?	¿Dónde está el teléfono más próximo?
Help!	¡Socorro!
Call a doctor!	¡Llame a un médico!
Call the police!	¡Llame a la policía!
Call the fire brigade!	¡Llame a los bomberos!
Stop!	¡Pare!

COMMUNICATION ESSENTIALS

Yes	Sí
No	No
Please	Por favor
Thank you	Gracias
Excuse me	Perdone
Hello	Hola
Goodbye	Adiós
Good morning	Buenos días
Good night	Buenas noches
In the morning	Por la mañana
In the afternoon	Por la tarde
afternoon	La tarde
today	Hoy
tomorrow	Mañana
yesterday	Ayer
here	Aquí
there	Allí
What?	¿Qué?
When??	¿Cuándo?
Where?	¿Dónde?
Why?	¿Por qué?

USEFUL PHRASES

How are you?	¿Cómo estás?
Very well, thanks	Muy bien, gracias
Pleased to meet you	Encantado de conocerle
See you soon	Hasta pronto
Where is/are...?	¿Dónde está/ están...?
How far is it to...?	¿Cuántos metros/kilómetros hay de aquí a...?
Which way to...?	¿Por dónde se va a...?
Do you speak English?	¿Habla inglés?
I don't understand	No comprendo
Could you speak more slowly please?	¿Puede hablar más despacio por favor?
I'm sorry	Lo siento

USEFUL WORDS

large	grande
small	pequeño
hot	caliente
cold	frío
good	bueno
bad	mal
well	bien
open	abierto
closed	cerrado
to the left	a la izquierda
to the right	a la derecha
straight ahead	todo recto
near	cerca
far	lejos
above	arriba
below	abajo
early	temprano
late	tarde
more	más
less	menos
entrance	entrada
exit	salida
toilets	servicios

SIGHTSEEING

church	la basílica
library	la biblioteca
ticket	el billete
train station	la estación de trenes
tourist information office	la oficina de turismo
cathedral	la catedral
church	la iglesia
museum	el museo
garden	el jardín
palace	el palacio
bus station	la estación de autobuses
town hall	el ayuntamiento

SHOPPING

I would like...	Me gustaría...
Do you have...?	¿Tienen...?
Do you accept credit cards?	¿Aceptan tarjetas de crédito?
How much does this cost?	¿Cuánto cuesta esto?
What time do you open/close?	A qué hora abren/cierran?
This one	Éste
That one	Ése
expensive	caro
cheap	barato
size (clothes)	talla
size (shoes)	número
colour	color
white	blanco
brown	marrón
black	negro
red	rojo
blue	azul
green	verde
yellow	amarillo

SHOPS

antiques shop	la tienda de antigüedades
pharmacy	la farmacia
bank	el banco
market	el mercado
travel agency	la agencia de viajes
supermarket	supermercado
hairdresser	la peluquería
newsagent	el kiosko de prensa
bookshop	la librería
bakery	la panadería
post office	la oficina de correos
shop	la tienda
shoe store	la zapatería
fish monger	la pescadería
petrol station	la gasolinera

STAYING IN A HOTEL

Do you have a vacant room?	¿Tienen una habitación libre?
double room	habitación doble
single room	habitación individual
room with a double bed	habitación con cama de matrimonio
room with two beds	habitación con dos camas
room with a bath	habitación con baño
room with a shower	habitación con ducha
porter	el botones
key	la llave
I have a reservation	Tengo una habitación reservada

EATING OUT

Do you have a table for...?	¿Tienen mesa para...?
I would like to reserve a table	Quiero reservar una mesa
The bill, please	La cuenta por favor
I am a vegetarian	Soy vegetariano/a
waitress/waiter	camarera/camarero
tip	propina
fixed-price menu	menú del día
menu	la carta
breakfast	el desayuno
lunch	la comida/el almuerzo
dinner	la cena
starters	los entremeses
soup	la sopa
main course	el primer plato
dish of the day	el plato del día
dessert	el postre
well done	muy hecho
medium	medio hecho
rare	poco hecho
wine list	la carta de vinos
coffee	el café
juice	el zumo

bottle	una botella
glass (with a stem)	una copa
cup	una taza
glass (without a stem)	un vaso
plate	un plato
spoon	una cuchara
teaspoon	una cucharita
knife	un cuchillo
fork	un tenedor

MENU

al horno	baked
asado	roast
el aceite	oil
las aceitunas	olives
el agua mineral sin gas/con gas	mineral water still/sparkling
el ajo	garlic
el arroz	rice
el azúcar	sugar
el bogavente	lobster
la cabra	goat
los calamares	calamari (squid)
la carne	meat
la cebolla	onion
la cerveza	beer
el cerdo	pork
el chocolate	chocolate
el chorizo	red sausage
el cordero	lamb
fiambres	cold cuts
frito	smażony
la fruta	fruit
los frutos secos	dried fruit
las gambas	prawns
el helado	ice cream
el huevo	egg
el jamón serrano	cured ham
el jerez	sherry
la langosta	lobster
la leche	milk
el limón	lemon
la mantequilla	butter
la manzana	apple
los mariscos	seafood
la naranja	orange
el pan	bread
el pastel	cake
las patatas	potatoes
el pescado	fish
la pimienta	pepper
el plátano	banana
el pollo	chicken
el queso	cheese
las salchichas	sausages
la salsa	sauce
el solomillo	sirloin
la tarta	pie/cake
el té	tea

la ternera	beef
las tostadas	toast
el vino blanco	white wine
el vino rosado	rosé wine
el vino tinto	red wine
el vino seco	dry wine

NUMBERS

0	cero
1	uno
2	dos
3	tres
4	cuarto
5	cinco
6	seis
7	siete
8	ocho
9	nueve
10	diez
11	once
12	doce
13	trece
14	catorce
15	quince
16	dieciséis
17	diecisiete
18	dieciocho
19	diecinueve
20	veinte
21	veintiuno
22	veintidós
30	treinta
31	treina y uno
40	cuarenta
50	cincuenta
60	sesenta
70	setenta
80	ochenta
90	noventa
100	cien

101	ciento uno
102	ciento dos
200	doscientos
900	novecientos
1000	mil
1001	mil uno

TIME

one minute	un minuto
one hour	una hora
half an hour	media hora
a day	un día
a month	un mes
a year	un año
a century	un siglo
Monday	lunes
Tuesday	martes
Wednesday	miércoles
Thursday	jueves
Friday	viernes
Saturday	sábado
Sunday	domingo
January	enero
February	febrero
March	marzo
April	abril
May	mayo
June	junio
July	julio
August	agosto
September	septiembre
October	octubre
November	noviembre
December	diciembre

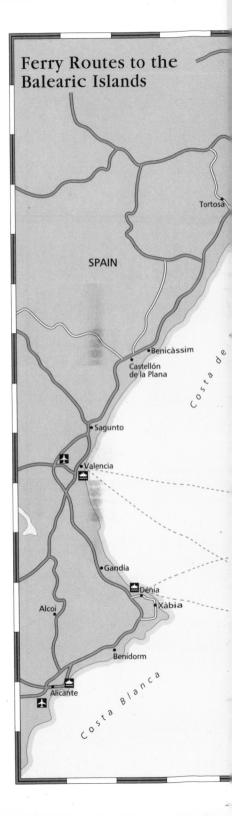

Ferry Routes to the Balearic Islands

SPAIN

Tortosa

Benicàssim

Castellón de la Plana

Costa de

Sagunto

Valencia

Gandía

Dénia

Alcoi

Xàbia

Benidorm

Alicante

Costa Blanca

SHOPS

antiques shop	la tienda de antigüedades
pharmacy	la farmacia
bank	el banco
market	el mercado
travel agency	la agencia de viajes
supermarket	supermercado
hairdresser	la peluquería
newsagent	el kiosko de prensa
bookshop	la librería
bakery	la panadería
post office	la oficina de correos
shop	la tienda
shoe store	la zapatería
fish monger	la pescadería
petrol station	la gasolinera

STAYING IN A HOTEL

Do you have a vacant room?	¿Tienen una habitación libre?
double room	habitación doble
single room	habitación individual
room with a double bed	habitación con cama de matrimonio
room with two beds	habitación con dos camas
room with a bath	habitación con baño
room with a shower	habitación con ducha
porter	el botones
key	la llave
I have a reservation	Tengo una habitación reservada

EATING OUT

Do you have a table for...?	¿Tienen mesa para...?
I would like to reserve a table	Quiero reservar una mesa
The bill, please	La cuenta por favor
I am a vegetarian	Soy vegetariano/a
waitress/waiter	camarera/camarero
tip	propina
fixed-price menu	menú del dia
menu	la carta
breakfast	el desayuno
lunch	la comida/el almuerzo
dinner	la cena
starters	los entremeses
soup	la sopa
main course	el primer plato
dish of the day	el plato del día
dessert	el postre
well done	muy hecho
medium	medio hecho
rare	poco hecho
wine list	la carta de vinos
coffee	el café
juice	el zumo

bottle	una botella
glass (with a stem)	una copa
cup	una taza
glass (without a stem)	un vaso
plate	un plato
spoon	una cuchara
teaspoon	una cucharita
knife	un cuchillo
fork	un tenedor

MENU

al horno	baked
asado	roast
el aceite	oil
las aceitunas	olives
el agua mineral sin gas/con gas	mineral water still/sparkling
el ajo	garlic
el arroz	rice
el azúcar	sugar
el bogavente	lobster
la cabra	goat
los calamares	calamari (squid)
la carne	meat
la cebolla	onion
la cerveza	beer
el cerdo	pork
el chocolate	chocolate
el chorizo	red sausage
el cordero	lamb
fiambres	cold cuts
frito	smażony
la fruta	fruit
los frutos secos	dried fruit
las gambas	prawns
el helado	ice cream
el huevo	egg
el jamón serrano	cured ham
el jerez	sherry
la langosta	lobster
la leche	milk
el limón	lemon
la mantequilla	butter
la manzana	apple
los mariscos	seafood
la naranja	orange
el pan	bread
el pastel	cake
las patatas	potatoes
el pescado	fish
la pimienta	pepper
el plátano	banana
el pollo	chicken
el queso	cheese
las salchichas	sausages
la salsa	sauce
el solomillo	sirloin
la tarta	pie/cake
el té	tea

la ternera	beef	101	ciento uno
las tostadas	toast	102	ciento dos
el vino blanco	white wine	200	doscientos
el vino rosado	rosé wine	900	novecientos
el vino tinto	red wine	1000	mil
el vino seco	dry wine	1001	mil uno

NUMBERS

0	cero
1	uno
2	dos
3	tres
4	cuarto
5	cinco
6	seis
7	siete
8	ocho
9	nueve
10	diez
11	once
12	doce
13	trece
14	catorce
15	quince
16	dieciséis
17	diecisiete
18	dieciocho
19	diecinueve
20	veinte
21	veintiuno
22	veintidós
30	treinta
31	treina y uno
40	cuarenta
50	cincuenta
60	sesenta
70	setenta
80	ochenta
90	noventa
100	cien

TIME

one minute	un minuto
one hour	una hora
half an hour	media hora
a day	un día
a month	un mes
a year	un año
a century	un siglo
Monday	lunes
Tuesday	martes
Wednesday	miércoles
Thursday	jueves
Friday	viernes
Saturday	sábado
Sunday	domingo
January	enero
February	febrero
March	marzo
April	abril
May	mayo
June	junio
July	julio
August	agosto
September	septiembre
October	octubre
November	noviembre
December	diciembre

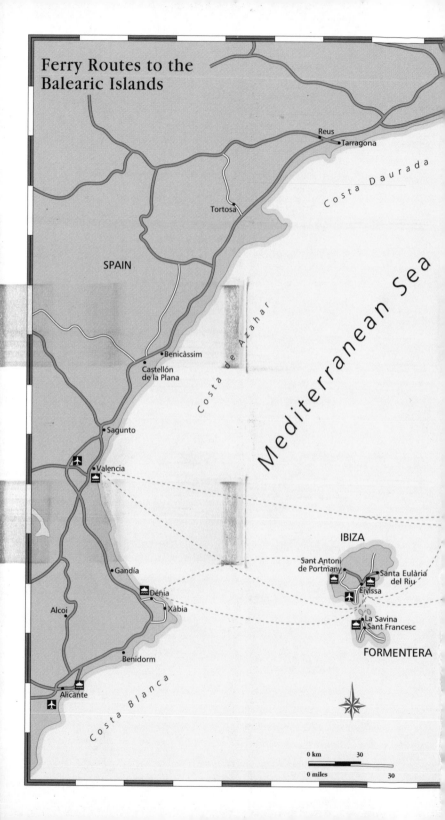

Ferry Routes to the Balearic Islands

SPAIN

Reus
Tarragona

Costa Daurada

Tortosa

Costa de Azahar

Benicàssim
Castellón de la Plana

Sagunto

Valencia

Mediterranean Sea

Gandía

Dénia

Xàbia

Alcoi

Benidorm

Alicante

Costa Blanca

IBIZA

Sant Antoni de Portmany

Santa Eulària del Riu

Eivissa

La Savina
Sant Francesc

FORMENTERA

0 km   30
0 miles   30